Voltaire, P. Dodsley

Romances, Tales and Smaller Pieces of Voltaire

Voltaire, P. Dodsley

Romances, Tales and Smaller Pieces of Voltaire

ISBN/EAN: 9783337345518

Printed in Europe, USA, Canada, Australia, Japan

Cover: Foto ©Thomas Meinert / pixelio.de

More available books at **www.hansebooks.com**

AND

SMALLER PIECES,

OF

M. DE VOLTAIRE.

VOLUME THE FIRST.

VOL. I. contains

ZADIG,
The WORLD as it goes,
MICROMEGAS,
The WHITE BULL,
TRAVELS of SCARMENTADO,
How far we ought to impose
  upon the PEOPLE,
The Two COMFORTERS,
PRINCESS of BABYLON,
MAMMON the PHILOSOPHER,
PLATO's DREAM,
BABABEC,
The BLACK and the WHITE,
  &c. &c.

VOL. II. contains

CANDID, or the OPTIMIST,
The HURON, or PUPIL of
  NATURE,
JEANNOT and COLIN,
What pleases the LADIES,
The EDUCATION of a
  PRINCE,
The EDUCATION of a
  DAUGHTER,
The THREE MANNERS,
THELEMA and MACAREUS,
AZOLAN,
  And
The ORIGIN of TRADES.

LONDON:

PRINTED FOR P. DODSLEY.

1794.

Price, in Boards, 11 s.—*in plain Binding,* 13 s.

CONTENTS

OF

VOLUME FIRST.

ZADIG.   Page

   Epiſtle Dedicatory,   -   -   -   5
   The Blind of one Eye,   -   -   9
   The Noſe,   -   -   -   -   13
   The Dog and Horſe,   -   -   15
   The Envious man,   -   -   -   20
   The Generous,   -   -   -   26
   The Miniſter,   -   -   -   29
   The Diſputes and the Audiences   -   31
   Jealouſy,   -   -   -   -   35
   The Woman beaten,   -   -   41
   Slavery,   -   -   -   -   45
   The funeral Pile,   -   -   -   48
   The Supper,   -   -   -   52
   The Rendezvous,   -   -   57
   The Robber,   -   -   -   60
   The Fiſherman,   -   -   64
   The Baſiliſk,   -   -   -   69
   The Combats,   -   -   78
   The Hermit,   -   -   -   83
   The Ænigmas,   -   -   91
The WORLD AS IT GOES, the viſion of Babouc, 96
MICROMEGAS, a Satire on the Philoſophy, Igno-
   rance and Self-conceit of Mankind,   121

Contents of Volume First.

The WHITE BULL,   -   -   P. 151

The TRAVELS of SCARMENTADO,   -   195

How far we ought to impose upon the PEO-
PLE,   -   -   -   206

The Two COMFORTERS,   -   -   210

PRINCESS of BABYLON,   -   -   213

MEMNON the PHILOSOPHER,   -   303

PLATO's DREAM,   -   -   311

BABABEC,   -   -   -   315

A Conversation with a CHINESE,   -   319

The BLACK and the WHITE,   -   323

1

ZADIG;

OR,

FATE.

AN

ORIENTAL HISTORY.

Pl. I.   A

APPROBATION.

I The underwritten, who have obtained the character of a learned, and even of an ingenious man, have read this manuscript, which, in spite of myself, I have found to be curious, entertaining, moral, philosophical, and capable of affording pleasure even to those who hate romances. I have therefore decried it; and have assured the Cadi-lesquier that it is an abominable performance.

EPISTLE DEDICATORY

TO THE

SULTANA SHERAA.

By SADI.

———————

The 18th of the Month SCHEWAL, *in the 837th Year of the* HEGIRA.

DELIGHT of the eyes, torment of the heart, and light of the mind, I kifs not the duft of thy feet, becaufe thou never walkeft; or walkeft only on the carpets of Iran, or in paths ftrewed with rofes. I offer thee the tranflation of a book, written by an ancient fage; who, having the happinefs to have nothing to do, amufed himfelf in compofing the hiftory of Zadig; a work which performs more than it promifes. I befeech thee to read and examine it; for, though thou art in the fpring of life, and every pleafure courts thee to its embrace; though thou art beautiful, and thy beauty be embellifhed by thy admirable talents; tho' thou art praifed from evening to morning, and, on all thefe accounts, haft a right to be devoid of common fenfe; yet thou haft a found judgment, and a fine tafte; and I have heard thee reafon with more accuracy than the old dervifes, with their long beards and pointed bonnets.

Thou

Thou art discreet, without being distrustful; gentle without weakness; and beneficent with discernment. Thou lovest thy friends, and makest thyself no enemies. Thy wit never borrows its charms from the shafts of detraction; thou neither sayest nor doest any ill, notwithstanding that both are so much in thy power. In a word, thy soul hath always appeared to me to be as pure and unsullied as thy beauty. Besides, thou hast some little knowledge in philosophy, which makes me believe that thou wilt take more pleasure than others of thy sex in perusing the work of this venerable sage.

It was originally written in the ancient Chaldee, a language which neither thou nor I understand. It was afterwards translated into the Arabic, to amuse the famous sultan Oulougbeg, much about the time that the Arabians and the Persians began to write the Thousand and One Nights, the Thousand and One Days, &c. Ouloug was fond of reading Zadig, but the sultanas were fonder of the Thousand and One. "How can you prefer (would the wise Ouloug say to them) those stories which have neither sense nor meaning?" "It is for that very reason (replied the sultanas) that we like them."

I flatter myself that thou wilt not resemble these thy predecessors; but that thou wilt be a true Ouloug. I even hope, that when thou art tired
with

with thofe general converfations, which differ from the Thoufand and One in nothing but in being lefs agreeable, I fhall have the honour to entertain thee for a moment with a rational difcourfe, Hadft thou been Thaleftris, in the time of Scander the fon of Philip; hadft thou been the queen of Sheba in the time of Solomon, thefe are the very kings that would have paid thee a vifit.

I pray the heavenly powers, that thy pleafures may be unmixed, thy beauty never fading, and thy happinefs without end.

SADI.

Z A D I G *.

AN

ORIENTAL HISTORY.

The BLIND of One EYE.

THERE lived at Babylon, in the reign of king
Moabdar, a young man, named Zadig, of a
good natural difpofition, ftrengthened and improved by education. Tho' rich and young, he had
learned to moderate his paffions : he had nothing
ftiff or affected in his behaviour; he did not pretend
to examine every action by the ftrict rules of reafon, but was always ready to make proper allow-
ances for the weaknefs of mankind. It was matter of furprize, that, notwithftanding his fprightly
wit, he never expofed by his raillery thofe vague,
incoherent, and noify difcourfes, thofe rafh cen-
fures, ignorant decifions, coarfe jefts, and all that
empty jingle of words which at Babylon went by
the name of Converfation. He had learned, in the
firft book of Zoroafter, that felf-love is a foot-ball
fwelled with wind, from which, when pierced, the
moft terrible tempefts iffue forth. Above all,

* The reader will at once perceive that this piece is a divert-
ing picture of human life, in which the author has ingenioufly
contrived to ridicule and ftigmatize the follies and vices that
abound in every ftation.

Zadig never boasted of his conquests among the women, nor affected to entertain a contemptible opinion of the fair sex. He was generous, and was never afraid of obliging the ungrateful; remembering the grand precept of Zoroaster, " When thou eatest, give to the dogs, should they even bite thee." He was as wise as it is possible for man to be; for he sought to live with the wife. Instructed in the sciences of the ancient Chaldeans, he understood the principles of natural philosophy, such as they were then supposed to be; and knew as much of metaphysics as hath ever been known in any age, that is, little or nothing at all. He was firmly persuaded, notwithstanding the new philosophy of the times, that the year consisted of three hundred and sixty-five days and six hours, and that the sun was in the center of the world. But when the principal magi told him, with a haughty and contemptuous air, that his sentiments were of a dangerous tendency, and that it was to be an enemy to the state to believe that the sun revolved round its own axis, and that the year had twelve months, he held his tongue with great modesty and meekness*.

Possessed as he was of great riches, and consequently of many friends, blessed with a good constitution, a handsome figure, a mind just and moderate, and a heart noble and sincere, he fondly imagined that he might easily be happy. He was going to be married to Semira, who, in point of beauty, birth, and fortune, was the first match in Babylon. He had a real and virtuous affection

---

* Alluding to the story of Galileo, who was imprisoned in the inquisition at Rome under Pope Urban VIII. for having taught the motion of the earth, and obliged to retract that doctrine.

for this lady, and she loved him with the most passionate fondness. The happy moment was almost arrived, that was to unite them for ever in the bands of wedlock, when happening to take a walk together towards one of the gates of Babylon, under the palm-trees that adorn the banks of the Euphrates, they saw some men approaching, armed with sabres and arrows. These were the attendants of young Orcan, the minister's nephew, whom his uncle's creatures had flattered into an opinion that he might do every thing with impunity. He had none of the graces nor virtues of Zadig; but thinking himself a much more accomplished man, he was enraged to find that the other was preferred before him. This jealousy, which was merely the effect of his vanity, made him imagine that he was desperately in love with Semira; and accordingly he resolved to carry her off. The ravishers seized her; in the violence of the outrage they wounded her, and made the blood flow from a person, the sight of which would have softened the tygers of mount Imaus. She pierced the heavens with her complaints. She cried out, " My dear husband! they tear me from the man I adore." Regardless of her own danger, she was only concerned for the fate of her dear Zadig, who, in the mean time, defended himself with all the strength that courage and love could inspire. Assisted only by two slaves, he put the ravishers to flight, and carried home Semira, insensible and bloody as she was. On opening her eyes, and beholding her deliverer, " O Zadig, (said she,) I loved thee formerly as my intended husband; I now love thee as the preserver of my honour and my life." Never was heart more deeply affected than that of Semira. Never did a more charming mouth express more moving

senti-

sentiments, in those glowing words inspired by a
sense of the greatest of all favours, and by the most
tender transports of a lawful passion. Her wound
was slight, and was soon cured. Zadig was more
dangerously wounded; an arrow had pierced him
near his eye, and penetrated to a considerable
depth. Semira wearied heaven with her prayers
for the recovery of her lover. Her eyes were constantly bathed in tears; she anxiously waited the
happy moment when those of Zadig should be able
to meet her's; but an abscess growing on the
wounded eye, gave every thing to fear. A messenger
was immediately dispatched to Memphis, for the
great physician Hermes, who came with a numerous retinue. He visited the patient, and declared
that he would lose his eye. He even foretold the
day and hour when this fatal event would happen.
" Had it been the right eye, (said he) I could easily
have cured it; but the wounds of the left eye are
incureable." All Babylon lamented the fate of
Zadig, and admired the profound knowledge of
Hermes. In two days the abscess broke of its own
accord, and Zadig was perfectly cured. Hermes
wrote a book, to prove that it ought not to have
been cured. Zadig did not read it: but, as soon
as he was able to go abroad, he went to pay a visit
to her in whom all his hopes of happiness were
centered, and for whose sake alone he wished to
have eyes. Semira had been in the country for
three days past. He learned on the road, that
that fine lady, having openly declared that she had
an unconquerable aversion to one-eyed men, had
the night before given her hand to Orcan. At
this news he fell speechless to the ground. His
sorrows brought him almost to the brink of the
grave. He was long indisposed; but reason at
last

laft got the better of his affliction; and the feverity of his fate ferved even to confole him.

" Since (faid he) I have fuffered fo much from the cruel caprice of a woman educated at court, I muft now think of marrying the daughter of a citizen." He pitched upon Azora, a lady of the greateft prudence, and of the beft family in town. He married her, and lived with her for three months in all the delights of the moft tender union. He only obferved that fhe had a little levity; and was too apt to find that thofe young men who had the moft handfome perfons were likewife poffeffed of moft wit and virtue.

The N O S E.

ONE morning Azora returned from a walk in a terrible paffion, and uttering the moft violent exclamations. " What aileth thee, (faid he) my dear fpoufe? what is it that can thus have difcompofed thee?" " Alas, (faid fhe) thou wouldeft be as much enraged as I am, hadft thou feen what I have juft beheld. I have been to comfort the young widow Cofrou, who, within thefe two days, hath raifed a tomb to her young hufband, near the rivulet that wafhes the fkir's of this meadow. She vowed to heaven, in the bitternefs of her grief, to remain at this tomb, while the water of the rivulet fhould continue to run near it." " Well, (faid Zadig) fhe is an excellent woman, and loved her hufband with the moft fincere affection." " Ah, (replied Azora) didft thou but know in what fhe was employed when I went to wait upon her !" " In what, pray, beautiful Azora? was fhe turning the courfe of the rivulet?" Azora broke out into

fuch

such long invectives, and loaded the young widow
with such bitter reproaches, that Zadig was far
from being pleased with this oftentation of virtue.

Zadig had a friend, named Cador, one of those
young men in whom his wife difcovered more probity and merit than in others. He made him his
confident, and fecured his fidelity as much as poffible, by a confiderable prefent. Azora having
pafled two days with a friend in the country, returned home on the third. The fervants told her, with
tears in their eyes, that her hufband died fuddenly
the night before: that they were afraid to fend
her an account of this mournful event; and that
they had juft been depofiting his corps in the tomb
of his anceftors, at the end of the garden. She
wept, fhe tore her hair, and fwore fhe would follow him to the grave. In the evening, Cador
begged leave to wait upon her, and joined his tears
with her's. Next day they wept lefs, and dined
together. Cador told her, that his friend had left
him the greateft part of his eftate; and that he
fhould think himfelf extremely happy in fharing
his fortune with her. The lady wept, fell into a
paffion, and at laft became more mild and gentle.
They fat longer at fupper than at dinner. They
now talked with greater confidence. Azora prait-
ed the deceafed; but owned that he had many fail-
ings from which Cador was free.

During fupper, Cador complained of a violent
pain in his fide. The lady, greatly concerned, and
eager to ferve him, caufed all kinds of effences to
be brought, with which fhe anointed him, to try if
fome of them might not poffibly eafe him of his
pain. She lamented that the great Hermes was
not ftill in Babylon. She even condefcended to
touch the fide in which Cador felt fuch exquifite
                                              pain.

pain. "Art thou fubject to this cruel diforder?" faid fhe to him with a compaffionate air. "It fometimes brings me (replied Cador) to the brink of the grave; and there is but one remedy that can give me relief, and that is, to apply to my fide the nofe of a man who is lately dead." "A ftrange remedy, indeed!" faid Azora. "Not more ftrange (replied he) than the fachels of Arnou againft the apoplexy*." This reafon, added to the great merit of the young man, at laft determined the lady. "After all, (fays fhe) when my hufband fhall crofs the bridge Tchinavar, in his journey to the other world, the angel Afrael will not refufe him a paffage, becaufe his nofe is a little fhorter in the fecond life than it was in the firft." She then took a razor, went to her hufband's tomb, bedewed it with her tears, and drew near to cut off the nofe of Zadig, whom fhe found extended at full length in the tomb. Zadig arofe, holding his nofe with one hand, and putting back the razor with the other, "Madam, (faid he) don't exclaim fo violently againft young Cofrou: the project of cutting off my nofe is equal to that of turning the courfe of a rivulet †."

The Dog and the Horse.

ZADIG found by experience, that the firft month of marriage, as it is written in the

---

* There was at that time a Babylonian named Arnou, who, according to his advertifements in the Gazettes, cured and prevented all kinds of apoplexies, by a little bag hung about the neck.

† One fees the author had in his eye the well-known fable of the Ephefian matron.

book of Zend, is the moon of honey, and that the second is the moon of wormwood. He was some time after obliged to repudiate Azora, who became too difficult to be pleafed; and he then fought for happinefs in the ftudy of nature. "No man (faid he) can be happier than a philofopher, who reads in this great book, which God hath placed before our eyes. The truths he difcovers are his own, he nourifhes and exalts his foul; he lives in peace; he fears nothing from men; and his tender fpoufe will not come to cut off his nofe."

Poffeffed of thefe ideas, he retired to a country-houfe on the banks of the Euphrates. There he did not employ himfelf in calculating how many inches of water flow in a fecond of time under the arches of a bridge, or whether there fell a cube-line of rain in the month of the Moufe more than in the month of the Sheep. He never dreamed of making filk of cobwebs, or porcelain of broken bottles; but he chiefly ftudied the properties of plants and animals; and foon acquired a fagacity that made him difcover a thoufand differences where other men fee nothing but uniformity.

One day, as he was walking near a little wood, he faw one of the queen's eunuchs running towards him, followed by feveral officers, who appeared to be in great perplexity, and who ran to and fro like men diftracted, eagerly fearching for fomething they had loft of great value. "Young man, (faid the firft eunuch) haft thou feen the queen's dog?" "It is a bitch, (replied Zadig with great modefty) and not a dog." "Thou art in the right," returned the firft eunuch. "It is a very fmall fhe-fpaniel, (added Zadig); fhe has lately whelped; fhe limps on the left fore-foot, and has very long ears." "Thou haft feen her," faid the
first

firft eunuch, quite out of breath. " No, (replied Zadig) I have not feen her, nor did I fo much as know that the queen had a bitch."

Exactly at the fame time, by one of the common freaks of fortune, the fineft horfe in the king's ftable had efcaped from the jockey in the plains of Babylon. The principal huntfman, and all the other officers, run after him with as much eager-nefs and anxiety as the firft eunuch had done after the bitch. The principal huntfman addreffed himfelf to Zadig, and afked him if he had not feen the king's horfe paffing by. " He is the fleeteft horfe in the king's ftable, (replied Zadig); he is five feet high, with very fmall hoofs, and a tail three feet and an half in length; the ftuds on his bit are gold of twenty-three carats, and his fhoes are filver of eleven penny-weights." " What way did he take? where is he?" demanded the chief huntf-man. " I have not feen him, (replied Zadig) and never heard talk of him before."

The principal huntfman and the firft eunuch never doubted but that Zadig had ftolen the king's horfe and the queen's bitch. They there-fore had him conducted before the affembly of the grand defterham, who condemned him to the knout, and to fpend the reft of his days in Siberia *. Hardly was the fentence paffed when the horfe and the bitch were both found. The judges were reduced to the difagreeable neceffity of reverfing

---

* Here the author feems to have forgot himfelf; otherwife he would never have dreamed of inflicting a Ruffian punifhment on a Babylonian criminal; far lefs of fending him in exile from the banks of the Euphrates into the deferts of Siberia.

their fentence; but they condemned Zadig to pay
four hundred ounces of gold, for having faid that
he had not feen what he had feen. This fine he
was obliged to pay; after which he was permit-
ed to plead his caufe before the counfel of the
grand defterham, when he fpoke to the following
effect:

" Ye ftars of juftice, abyfs of fciences, mirrors
of truth, who have the weight of lead, the hardnefs of iron, the fplendour of the diamond, and
many of the properties of gold: Since I am permitted to fpeak before this auguft affembly, I fwear to
you by Oromades, that I have never feen the
queen's refpectable bitch, nor the facred horfe of
the king of kings. The truth of the matter was
as follows: I was walking towards the little wood,
where I afterwards met the venerable eunuch, and
the moft illuftrious chief huntfman. I obferved
on the fand the traces of an animal, and could eafily perceive them to be thofe of a little dog. The
light and long furrows impreffed on little emi-
nences of fand between the marks of the paws,
plainly difcovered that it was a bitch, whofe dugs
were hanging down, and that therefore fhe muft
have whelped a few days before. Other traces of
a different kind, that always appeared to have gently brufhed the furface of the fand near the marks
of the fore-feet, fhewed me that fhe had very long
ears; and as I remarked that there was always a
flighter impreffion made on the fand by one foot
than by the other three, I found that the bitch of
our auguft queen was a little lame, if I may be allowed the expreffion.

" With regard to the horfe of the king of kings,
you will be pleafed to know, that walking in the
lanes of this wood, I obferved the marks of a
                                        horfe's

horfe's fhoes, all at equal diftances. This muft be a horfe, faid I to myfelf, that gallops excellently. The duft on the trees in a narrow road that was but feven feet wide was a little brufhed off, at the diftance of three feet and a half from the middle of the road. This horfe, faid I, has a tail three feet and a half long, which being whifked to the right and left, has fwept away the duft. I obferv, ed under the trees that formed an arbour five feet in height, that the leaves of the branches were newly fallen; from whence I inferred that the horfe had touched them, and that he muft therefore be five feet high. As to his bit, it muft be gold of twenty-three carats, for he had rubbed its boffes againft a ftone which I knew to be a touchftone, and which I have tried. In a word, from the marks made by his fhoes on flints of another kind, I concluded that he was fhod with filver eleven deniers fine." All the judges admired Zadig for his acute and profound difcernment. The news of this fpeech was carried even to the king and queen. Nothing was talked of but Zadig in the antichambers, the chambers, and the cabinet; and though many of the Magi were of opinion that he ought to be burnt as a forcerer, the king ordered his officers to reftore him the four hundred ounces of gold which he had been obliged to pay. The regifter, the attornies, and bailiffs, went to his houfe with great formality, to carry him back his four hundred ounces. They only retained three hundred and ninety-eight of them to defray the expen- ces of juftice ; and their fervants demanded their fees.

Zadig faw how extremely dangerous it fometimes is to appear too knowing, and therefore refolved,

that

that on the next occasion of the like nature he
would not tell what he had seen.

Such an opportunity soon offered. A prisoner
of state made his escape, and passed under the windows of Zadig's house. Zadig was examined and
made no answer. But it was proved that he had
looked at the prisoner from this window. For
this crime he was condemned to pay five hundred
ounces of gold; and, according to the polite custom of Babylon, he thanked his judges for their indulgence. " Great God! said he to himself, what
a misfortune it is to walk in a wood through which
the queen's bitch or the king's horse have passed!
how dangerous to look out at a window! and how
difficult to be happy in this life!"

The Envious Man.

ZADIG resolved to comfort himself by philosophy and friendship, for the evils he had suffered from fortune. He had in the suburbs of Babylon a house elegantly furnished, in which he af-
sembled all the arts and all the pleasures worthy the
pursuit of a gentleman. In the morning his library was open to the learned. In the evening, his
table was surrounded by good company. But he
soon found what very dangerous guests these men
of letters are. A warm dispute arose on one of
Zoroaster's laws, which forbids the eating of a
griffin. " Why, said some of them, prohibit the
eating of a griffin, if there is no such animal in nature?" " There must necessarily be such an animal, (said the others,) since Zoroaster forbids
us to eat it." Zadig would fain have reconciled them by saying, " If there are no griffins,
                                                    we

we cannot poffibly eat them; and thus either way we fhall obey Zoroafter."

A learned man, who had compofed thirteen volumes on the properties of the griffin, and was befides the chief theurgite, hafted away to accufe Zadig before one of the principal Magi, named Yebor, the greateft blockhead, and therefore the greateft fanatick among the Chaldeans. This man would have empaled Zadig to do honour to the fun, and would then have recited the breviary of Zoroafter with greater fatisfaction. The friend Cador (a friend is better than a hundred priefts) went to Yebor, and faid to him, "Long live the fun and the griffins; beware of punifhing Zadig; he is a faint; he has griffins in his inner court, and does not eat them; and his accufer is an heretic, who dares to maintain that rabbits have cloven feet, and are not unclean." "Well, (faid Yebor, fhaking his bald pate) we muft empale Zadig for having thought contemptuoufly of griffins, and the other for having fpoke difrefpectfully of rabbits." Cador hufhed up the affair by means of a maid of honour who had bore him a child, and who had great intereft in the college of the Magi. No body was empaled. This lenity occafioned a great murmuring among fome of the doctors, who from thence predicted the fall of Babylon *. "Upon what does happinefs depend, (faid Zadig) I am perfecuted by every thing in the world, even on account of beings that have no exiftence." He curfed thofe men of learning, and refolved for the future to live with none but good company.

---

* This is a fevere fatire upon thofe cruel bigots who perfecute all fuch as prefume to differ from eftablifhed opinions, though purely fpeculative.

He

He affembled at his houfe the moft worthy men,
and the moft beautiful ladies of Babylon. He
gave them delicious fuppers, often preceded by
concerts of mufick, and always animated by polite
converfation, from which he knew how to banifh
that affectation of wit, which is the fureft method
of preventing it entirely, and of fpoiling the pleafure of the moft agreeable fociety. Neither the
choice of his friends, nor that of the difhes, was
made by vanity; for in every thing he preferred the
fubftance to the fhadow; and by thefe means he
procured that real refpect to which he did not afpire.

Oppofite to his houfe lived one Arimazes, a
man whofe deformed countenance was but a faint
picture of his ftill more deformed mind. His heart
was a mixture of malice, pride, and envy. Having never been able to fucceed in any of his under-
takings, he revenged himfelf on all around him, by
loading them with the blackeft calumnies. Rich
as he was, he found it difficult to procure a fet of
flatterers. The rattling of the chariots that entered
Zadig's court in the evening filled him with uneafinefs; the found of his praifes enraged him ftill
more. He fometimes went to Zadig's houfe, and
fat down at table without being defired ; where he
fpoiled all the pleafure of the company, as the har-
pies are faid to infect the viands they touch. It
happened that one day he took it in his head to
give an entertainment to a lady, who, inftead of
accepting it, went to fup with Zadig. At another
time, as he was talking with Zadig at Court, a Minifter of State came up to them, and invited Zadig to
fupper, without inviting Arimazes. The moft im-
placable hatred has feldom a more folid foundation.
This man, who in Babylon was called the *Envious*,
refolved to ruin Zadig, becaufe he was called the
Happy.

Happy. " The opportunity of doing mischief occurs a hundred times in a day, and that of doing good but once a year," as sayeth the wise Zoroaster.

The envious man went to see Zadig, who was walking in his garden with two friends and a lady, to whom he said many gallant things, without any other intention than that of saying them. The conversation turned upon a war which the king had just brought to a happy conclusion against the prince of Hircania, his vassal. Zadig, who had signalized his courage in this short war, bestowed great praises on the king, but greater still on the lady. He took out his pocket-book, and wrote four lines extempore, which he gave to this amiable person to read. His friends begged they might see them; but modesty, or rather a well-regulated self-love, would not allow him to grant their request. He knew that extemporary verses are never approved by any but by the person in whose honour they are written. He therefore tore in two the leaf on which he had wrote them, and threw both the pieces into a thicket of rose bushes where the rest of the company sought for them in vain. A slight shower falling soon after, obliged them to return to the house. The envious man, who staid in the garden, continued to search, till at last he found a piece of the leaf. It had been torn in such a manner, that each half of a line formed a complete sense, and even a verse of a shorter measure; but what was still more surprising, these short verses were found to contain the most injurious reflections on the king; they ran thus:

> To flagrant crimes
> His Crown he owes,

To

To peaceful times
The worst of foes.

The envious man was now happy for the first time
of his life.   He had it in his power to ruin a person of virtue and merit.   Filled with this fiend-
like joy, he found means to convey to the king the
satire written by the hand of Zadig, who, together
with the lady and his two friends, was thrown into
prison.

His trial was soon finished, without his being
permitted to speak for himself.   As he was going to receive his sentence, the envious man threw
himself in his way, and told him with a loud voice,
that his verses were good for nothing.   Zadig did
not value himself on being a good poet; but it filled him with inexpressible concern to find that he
was condemned for high treason; and that the fair
lady and his two friends were confined in prison
for a crime of which they were not guilty.   He
was not allowed to speak because his writing spoke
for him.   Such was the law of Babylon.   Accordingly he was conducted to the place of execution,
through an immense crowd of spectators, who durst
not venture to express their pity for him, but who
carefully examined his countenance, to see if he
died with a good grace.   His relations alone were
inconsolable; for they could not succeed to his
estate.   Three fourths of his wealth were confiscated
into the king's treasury, and the other fourth was
given to the envious man.

Just as he was preparing for death, the king's
parrot flew from its cage, and alighted on a rose
bush in Zadig's garden.   A peach had been driven
thither by the wind from a neighbouring tree, and
had

had fallen on a piece of the written leaf of the pocket-book to which it ftuck. The bird carried off the peach and the paper, and laid them on the king's knee. The king took up the paper with great eagernefs, and read the words, which formed no fenfe, and feemed to be the endings of verfes. He loved poetry; and there is always fome mercy to be expected from a prince of that difpofition. The adventure of the parrot fet him a think-ing.

The queen, who remembered what had been writ-ten on the piece of Zadig's pocket-book, caufed it to be brought. They compared the two pieces to-gether, and found them to tally exactly: they then read the verfes as Zadig had wrote them.

Tyrants are prone to flagrant Crimes;
To Clemency his Crown he owes;
To Concord and to peaceful Times,
Love only is the worft of Foes.

The king gave immediate orders that Zadig fhould be brought before him, and that his two friends and the lady fhould be fet at liberty. Zadig fell proftrate on the ground before the king and queen; humbly begged their pardon for having made fuch bad verfes, and fpoke with fo much propriety, wit, and good fenfe, that their majefties defired they might fee him again. He did himfelf that honour, and infinuated himfelf ftill farther into their good graces. They gave him all the wealth of the en-vious man; but Zadig reftored him back the whole of it; and this inftance of generofity gave no other pleafure to the envious man than that of having preferved his eftate. The king's efteem

for Zadig increafed every day. He admitted him
into all his parties of pleafure, and confulted him
in all affairs of ftate. From that time the queen
began to regard him with an eye of tendernefs,
that might one day prove dangerous to herfelf, to
the king her auguft confort, to Zadig, and to the
kingdom in general. Zadig now began to think
that happinefs was not fo unattainable as he had formerly imagined.

The GENEROUS.

THE time was now arrived for celebrating a
grand feftival, which returned every five
years. It was a cuftom in Babylon folemnly to
declare, at the end of every five years, which of
the citizens had performed the moft generous action. The grandees and the magi were the judges.
The firft fatrape, who was charged with the government of the city, publifhed the moft noble actions
that had paffed under his adminiftration. The
competition was decided by votes; and the king
pronounced the fentence. People came to this fo-
lemnity from the extremities of the earth. The
conqueror received from the monarch's hands a
golden cup adorned with precious ftones, his majefty at the fame time making him this compliment:
" Receive this reward of thy generofity; and may
the gods grant me many fubjects like to thee."

This memorable day being come, the king appeared on his throne, furrounded by the grandees,
the magi, and the deputies of all the nations that
came

came to thefe games, where glory was acquired not by the fwiftnefs of horfes, nor by ftrength of body, but by virtue. The firft fatrape recited, with an audible voice, fuch actions as might entitle the authors of them to this invaluable prize. He did not mention the greathefs of foul with which Zadig had reftored the envious man his fortune, becaufe it was not judged to be an action worthy of difputing the prize.

He firft prefented a judge, who having made a citizen lofe a confiderable caufe by a miftake, for which, after all, he was not accountable, had given him the whole of his own eftate, which was juft equal to what the other had loft.

He next produced a young man, who being defperately in love with a lady whom he was going to marry, had yielded her up to his friend, whofe paffion for her had almoft brought him to the brink of the grave, and at the fame time had given him the lady's fortune.

He afterwards produced a foldier, who, in the wars of Hircania, had given a ftill more noble inftance of generofity. A party of the enemy having feized his miftrefs, he fought in her defence with great intrepidity. At that very inftant he was informed that another party, at the diftance of a few paces, were carrying off his mother; he therefore left his miftrefs with tears in his eyes, and flew to the affiftance of his mother. At laft, he returned to the dear object of his love, and found her expiring. He was juft going to plunge his fword in his own bofom; but his mother remonftrating againft fuch a defperate deed, and telling him that he was the only fupport of her life, he had the courage to endure to live.

The judges were inclined to give the prize to

the

the foldier. But the king took up the difcourfe
and faid, " The action of the foldier, and thofe of
the other two, are doubtlefs very great, but they
have nothing in them furprifing. Yefterday Zadig
performed an action that filled me with wonder.
I had a few days before difgraced Coreb, my
minifter and favourite. I complained of him in the
moft violent and bitter terms ; all my courtiers affured me that I was too gentle, and feemed to vie
with each other in fpeaking ill of Coreb. I afked
Zadig what he thought of him, and he had the courage to commend him. I have read in our hiftories of many people who have atoned for an error
by the furrender of their fortune ; who have refigned a miftrefs; or preferred a mother to the object of their affection ; but never before did I hear
of a courtier who fpoke favourably of a difgraced
minifter, that laboured under the difpleafure of his
fovereign. I give to each of thofe whofe generous
actions have been now recited, twenty thoufand
pieces of gold ; but the cup I give to Zadig."

" May it pleafe your majefty, (faid Zadig,) thyfelf alone deferveft the cup; thou haft performed
an action of all others the moft uncommon and
meritorious, fince, notwithftanding thy being a
powerful king, thou waft not offended at thy flave,
when he prefumed to oppofe thy paffion." The
king and Zadig were equally the object of admiration. The judge who had given his eftate to his
client ; the lover who had refigned his miftrefs to
his friend ; and the foldier, who had preferred the
fafety of his mother to that of his miftrefs, received
the king's prefents, and faw their names inrolled in
the catalogue of generous men. Zadig had the
cup, and the king acquired the reputation of a
good prince, which he did not long enjoy. The
day

day was celebrated by feafts that lafted longer than the law enjoined; and the memory of it is ftill preferved in Afia. Zadig faid, " Now I am happy at laft ;" but he found himfelf fatally deceived.

The MINISTER.

THE king had loft his firft minifter, and chofe Zadig to fupply his place. All the ladies in Babylon applauded the choice ; for fince the foundation of the empire there had never been fuch a young minifter. But all the courtiers were filled with jealoufy and vexation. The envious man, in particular, was troubled with a fpitting of blood, and a prodigious inflammation in his nofe. Zadig having thanked the king and queen for their goodnefs, went likewife to thank the parrot.. " Beautiful bird, (faid he) 'tis thou that haft faved my life, and made me firft minifter. The queen's bitch and the king's horfe did me a great deal of mifchief ; but thou haft done me much good. Upon fuch flender threads as thefe do the fates of mortals hang ! but (added he) this happinefs perhaps will vanifh very foon." " Soon," replied the parrot. Zadig was fomewhat ftartled at this word. But as he was a good natural philofopher, and did not believe parrots to be prophets, he quickly recovered his fpirits, and refolved to execute his duty to the beft of his power.

He made every one feel the facred authority of the laws, but no one felt the weight of his dignity. He never checked the deliberations of the divan ; and every vizier might give his opinion without the fear of incurring the minifter's difpleafure. When he gave judgment, it was not he that gave
it,

it, it was the law ; the rigour of which, however, whenever it was too fevere, he always took care to foften; and when laws were wanting, the equity of his decifions was fuch as might eafily have made them pafs for thofe of Zoroafter.

It is to him that the nations are indebted for this grand principle, to wit, that it is better to run the rifk of fparing the guilty than to condemn the innocent. He imagined that laws were made as well to fecure the people from the fuffering of injuries as to reftrain them from the commiffion of crimes. His chief talent confifted in difcovering the truth, which all men feek to obfcure. This great talent he put in practice from the very beginning of his adminiftration. A famous merchant of Babylon, who died in the Indies, divided his eftate equally between his two fons, after having difpofed of their fifter in marriage, and left a prefent of thirty thoufand pieces of gold to that fon who fhould be found to have loved him beft. The eldeft raifed a tomb to his memory; the youngeft increafed his fifter's portion, by giving her a part of his inheritance. Every one faid that the eldeft fon loved his father beft, and the youngeft his fifter ; and that the thirty thoufand pieces belonged to the eldeft.

Zadig fent for both of them, the one after the other. To the eldeft he faid, " Thy father is not dead ; he is recovered of his laft illnefs, and is returning to Babylon." " God be praifed, (replied the young man,) but his tomb coft me a confiderable fum." Zadig afterwards faid the fame thing to the youngeft. " God be praifed, (faid he) I will go and reftore to my father all that I have ; but I could wifh that he would leave my fifter what I have given her." " Thou fhalt reftore nothing,

thing, replied Zadig, and thou fhalt have the thirty thoufand pieces, for thou art the fon who loves his father beft."

A young lady poffeffed of a handfome fortune had given a promife of marriage to two magi; and after having, for fome months, received the inftructions of both, fhe, proved with child. They were both defirous of marrying her. " I will take for my hufband, faid fhe, the man who has put me in a condition to give a fubject to the ftate." " I am the man that has done the work," faid the one. " I am the man that has done it," faid the other. " Well, replied the lady, I will acknowledge for the infant's father him that can give it the beft education." The lady was delivered of a fon. The two magi contended who fhould bring him up, and the caufe was carried before Zadig. Zadig fummoned the two magi to attend him. " What will you teach your pupil?" faid he to the firft. " I will teach him, (faid the doctor) the eight parts of fpeech, logick, aftrology, pneumatics, what is meant by fubftance and accident, abftract and concrete, the doctrine of the monades, and the pre-eftablifhed harmony." " For my part, (faid the fecond) I will endeavour to give him a fenfe of juftice, and to make him worthy the friendfhip of good men." Zadig then cried, " Whether thou art his father or not, thou fhalt have his mother.

The Disputes and the Audiences.

IN this manner he daily difcovered the fubtilty of his genius and the goodnefs of his heart. The people at once admired and loved him. He paffed for the happieft man in the world. The
whole

whole empire refounded with his name. All the
ladies ogled him. All the men praifed him for his
juftice. The learned regarded him as an oracle;
and even the priefts confeffed that he knew more
than the old archmagi Yebor. They were now
fo far from profecuting him on account of the griffins, that they believed nothing but what he thought
credible.

There had reigned in Babylon, for the fpace of
fifteen hundred years, a violent conteft that had
divided the empire into two fects. The one pretended that they ought to enter the temple of Mitra with the left foot foremoft * ; the other held
this cuftom in deteftation, and always entered with
the right foot firft. The people waited with great
impatience for the day on which the folemn feaft
of the facred fire was to be celebrated, to fee which
fect Zadig would favour. All the world had their
eyes fixed on his two feet, and the whole city was
in the utmoft fufpence and perturbation. Zadig
jumped into the temple with his feet joined together; and afterwards proved, in an eloquent difcourfe, that the Sovereign of heaven and earth, who
accepteth not the perfons of men, makes no diftinction between the right and the left foot. The
envious man and his wife alledged that his difcourfe was not figurative enough, and that he did
not make the rocks and mountains to dance with
fufficient agility. " He is dry, (faid they) and
void of genius: he does not make the fea to fly,
and ftars to fall, nor the fun to melt like wax : he
has not the true oriental ftile." Zadig contented
himfelf with having the ftile of reafon. All the

* This is probably a glance at the difputes about Janfenifm,
which, though in themfelves infignificant, have divided France
into two inveterate factions.

world favoured him, not becaufe he was in the right road, or followed the dictates of reafon, or was a man of real merit, but becaufe he was prime vizier.

He terminated with the fame happy addrefs the grand difference between the white and the black magi. The former maintained that it was the height of impiety to pray to God with the face turned towards the eaft in winter; the latter affferted that God abhorred the prayers of thofe who turned towards the weft in fummer. Zadig decreed that every man fhould be allowed to turn as he pleafed.

Thus he found out the happy fecret of finifhing all affairs, whether of a private or public nature, in the morning. The reft of the day he employed in fuperintending and promoting the embellifhments of Babylon. He exhibited tragedies that drew tears from the eyes of the fpectators, and comedies that fhook their fides with laughter; a cuftom which had long been difufed, and which his good tafte now induced him to revive. He never affected to be more knowing in the polite arts than the artifts themfelves; he encouraged them by rewards and honours, and was never jealous of their talents. In the evening the king was highly entertained with his converfation, and the queen ftill more. "Great minifter!" faid the king. "Amiable minifter!" faid the queen; and both of them added, "it would have been a great lofs to the ftate had fuch a man been hanged."

Never was man in power obliged to give fo many audiences to the ladies. Moft of them came to confult him about——no bufinefs at all, that fo they might have fome bufinefs with him. The wife of the envious man was among the firft. She fwore to him by Mitra, by Zenda Vefta, and by

the facred fire, that fhe detefted her hufband's conduct: fhe then told him in confidence that he was a
jealous brutal wretch; and gave him to underftand
that heaven punifhed him for his crimes, by re-
fufing him the precious effects of the facred fire,
by which alone man can be rendered like the gods.
At laft fhe concluded by dropping her garter. Zadig took it up with his ufual politenefs, but did
not tie it about the lady's leg; and this flight
fault, if it may be called a fault, was the caufe of
the moft terrible misfortunes. Zadig never thought
of it more; but the lady thought of it with great
attention.

    Never a day paffed without feveral vifits from the
ladies. The fecret annals of Babylon pretend
that he once yielded to the temptation, but that
he was furprifed to find that he enjoyed his
miftrefs without pleafure, and embraced her without diftraction. The lady to whom he gave, almoft without being fenfible of it, thefe marks of
his favour, was a maid of honour to queen Aftarte.
This tender Babylonian faid to herfelf by way of
comfort, " This man muft have his head filled
with a prodigious heap of bufinefs, fince even in
making love he cannot avoid thinking on public
affairs." Zadig happened, at the very inftant when
moft people fay nothing at all, and others only
pronounce a few facred words, to cry out, " The
queen." The Babylonian thought that he was at
laft happily come to himfelf, and that he faid, "My
queen." But Zadig, who was always too abfent,
pronounced the name of Aftarte. The lady, who
in this happy fituation interpreted every thing in
her own favour, imagined that he meant to fay,
" Thou art more beautiful than queen Aftarte."
After receiving fome handfome prefents, fhe left
the

the feraglio of Zadig, and went to relate her adventure to the envious woman, who was her intimate friend, and who was greatly piqued at the
preference given to the other. " He would not
fo much as deign, faid fhe, to tie this garter about
my leg, and I am therefore refolved never to wear
it more." " O ho, faid the happy lady to the
envious one, your garters are the fame with the
queen's! do you buy them from the fame weaver?"
This hint fet the envious lady a-thinking; fhe
made no reply, but went to confult with her envious hufband.

Meanwhile Zadig perceived that his thoughts
were always diftracted, as well when he gave audience as when he fat in judgment. He did not
know to what to attribute this abfence of mind;
and that was his only forrow.

He had a dream, in which he imagined that he
laid himfelf down upon a heap of dry herbs, among
which there were many prickly ones that gave him
great uneafinefs, and that he afterwards repofed
himfelf on a foft bed of rofes, from which there
fprung a ferpent that wounded him to the heart
with its fharp and venomed tongue. " Alas, faid
he, I have long lain on thefe dry and prickly herbs,
I am now on the bed of rofes; but what fhall be
the ferpent ?"

JEALOUSY.

ZADIG's calamities fprung even from his happinefs, and efpecially from his merit. He
every day converfed with the king, and Aftarte his
auguft confort. The charms of his converfation
were greatly heightened by that defire of pleafing,

which is to the mind what drefs is to beauty. His youth and graceful appearance infenfibly made an impreffion on Aftarte, which fhe did not at firft perceive. Her paffion grew and flourifhed in the bofom of innocence. Without fear or fcruple, fhe indulged the pleafing fatisfaction of feeing and hearing a man, who was fo dear to her hufband, and to the empire in general. She was continually praifing him to the king. She talked of him to her women, who were always fure to improve on her praifes. And thus every thing contributed to pierce her heart with a dart, o which fhe did not feem to be fenfible. She made feveral prefents to Zadig, which difcovered a greater fpirit of gallantry than fhe imagined. She intended to fpeak to him only as a queen fatisfied with his fervices; and her expreffions were fometimes thofe of a woman in love.

Aftarte was much more beautiful than that Semira who had fuch a ftrong averfion to one-eyed men, or that other woman who had refolved to cut off her hufband's nofe. Her unreferved familiarity, her tender expreffions, at which fhe began to blufh; and her eyes, which, though fhe endeavoured to divert them to other objects, were always fixed upon his, infpired Zadig with a paffion that filled him with aftonifhment. He ftruggled hard to get the better of it. He called to his aid the precepts of philofophy, which had always ftood him in ftead; but from thence, though he could derive the light of knowledge, he could procure no remedy to cure the diforders of his love-fick-heart. Duty, gratitude, and violated majefty, prefented themfelves to his mind, as fo many avenging gods. He ftruggled; he conquered; but this victory, which he was obliged to purchafe afrefh every mo-

ment,

ment, coft him many fighs and tears. He no
longer dared to fpeak to the queen with that fweet
and charming familiarity which had been fo agreeable to them both. His countenance was covered
with a cloud. His converfation was conftrained
and incoherent. His eyes were fixed on the ground ;
and when, in fpite of all his endeavours to the contrary, they encountered thofe of the queen, they
found them bathed in tears, and darting arrows of
flame. They feemed to fay, We adore each other,
and yet are afraid to love : we both burn with a
fire which we both condemn.

Zadig left the royal prefence full of perplexity
and defpair, and having his heart oppreffed with a
burden which he was no longer able to bear. In
the violence of his perturbation he involuntarily
betrayed the fecret to his friend Cador, in the fame
manner as a man, who, having long fupported the
fits of a cruel difeafe, difcovers his pain by a cry
extorted from him by a more fevere fit, and by the
cold fweat that covers his brow.

" I have already difcovered, faid Cador, the fentiments which thou wouldeft fain conceal from
thyfelf. The fymptoms by which the paffions fhew
themfelves are certain and infallible. Judge, my
dear Zadig, fince I have read thy heart, whether
the king will not difcover fomething in it that may
give him offence. He has no other fault but that
of being the moft jealous man in the world. Thou
canft refift the violence of thy paffion with greater
fortitude than the queen, becaufe thou art a philofopher, and becaufe thou art Zadig. Aftarte is a
woman: fhe fuffers her eyes to fpeak with fo much
the more imprudence, as fhe does not as yet think
herfelf guilty. Confcious of her own innocence,
fhe unhappily neglects thofe external appearances
which

which are so necessary. I shall tremble for her so long as she has nothing wherewithal to reproach herself. Were ye both of one mind, ye might easily deceive the whole world. A growing passion which we endeavour to suppress, discovers itself in spite of all our efforts to the contrary; but love, when gratified, is easily concealed." Zadig trembled at the proposal of betraying the king, his benefactor; and never was he more faithful to his prince, than when guilty of an involuntary crime against him. Meanwhile, the queen mentioned the name of Zadig so frequently, and with such a blushing and downcast look; she was sometimes so lively, and sometimes so perplexed, when she spoke to him in the king's presence, and was seized with such a deep thoughtfulness at his going away, that the king began to be troubled. He believed all that he saw, and imagined all that he did not see. He particularly remarked, that his wife's shoes were blue, and that Zadig's shoes were blue; that his wife's ribbands were yellow; and that Zadig's bonnet was yellow; and these were terrible symptoms to a prince of so much delicacy. In his jealous mind suspicions were turned into certainty.

All the slaves of kings and queens are so many spies over their hearts. They soon observed that Astarte was tender, and that Moabdar was jealous. The envious man persuaded his wife to send the king her garter, which resembled those of the queen; and to complete the misfortune, this garter was blue. The monarch now thought of nothing but in what manner be might best execute his vengeance. He one night resolved to poison the queen, and in the morning to put Zadig to death by the bowstring. The orders were given to a merciless eunuch, who commonly executed his acts of vengeance.

geance. There happened at that time to be in the king's chamber a little dwarf, who, tho' dumb, was not deaf. He was allowed, on account of his infignificance, to go wherever he pleafed; and, as a domeftic animal, was a witnefs of what paffed in the moft profound fecrecy. This little mute was ftrongly attached to the queen and Zadig. With equal horror and furprife he heard the cruel orders given. But how prevent the fatal fentence that in a few hours was to be carried into execution. He could not write, but he could paint; and excelled particularly in drawing a ftriking refemblance. He employed a part of the night in fketching out with his pencil what he meant to impart to the queen. The piece reprefented the king in one corner, boiling with rage, and giving orders to the eunuch; a blue bowftring, and a bowl on a table, with blue garters and yellow ribbands; the queen in the middle of the picture, expiring in the arms of her woman, and Zadig ftrangled at her feet. The horizon reprefented a rifing fun, to exprefs that this fhocking execution was to be performed in the morning. As foon as he had finifhed the picture, he ran to one of Aftarte's women, awaked her, and made her underftand that fhe muft immediately carry it to the queen.

At midnight a meffenger knocks at Zadig's door, awakes him, and gives him a note from the queen. He doubts whether it is not a dream; and opens the letter with a trembling hand. But how great was his furprife! and who can exprefs the confternation and defpair into which he was thrown upon reading thefe words: " Fly, this inftant, or thou art a dead man. Fly, Zadig, I conjure thee by our mutual love and my yellow ribbands. I have not been

been guilty, but I find that I muſt die like a criminal."

Zadig was hardly able to ſpeak. He ſent for Cador, and, without uttering a word, gave him the note. Cador forced him to obey, and forthwith to take the road to Memphis. "Shouldeſt thou dare (ſaid he) to go in ſearch of the queen, thou wilt haſten her death. Shouldeſt thou ſpeak to the king, thou wilt infallibly ruin her. I will take upon me the charge of her deſtiny; follow thy own. I will ſpread a report that thou haſt taken the road to India. I will ſoon follow thee, and inform thee of all that ſhall have paſſed in Babylon." At that inſtant, Cador cauſed two of the ſwifteſt dromedaries to be brought to a private gate of the palace. Upon one of theſe he mounted Zadig, whom he was obliged to carry to the door, and who was ready to expire with grief. He was accompanied by a ſingle domeſtic; and Cador, plunged in ſorrow and aſtoniſhment, ſoon loſt ſight of his friend.

This illuſtrious fugitive arriving on the ſide of a hill, from whence he could take a view of Babylon, turned his eyes towards the queen's palace, and fainted away at the ſight; nor did he recover his ſenſes but to ſhed a torrent of tears, and to wiſh for death. At length, after his thoughts had been long engroſſed in lamenting the unhappy fate of the lovelieſt woman and the greateſt queen in the world, he for a moment turned his views on himſelf, and cried, "What then is human life? O virtue, how haſt thou ſerved me! Two women have baſely deceived me; and now a third, who is innocent, and more beautiful than both the others, is going to be put to death! Whatever good I have done hath been to me a continual ſource of cala-mity

mity and affliction ; and I have only been raifed
to the height of grandeur, to be tumbled down the
moft horrid precipice of misfortune." Filled with
thefe gloomy reflections, his eyes overfpread with
the veil of grief, his countenance covered with the
palenefs of death, and his foul plunged in an abyfs
of the blackeft defpair, he continued his journey towards Egypt.

The WOMAN beaten.

ZADIG directed his courfe by the ftars. The
conftellation of Orion, and the fplendid Dog-
ftar, guided his fteps towards the pole of Cano-
pæa.   He admired thofe vaft globes of light, which
appear to our eyes but as fo many little fparks,
while the earth, which in reality is only an imperceptible point in nature, appears to our fond ima-
ginations as fomething fo grand and noble.   He
then reprefented to himfelf the human fpecies, as it
really is, as a parcel of infects devouring one another on a little atom of clay.   This true image
feemed to annihilate his misfortunes, by making
him fenfible of the nothingnefs of his own being,
and of that of Babylon.   His foul launched out
into infinity, and detached from the fenfes, contem-
plated the immutable order of the univerfe.   But
when afterwards, returning to himfelf, and entering into his own heart, he confidered that Aftarte
had perhaps died for him, the univerfe vanifhed
from his fight, and he beheld nothing in the whole
compafs of nature but Aftarte expiring, and Zadig
unhappy.   While he thus alternately gave up his
mind to this flux and reflux of fublime philofophy

and intolerable grief, he advanced towards the frontiers of Egypt; and his faithful domeftic was already in the firft village, in fearch of a lodging. Meanwhile, as Zadig was walking towards the gardens that fkirted the village, he faw, at a fmall diftance from the highway, a woman bathed in tears, and calling heaven and earth to her affiftance, and a man in a furious paffion, purfuing her. This madman had already overtaken the woman, who embraced his knees, notwithftanding which he loaded her with blows and reproaches. Zadig judged by the frantic behaviour of the Egyptian, and by the repeated pardons which the lady afked him, that the one was jealous, and the other unfaithful. But when he furveyed the woman more narrowly, and found her to be a lady of exquifite beauty, and even to have a ftrong refemblance to the unhappy Aftarte, he felt himfelf infpired with compaffion for her, and horror towards the Egyptian. " Affift me, (cried fhe to Zadig with the deepeft fighs) deliver me from the hands of the moft barbarous man in the world; fave my life." Moved by thefe pitiful cries, Zadig ran and threw himfelf between her and the barbarian. As he had fome knowledge of the Egyptian language, he addreffed him in that tongue: " If (faid he) thou haft any humanity, I conjure thee to pay fome regard to her beauty and weaknefs. How canft thou behave in this outrageous manner to one of the mafter-pieces of nature, who lies at thy feet, and has no defence but her tears? " Ah, ah! (replied the madman) thou art likewife in love with her; I muft be revenged on thee too." So faying, he left the lady, whom he had hitherto held with his hand twifted in her hair, and taking his lance, attempted to ftab the ftranger. Zadig, who was

in

in cold blood, eafily eluded the blow aimed by the
frantic Egyptian.   He feized the lance near the iron
with which it was armed.   The Egyptian ftrove to
draw it back; Zadig to wreft it from the Egyptian ;
and in the ftruggle it was broke in two.   The
Egyptian draws his fword; Zadig does the fame.
They attack each other.   The former gives a hundred blows at random ; the latter wards them off
with great dexterity.   The lady, feated on a turf,
re-adjufts her head-drefs, and looks at the combatants.   The Egyptian excelled in ftrength; Zadig
in addrefs.   The one fought like a man whofe arm
was directed by his judgment; the other like a madman, whofe blind rage made him deal his blows
at random.   Zadig clofes with him, and difarms
him ; and while the Egyptian, now become more
furious, endeavours to throw himfelf upon him, he
feizes him, preffes him clofe, and throws him down;
and then holding his fword to his breaft, offers
him his life.   The Egyptian, frantic with rage,
draws his poniard, and wounds Zadig at the very
inftant that the conqueror was granting a pardon.
Zadig, provoked at fuch a brutal behaviour, plunged his fword in the bofom of the Egyptian, who
giving a horrible fhriek and a violent ftruggle, inftantly expired.   Zadig then approached the lady,
and faid to her with a gentle tone, " He hath forced me to kill him ; I have avenged thy caufe;
thou art now delivered from the moft violent man
I ever faw ; what further, madam, wouldeft thou
have me to do for thee?" " Die, villain, (replied
fhe) die; thou haft killed my lover; O that
I were able to tear out thy heart!"   " Why
truly, madam, (faid Zadig) thou hadft a ftrange
kind of a man for a lover ; he beat thee with
all his might, and would have killed me, be-

caufe thou hadft entreated me to give thee affiftance." " I wifh he were beating me ftill, (replied the lady, with tears and lamentation;) I well
deferved it; for I had given him caufe to be jealous. Would to heaven that he was now beating
me, and that thou waft in his place." Zadig, ftruck
with furprife, and inflamed with a higher degree of
refentment than he had ever felt before, faid,
" Beautiful as thou art, madam, thou deferveft
that I fhould beat thee in my turn for thy perverfe
and impertinent behaviour; but I fhall not give myfelf the trouble." So faying, he remounted his
camel, and advanced towards the town. He had
proceeded but a few fteps, when he turned back at
the noife of four Babylonian couriers, who came
riding at full gallop. One of them, upon feeing
the woman, cried, " It is the very fame; fhe refembles the defcription that was given us." They
gave themfelves no concern about the dead Egyptian,
but inftantly feized the lady. She called out to
Zadig; " Help me once more, generous ftranger;
I afk pardon for having complained of thy conduct;
deliver me again, and I will be thine for ever."
Zadig was no longer in the humour of fighting
for her. " Apply to another, (faid he) thou fhalt not
again enfnare me by thy wiles." Befides, he was
wounded; his blood was ftill flowing, and he himfelf had need of affiftance: and the fight of four
Babylonians, probably fent by king Moabdar, filled
him with apprehenfion. He therefore haftened
toward the village, unable to comprehend why
four Babylonian couriers fhould come to feize this
Egyptian woman, but ftill more aftonifhed at the
lady's behaviour.

SLAVERY

SLAVERY.

AS he entered the Egyptian village, he saw himself furrounded by the people. Every one faid, " This is the man that carried off the beautiful Miffouf, and affaffinated Clitofis." " Gentlemen, (faid he) God preferve me from carrying off your beautiful Miffouf ; fhe is too capricious for me : and with regard to Clitofis, I did not affaffinate him ; I only fought with him in my own defence. He endeavoured to kill me, becaufe I humbly interceded for the beautiful Miffouf, whom he beat moft unmercifully. I am a ftranger, come to feek refuge in Egypt ; and it is not likely, that in coming to implore your protection, I fhould begin by carrying off a woman, and affaffinating a man."

The Egyptians were then juft and humane. The people conducted Zadig to the town-houfe. They firft of all ordered his wound to be dreffed, and then examined him and his fervant apart, in order to difcover the truth. They found that Zadig was not an affaffin ; but as he was guilty of having killed a man, the law condemned him to be a flave. His two camels were fold for the benefit of the town : all the gold he had brought with him was diftributed among the inhabitants ; and his perfon, as well as that of the companion of his journey, was expofed to fale in the market-place. An Arabian merchant, named Setoc, made the purchafe ; but as the fervant was fitter for labour than the mafter, he was fold at a higher price. There was no comparifon between the two men. Thus Zadig became a flave fubordinate to his own fervant. They were linked together by a chain faftened to their feet, and in this condition they

followed

followed the Arabian merchant to his houfe. By the way Zadig comforted his fervant, and exhorted him to patience; but he could not help making, according to his ufual cuftom, fome reflections on human life. "I fee (faid he) that the unhappinefs of my fate hath an influence on thine. Hitherto every thing has turned out to me in a moft unaccountable manner. I have been condemned to pay a fine for having feen the marks of a bitch's feet. I thought that I fhould once have been empaled on account of a griffin. I have been fent to execution for having made fome verfes in praife of the king. I have been upon the point of being ftrangled, becaufe the queen had yellow ribbands; and now I am a flave with thee, becaufe a brutal wretch beat his miftrefs. Come, let us keep a good heart; all this perhaps will have an end. The Arabian merchants muft neceffarily have flaves; and why not me as well as another, fince, as well as another, I am a man? This merchant will not be cruel; he muft treat his flaves well, if he expects any advantage from them." But while he fpoke thus, his heart was entirely engroffed by the fate of the queen of Babylon.

Two days after, the merchant Setoc fet out for Arabia Deferta, with his flaves and his camels. His tribe dwelt near the defart of Oreb. The journey was long and painful. Setoc fet a much greater value on the fervant than the mafter, becaufe the former was more expert in loading the camels; and all the little marks of diftinction were fhewn to him. A camel having died within two days journey of Oreb, his burden was divided and laid on the backs of the fervants; and Zadig had his fhare among the reft. Setoc laughed to fee all his flaves walking with their bodies inclined. Zadig took the

the liberty to explain to him the caufe, and inform him of the laws of the balance. The merchant was aftonifhed, and began to regard him with other eyes. Zadig, finding he had raifed his curiofity, encreafed it ftill further by acquainting him with many things that related to commerce; the fpecific gravity of metals and commodities under an equal bulk; the properties of feveral ufeful animals; and the means of rendering thofe ufeful that are not naturally fo. At laft Setoc began to confider Zadig as a fage, and preferred him to his companion, whom he had formerly fo much efteemed. He treated him well, and had no caufe to repent of his kindnefs.

As foon as Setoc arrived among his own tribe, he demanded the payment of five hundred ounces of filver, which he had lent to a Jew in prefence of two witneffes; but as the witneffes were dead, and the debt could not be proved, the Hebrew appropriated the merchant's money to himfelf, and pioufly thanked God for putting it in his power to cheat an Arabian. Setoc imparted this troublefome affair to Zadig, who was now become his counfel. " In what place (faid Zadig) didft thou lend the five hundred ounces to this infidel?" " Upon a large ftone, (replied the merchant) that lies near mount Oreb." " What is the character of thy debtor?" faid Zadig. " That of a knave," returned Setoc. " But I afk thee, whether he is lively or phlegmatic; cautious or imprudent?" " He is, of all bad prayers, (faid Setoc) the moft lively fellow I ever knew." " Well, (refumed Zadig) allow me to plead thy caufe." In effect, Zadig having fummoned the Jew to the tribunal, addreffed the judge in the following terms: " Pillow of the throne of equity, I come to demand of this man,

iii

in the name of my mafter, five hundred ounces of
filver, which he refufes to repay." "Haft thou any
witneffes?" faid the judge. "No, they are dead;
but there remains a large ftone upon which the
money was counted ; and if it pleafe thy grandeur
to order the ftone to be fought for, I hope that it
will bear witnefs. The Hebrew and I will tarry
here till the ftone arrives : I will fend for it at my
mafter's expence." "With all my heart," replied
the judge, and immediately applied himfelf to the
difcuffion of other affairs.

When the court was going to break up, the
judge faid to Zadig, "Well, friend, is not thy
ftone come yet?" The Hebrew replied with a
fmile, "Thy grandeur may ftay here till the morrow, and after all not fee the ftone. It is more
than fix miles from hence; and it would require
fifteen men to move it." "Well, (cried Zadig)
did not I fay that the ftone would bear witnefs?
fince this man knows where it is, he thereby con-
feffes that it was upon it that the money was counted." The Hebrew was difconcerted, and was foon
after obliged to confefs the truth. The judge ordered him to be faftened to the ftone, without meat
or drink, till he fhould reftore the five hundred
ounces, which were foon after paid.

The flave Zadig and the ftone were held in great
repute in Arabia.

The FUNERAL PILE.

SETOC, charmed with the happy iffue of this
affair, made his flave his intimate friend. He
had now conceived as great an efteem for him as

ever the king of Babylon had done; and Zadig
was glad that Setoc had no wife. He difcovered
in his mafter a good natural difpofition, much probity of heart, and a great fhare of good fenfe; but
he was forry to fee, that, according to the ancient
cuftom of Arabia, he adored the hoft of heaven;
that is, the fun, moon, and ftars. He fometimes
fpoke to him on this fubject with great prudence
and difcretion. At laft he told him that thefe bodies were like all other bodies in the univerfe, and
no more deferving of our homage than a tree or a
rock. " But (faid Setoc,) they are eternal beings;
and it is from them we derive all we enjoy. They
animate nature; they regulate the feafons; and,
befides, are removed at fuch an immenfe diftance
from us, that we cannot help revering them."—
" Thou receiveft more advantage (replied Zadig,)
from the waters of the Red Sea, which carry thy
merchandize to the Indies. Why may not it be
as ancient as the ftars? and if thou adoreft what
is placed at a diftance from thee, thou oughteft to
adore the land of the Gangarides, which lies at the
extremity of the earth." " No (faid Setoc,) the
brightnefs of the ftars commands my adoration."

At night Zadig lighted up a great number of
candles in the tent where he was to fup with Setoc; and the moment his patron appeared, he fell
on his knees before thefe lighted tapers, and faid,
" Eternal and fhining luminaries! be ye always
propitious to me." Having thus faid, he fat down
at the table, without taking the leaft notice of Setoc. " What art thou doing?" faid Setoc to him
in amaze. " I act like thee (replied Zadig,) I a-
dore thefe candles, and neglect their mafter and
mine." Setoc comprehended the profound fenfe
of this apologue. The wifdom of his flave funk

deep into his foul; he no longer offered incenfe to the creatures, but adored the eternal Being who made them.

There prevailed at that time in Arabia a fhocking cuftom, fprung originally from Scythia, and which, being eftablifhed in the Indies by the credit of the Brachmans, threatened to over-run all the Eaft. When a married man died, and his beloved wife afpired to the character of a faint, fhe burned herfelf publickly on the body of her hufband. This was a folemn feaft, and was called the Funeral Pile of Widowhood; and that tribe in which moft women had been burned was the moft refpected.— An Arabian of Setoc's tribe being dead, his widow, whofe name was Almona, and who was very devout, publifhed the day and hour when fhe intended to throw herfelf into the fire, amidft the found of drums and trumpets. Zadig remonftrated againft this horrible cuftom; he fhewed Setoc how inconfiftent it was with the happinefs of mankind to fuffer young widows to burn themfelves every other day, widows who were capable of giving children to the ftate, or at leaft of educating thofe they already had; and he convinced him that it was his duty to do all that lay in his power to abolifh fuch a barbarous practice. " The women (faid Setoc,) have poffeffed the right of burning themfelves for more than a thoufand years; and who fhall dare to abrogate a law which time hath rendered facred? Is there any thing more refpectable than ancient abufes?" " Reafon is more ancient (replied Zadig;) meanwhile, fpeak thou to the chiefs of the tribes, and I will go to wait on the young widow."

Accordingly he was introduced to her; and, after having infinuated himfelf into her good graces by

by fome compliments on her beauty, and told her what a pity it was to commit fo many charms to the flames, he at laft praifed her for her conftancy and courage. " Thou muft furely have loved thy hufband (faid he to her,) with the moft paffionate fondnefs." " Who, I ? (replied the lady,) I loved him not at all. He was a brutal, jealous, infupportable wretch ; but I am firmly refolved to throw myfelf on his funeral pile." " It would appear then (faid Zadig,) that there muft be a very delicious pleafure in being burnt alive." " Oh ! it makes nature fhudder (replied the lady,) but that muft be overlooked. I am a devotee; I fhould lofe my reputation ; and all the world would defpife me, if I did not burn myfelf." Zadig having made her acknowledge that fhe burned herfelf to gain the good opinion of others, and to gratify her own vanity, entertained her with a long difcourfe, calculated to make her a little in love with life, and even went fo far as to infpire her with fome degree of good will for the perfon who fpoke to her.----
" And what wilt thou do at laft (faid he,) if the vanity of burning thyfelf fhould not continue ?"
" Alas ! (faid the lady,) I believe I fhould defire thee to marry me."

Zadig's mind was too much engroffed with the idea of Aftarte not to elude this declaration ; but he inftantly went to the chiefs of the tribes, told them what had paffed, and advifed them to make a law, by which a widow fhould not be permitted to burn herfelf, till fhe had converfed privately with a young man for the fpace of an hour. Since that time not a fingle woman hath burned herfelf in Arabia. They were indebted to Zadig alone for deftroying in one day a cruel cuftom, that had

lafted

lafted for fo many ages; and thus he became the benefactor of Arabia.

The S U P P E R.

SETOC, who could not feparate himfelf from this man, in whom dwelt wifdom, carried him to the great fair of Balzora, whither the richeft merchants in the earth reforted. Zadig was highly pleafed to fee fo many men of different countries united in the fame place. He confidered the whole univerfe as one large family affembled at Balzora. The fecond day he fat at table with an Egyptian, an Indian, an inhabitant of Cathay, a Greek, a Celtic, and feveral other ftrangers, who, in their frequent voyages to the Arabian gulph, had learned enough of the Arabic to make themfelves underftood.------ The Egyptian feemed to be in a violent paffion. "What an abominable country is Balzora! (faid he,) they refufe me a thoufand ounces of gold on the beft fecurity in the world." "How! (faid Setoc,) on what fecurity have they refufed thee this fum?" "On the body of my aunt (replied the Egyptian,) fhe was the moft notable woman in Egypt; fhe always accompanied me in my journies; fhe died on the road! I have converted her into one of the fineft mummies in the world; and, in my own country, I could have as much as I pleafe, by giving her as a pledge. It is very ftrange that they will not here lend me fo much as a thoufand ounces of gold on fuch a folid fecurity." Angry as he was, he was going to help himfelf to a bit of excellent boiled fowl, when the Indian, taking him by the hand, cried out in a forrowful tone, "Ah! what

art

art thou going to do?" "To eat a bit of this fowl,"
replied the man who owned the mummy. "Take
care that thou doeft not, (replied the Indian.) It
is poffible that the foul of the deceafed may have
paffed into this fowl, and thou wouldft not, furely,
expofe thyfelf to the danger of eating thy aunt*?
To boil fowls is a manifeft outrage on nature."----
"What doft thou mean by thy nature and thy
fowls? (replied the choleric Egyptian.) We a-
dore a bull, and yet we eat heartily of beef."
"You adore a bull! is it poffible?" faid the man
of Ganges. "Nothing is more poffible, (returned
the other;) we have done fo for thefe hundred and
thirty-five thoufand years; and no body amongft
us has ever found fault with it." A hundred and
thirty-five thoufand years! (faid the Indian.) This
account is a little exaggerated; it is but eighty
thoufand years fince India was firft peopled, and
we are furely more ancient than you: Brama† prohibited our eating of ox-flefh before you thought
of putting it on your fpits or altars." "This Brama
of your's (faid the Egyptian,) is a pleafant fort of
an animal truly to compare with our Apis; what
great things hath your Brama performed?" "It
was he (replied the Bramin,) that taught mankind
to read and write, and to whom the world is indebted for the game of chefs." "Thou art miftaken (faid a Chaldean who fat near him,) it is to the
fifh

---

* Many cafts or tribes of Indians, efpecially the Bramins,
believe in the metempfychofis, or tranfmigration of fouls.

† Brama, or Brahma, is one of the principal deities of the
Tonquinefe.

fifh Oannes* that we owe thefe great advantages;
and it is juft that we fhould render homage to none
but him.   All the world will tell thee, that he is a
divine being, with a golden tail and a beautiful
human head, and that for three hours every day he
left the water to preach on dry land.   He had feveral children who were kings, as every one knows.
I have a picture of him at home, which I worfhip
with becoming reverence.   We may eat as much
beef as we pleafe ; but it is furely a great fin to
drefs fifh for the table.   Befides, you are both of
an origin too recent and ignoble to difpute with
me.   The Egyptians reckon only a hundred and
thirty-five thoufand years, and the Indians but
eighty thoufand, while we have almanacks of four
thoufand ages. Believe me ; renounce your follies ;
and I will give to each of you a beautiful picture
of Oannes."

The man of Cathay took up the difcourfe, and
faid ; " I have a great refpect for the Egyptians,
the Chaldeans, the Greeks, the Celtics, Brama,
the bull Apis, and the beautiful fifh Oannes; but
I could think that Li, or Tien †, as he is commonly

---

* Berofus, in his account of the Babylonian antiquities, fays,
that in the beginning of the Chaldean empire, an animal called
Oannes came out of the Red Sea.   He had the body of a fifh,
with the head and feet of a man.   He converfed with the people, and imparted to them the knowledge of letters, arts, and
fciences.   He taught them to form focieties, build cities, erect
temples, meafure and cultivate lands ; in a word, civilized the
whole nation.   However, he neither ate nor drank with them;
and at fun-fet always retired into the fea.   The fable probably
alludes to fome ftrangers who arrived on the coaft in a fhip, and
took fome pains to humanize the barbarous inhabitants.

† Chinefe words. The firft properly fignifies Natural Light,
or Reafon ; and the laft Heaven, or God.

ly called, is superior to all the bulls in the earth, and all the fish in the sea. I shall say nothing of my native country; it is as large as Egypt, Chaldea, and the Indies, put together. Neither shall I dispute about the antiquity of our nation; because it is of little consequence whether we are ancient or not; it is enough if we are happy; but, were it necessary to speak of almanacks, I could say that all Asia takes ours, and that we had very good ones before Arithmetic was known in Chaldea."

"Ignorant men, as ye all are, (said the Greek;) do you not know that Chaos is the father of all; and that form and matter have put the world into its present condition?" The Greek spoke for a long time, but was at last interrupted by the Celtic, who, having drank pretty deeply while the rest were disputing, imagined he was now more knowing than all the others, and said with an oath, that there were none but Teutat * and the misletoe of the oak that were worth the trouble of a dispute; that, for his own part, he had always some misletoe in his pocket; and that the Scythians, his ancestors, were the only men of merit that had ever appeared in the world; that it was true they had sometimes ate human flesh, but that, notwithstanding that circumstance, his nation deserved to be held in great esteem; and that, in fine, if any one spoke ill of Teutat. he would teach him better manners. The quarrel was now become warm; and

---

* Teutat is the same with Mercury. *Teut,* in the Celtic language, signifies People, and *tat* a Father. The word Mercury, according to Pezron, comes from the Gaulish words *meres* and *ur;* the first importing Merchandize; the other signifying a Man; very little different from the Latin words *mer* and *vir.*

and Setoc faw the table ready to be ftained with
blood. Zadig, who had been filent during the
whole difpute, arofe at laft. He firft addreffed
himfelf to the Celtic, as the moft furious of
all the difputants ; he told him that he had reafon
on his fide, and begged a few mifletoes. He then
praifed the Greek for his eloquence ; and foftened
all their exafperated fpirits. He faid but little to
the man of Cathay, becaufe he had been the moft
reafonable of them all. At laft he faid ; " You
were going, my friends, to quarrel about nothing ;
for you are all of one mind." At this word they
all cried out together. " Is it not true (faid he to
the Celtic) that you adore not this mifletoe, but
him that made both the mifletoe and the oak ?"
" Moft undoubtedly," replied the Celtic. " And
thou, Mr Egyptian, doft not thou revere, in a certain bull, him who gave the bulls ?" " Yes," faid
the Egyptian. " The fifh Oannes (continued he,)
muft yield to him who made the fea and the fifhes.
The Indian and the Cathaian (added he,) acknowledge, like you, a firft principle. I did not fully
comprehend the admirable things that were faid by
the Greek ; but I am fure he will admit a fuperior
being, on whom form and matter depend." The
Greek, whom they all admired, faid that Zadig had
exactly taken his meaning. " You are all then
(replied Zadig,) of one opinion. and have no caufe
to quarrel." All the company embraced him.
Setoc, after having fold his commodities at a very
high price, returned to his own tribe with his
friend Zadig ; who learned, upon his arrival, that
he had been tried in his abfence, and was now going to be burned by a flow fire.

The RENDEZVOUS.

DURING his journey to Balzora, the priests
of the stars had resolved to punish him. The
precious stones and ornaments of the young widows
whom they sent to the funeral pile belonged to
them of right; and the least they could now do,
was to burn Zadig for the ill office he had done
them. Accordingly they accused him of entertaining
erroneous sentiments of the heavenly host. They
deposed against him, and swore, that they had
heard him say that the stars did not set in the sea.
This horrid blasphemy made the judges tremble;
they were ready to tear their garments upon hearing these impious words; and they would certainly
have tore them, had Zadig had wherewithal to
pay them for new ones. But, in the excess of their
zeal and indignation, they contented themselves
with condemning him to be burnt by a slow fire.
Setoc, filled with despair at this unhappy event,
employed all his interest to save his friend, but in
vain; he was soon obliged to hold his peace. The
young widow Almona, who had now conceived a
great fondness for life, for which she was obliged
to Zadig, resolved to deliver him from the funeral
pile, of the abuse of which he had fully convinced
her. She revolved the scheme in her own mind,
without imparting it to any person whatever. Zadig was to be executed the next day: if she could
save him at all, she must do it that very night; and
the method taken by this charitable and prudent
lady was as follows:

She perfumed herself; she heightened her beauty
by the richest and gayest apparel, and went to
demand a private audience of the chief priest of the

ſtars.   As ſoon as ſhe was introduced to the venerable old man, ſhe addreſſed him in theſe terms :
" Eldeſt ſon of the great bear; brother of the bull ;
and couſin of the great dog, (ſuch were the titles
of this pontiff,) I come to acquaint thee with my
ſcruples.   I am much afraid that I have committed
a heinous crime in not burning myſelf on the funeral pile of my dear huſband ; for, indeed, what had I
worth preſerving ? periſhable fleſh, thou ſeeſt, that
is already entirely withered."   So ſaying, ſhe drew
up her long-ſleeves of ſilk, and ſhewed her naked
arms, which were of an elegant ſhape and a dazzling whiteneſs. " Thou ſeeſt (ſaid ſhe,) that theſe
are little worth."   The prieſt found in his heart
that they were worth a great deal ; his eyes ſaid ſo,
and his mouth confirmed it : he ſwore that he had
never in his life ſeen ſuch beautiful arms.   " Alas !
(ſaid the widow,) my arms, perhaps, are not ſo bad
as the reſt ; but thou wilt confeſs that my neck is
not worthy of the leaſt regard." She then diſcovered the moſt charming boſom that nature had ever
formed.   Compared to it, a roſe-bud on an apple
of ivory would have appeared like madder on the
box-tree, and the whiteneſs of new-waſhed lambs
would have ſeemed of a duſky yellow.   Her neck ;
her large black eyes, languiſhing with the gentle
luſtre of a tender fire ; her cheeks animated with
the fineſt purple, mixed with the whiteneſs of the
pureſt milk ; her noſe, which had no reſemblance
to the tower of mount Lebanon ; her lips, like two
borders of coral, incloſing the fineſt pearls in the
Arabian Sea ; all conſpired to make the old man
believe that he was but twenty years of age.   Almona, ſeeing him enflamed, entreated him to pardon
Zadig. " Alas ! (ſaid he,) my charming lady, ſhould
I grant thee his pardon, it would be of no ſervice,

                                                    as

as it muſt neceſſarily be ſigned by three others, my brethren." "Sign it, however," ſaid Almona. "With all my heart (ſaid the prieſt,) on condition that thy favours ſhall be the price of my ready compliance." "Thou doeſt me too much honour (ſaid Almona;) be pleaſed only to come to my chamber after ſun-ſet, and when the bright ſtar of Sheat ſhall appear in the horizon, thou wilt find me on a roſe-coloured ſopha; and thou mayeſt then uſe thy ſervant as thou art able." So ſaying, ſhe departed with the ſignature, and left the old man full of love and diſtruſt of his own abilities. He employed the reſt of the day in bathing; he drank a liquor compoſed of the cinnamon of Ceylon, and of the precious ſpices of Tidor and Ternate; and waited with impatience till the ſtar Sheat ſhould make its appearance.

Meanwhile, Almona went to the ſecond pontiff. He aſſured her that the ſun, the moon, and all the luminaries of heaven, were but glimmering meteors in compariſon of her charms. She aſked the ſame favour of him; and he propoſed to grant it on the ſame terms. She ſuffered herſelf to be overcome; and appointed the ſecond pontiff to meet her at the riſing of the ſtar Algenib. From thence ſhe went to the third and fourth prieſt, always taking their ſignatures, and making an aſſignation from ſtar to ſtar. She then ſent a meſſage to the judges, entreating them to come to her houſe, on an affair of great importance. They obeyed her ſummons. She ſhewed them the four names, and told them at what price the prieſts had ſold the pardon of Zadig. Each of them arrived at the hour appointed. Each was ſurpriſed at finding his brethren there, but ſtill more at ſeeing the judges, before whom their ſhame was now mani-

feſt.

teſt. Zadig was ſaved ; and Setoc was ſo charmed
with the ingenuity and addreſs of Almona, that he
made her his wife. Zadig departed, after having
thrown himſelf at the feet of his fair deliverer.
Setoc and he took leave of each other with tears
in their eyes, ſwearing an eternal friendſhip, and promiſing, that the firſt of them that ſhould acquire a
large fortune ſhould ſhare it with the other.

Zadig directed his courſe along the frontiers of
Aſſyria, ſtill muſing on the unhappy Aſtarte, and
reflecting on the ſeverity of fortune, which ſeemed
determined to make him the ſport of her cruelty,
and the object of her perſecution. " What! (ſaid
he to himſelf,) four hundred ounces of gold for
having ſeen a bitch! condemned to loſe my head
for four bad verſes in praiſe of the king! ready to
be ſtrangled, becauſe the queen had ſhoes of the
colour of my bonnet! reduced to ſlavery for having
ſuccoured a woman who was beat! and on the
point of being burnt for having ſaved the lives of
all the young widows of Arabia !"

The ROBBER.

ARRIVING on the frontiers which divide Arabia Petræa from Syria, he paſſed by a pretty
ſtrong caſtle, from which a party of armed Arabians ſallied forth. They inſtantly ſurrounded him,
and cried, " All thou haſt belongs to us, and thy
perſon is the property of our maſter." Zadig replied by drawing his ſword; his ſervant, who was
a man of courage, did the ſame. They killed the
firſt Arabians that preſumed to lay hands on them;
and, though the number was redoubled, they were
not

not difmayed, but refolved to perifh in the conflict.
Two men defended themfelves againft a multitude;
and fuch a combat could not laft long. The mafter of the caftle, whofe name was Arbogad, having
obferved from a window the prodigies of valour
performed by Zadig, conceived a high efteem for
this heroic ftranger. He defcended in hafte, and
went in perfon to call off his men, and deliver the
two travellers. " All that paffes over my lands
(faid he,) belongs to me, as well as what I find upon
the lands of others; but thou feemeft to be a man
of fuch undaunted courage, that I will exempt thee
from the common law. He then conducted him
to his caftle, ordering his men to treat him well;
and in the evening Arbogad fupped with Zadig.
The lord of the caftle was one of thofe Arabians
who are commonly called robbers; but he now and
then performed fome good actions amidft a multitude of bad ones. He robbed with a furious ra-
pacity, and granted favours with great generofity;
intrepid in action; affable in company; a de-
bauchee at table, but gay in his debauchery; and
particularly remarkable for his frank and open behaviour. He was highly pleafed with Zadig, whofe
lively converfation lengthened the repaft. At laft
Arbogad faid to him; " I advife thee to enroll thy
name in my catalogue; thou canft not do better;
this is not a bad trade; and thou mayeft one day
become what I am at prefent." " May I take
the liberty of afking thee (faid Zadig,) how long
thou haft followed this noble profeffion?" " From
my moft tender youth (replied the lord.) I was
fervant to a pretty good-natured Arabian, but
could not endure the hardfhips of my fituation. I
was vexed to find that fate had given me no fhare
of the earth, which equally belongs to all men. I
impart-

imparted the cause of my uneasiness to an old Arabian, who said to me; ' My son, do not despair; ' there was once a grain of sand that lamented that ' it was no more than a neglected atom in the ' deserts; at the end of a few years it became a ' diamond; and it is now the brightest ornament ' in the crown of the king of the Indies.' This discourse made a deep impression on my mind; I was the grain of sand, and I resolved to become the diamond. I began by stealing two horses; I soon got a party of companions; I put myself in a condition to rob small caravans; and thus, by degrees, I destroyed the difference which had formerly subsisted between me and other men. I had my share of the good things of this world; and was even recompensed with usury for the hardships I had suffered. I was greatly respected, and became the captain of a band of robbers. I seized this castle by force. The satrape of Syria had a mind to dispossess me of it; but I was too rich to have any thing to fear. I gave the satrape a handsome present, by which means I preserved my castle, and increased my possessions. He even appointed me treasurer of the tributes which Arabia Petræa pays to the king of kings. I perform my office of receiver with great punctuality; but take the freedom to dispense with that of paymaster.

The grand Desterham of Babylon sent hither a petty satrape in the name of king Moabdar, to have me strangled. This man arrived with his orders: I was apprised of all; I caused to be strangled in his presence the four persons he had brought with him to draw the noose; after which I asked him how much his commission of strangling me might be worth. He replied, that his fees would amount to above three hundred pieces of gold. I
then

then convinced him that he might gain more by
ftaying with me. I made him an inferior robber ;
and he is now one of my beft and richeft officers.
If thou wilt take my advice, thy fuccefs may be
equal to his ; never was there a better feafon for
plunder, fince king Moabdar is killed, and all Babylon thrown into confufion.

" Moabdar killed ! (faid Zadig,) and what is become of queen Aftarte ?" " I know not (replied
Arbogad.) All I know is, that Moabdar loft his
fenfes, and was killed ; that Babylon is a fcene of
diforder and bloodfhed ; that all the empire is defolated ; that there are fome fine ftrokes to be
ftruck yet ; and that, for my own part, I have ftruck
fome that are admirable." " But the queen (faid
Zadig ;) for heaven's fake, knoweft thou nothing
of the queen's fate ?" " Yes (replied he,) I have
heard fomething of a prince of Hircania ; if fhe
was not killed in the tumult, fhe is probably one
of his concubines ; but I am much fonder of booty
than news. I have taken feveral women in my
excurfions ; but I keep none of them : I fell them
at a high price, when they are beautiful, without
enquiring who they are. In commodities of this
kind rank makes no difference, and a queen that
is ugly will never find a merchant. Perhaps I may
have fold queen Aftarte ; perhaps fhe is dead ; but,
be it as it will, it is of little confequence to me,
and I fhould imagine of as little to thee." So
faying, he drank a large draught, which threw all
his ideas into fuch confufion, that Zadig could obtain
no farther information.

Zadig remained for fome time without fpeech,
fenfe, or motion. Arbogad continued drinking ;
told ftories ; conftantly repeated that he was the
happieft man in the world ; and exhorted Zadig
to

to put himfelf in the fame condition.   At laft the
foporiferous fumes of the wine lulled him into a
gentle repofe.   Zadig paffed the night in the moft
violent perturbation.   "What! (faid he,) did the
king lofe his fenfes? and is he killed? I cannot
help lamenting his fate.   The empire is rent in
pieces : and this robber is happy.   O fortune! O
deftiny! A robber is happy, and the moft beautiful of
nature's works hath perhaps perifhed in a barbarous
manner, or lives in a ftate worfe than death.   O
Aftarte! what is become of thee ?"

At day break, he queftioned all thofe he met
in the caftle; but they were all bufy, and he
received no anfwer.   During the night they had
made a new capture, and they were now employed in dividing the fpoil.   All he could obtain in this hurry and confufion was an opportunity of departing, which he immediately embraced,
plunged deeper than ever in the moft gloomy and
mournful reflections.

Zadig proceeded on his journey with a mind
full of difquiet and perplexity, and wholly employed on the unhappy Aftarte, on the king of
Babylon, on his faithful friend Cador, on the
happy robber Arbogad, on that capricious woman whom the Babylonians had feized on the
frontiers of Egypt; in a word, on all the misfortunes and difappointments he had hitherto fuffered.

The FISHERMAN.

AT a few leagues diftance from Arbogad's
caftle, he came to the banks of a fmall river, ftill deploring his fate, and confidering himfelf

felf as the moft wretched of mankind. He faw a fifherman lying on the brink of the river, fcarcely holding, in his weak and feeble hand, a net which he feemed ready to drop, and lifting up his eyes to heaven.

" I am certainly (faid the fifherman,) the moft unhappy man in the world. 1 was univerfally allowed to be the moft famous dealer in cream-cheefe in Babylon, and yet I am ruined. I had the moft handfome wife that any man in my ftation could have ; and by her I have been betrayed. I had ftill left a paltry houfe, and that I have feen pillaged and deftroyed. At laft I took refuge in this cottage, where I have no other refource than fifhing, and yet I cannot catch a fingle fifh. Oh, my net ! no more will I throw thee into the water ; I will throw myfelf in thy place." So faying, he arofe and advanced forward, in the attitude of a man ready to throw himfelf into the river, and thus to finifh his life.

" What ! faid Zadig to himfelf, are there men as wretched as I ?" His eagernefs to fave the fifherman's life was as fudden as this reflection. He runs to him, ftops him, and fpeaks to him with a tender and compaffionate air. It is commonly fuppofed that we are lefs miferable when we have companions in our mifery. This, according to Zoroafter, does not proceed from malice, but neceffity. We feel ourfelves infenfibly drawn to an unhappy perfon as to one like ourfelves. The joy of the happy would be an infult ; but two men in diftrefs are like two flender trees, which mutually fupporting each other, fortify themfelves againft the ftorm. " Why, faid Zadig to the fifherman, doft thou fink under thy misfortunes ?" " Becaufe (replied he,) I fee no means of relief. I was the

moſt conſiderable man in the village of Derlback,
near Babylon, and with the aſſiſtance of my wife
I made the beſt cream-cheeſe in the empire. Queen
Aſtarte, and the famous miniſter Zadig, were extremely fond of them. I had ſent them ſix hundred
cheeſes, and one day went to the city to receive my
money ; but, on my arrival at Babylon, was informed that the queen and Zadig had diſappeared. I ran
to the houſe of lord Zadig, whom I had never
ſeen ; but found there the inferior officers of the
grand Deſterham, who being furniſhed with a royal licence, were plundering it with great loyalty
and order. From thence I flew to the queen's kit-
chen, ſome of the lords of which told me that the
queen was dead ; ſome ſaid ſhe was in priſon ; and
others pretended that ſhe had made her eſcape ;
but they all agreed in aſſuring me that I would not
be paid for my cheeſe. I went with my wife to
the houſe of lord Orcan, who was one of my cuſ-
tomers, and begged his protection in my preſent
diſtreſs. He granted it to my wife, but refuſed it
to me. She was whiter than the cream-cheeſes
that began my misfortune ; and the luſtre of the
Tyrian purple was not more bright than the car-
nation which animated this whiteneſs. For this
reaſon Orcan detained her, and drove me from his
houſe. In my deſpair I wrote a letter to my dear
wife. She ſaid to the bearer, ' Ha, ha ! I know
the writer of this a little ; I have heard his name
mentioned ; they ſay he makes excellent cream-
cheeſe ; deſire him to ſend me ſome, and he ſhall
be paid.'

" In my diſtreſs I reſolved to apply to juſtice. I
had ſtill ſix ounces of gold remaining : I was obliged to give two to the lawyer whom I conſulted,
two to the procurator who undertook my cauſe,
                                                        and

and two to the fecretary of the firft judge. When
all this was done, my bufinefs was not begun; and
I had already expended more money than my
cheefe and my wife were worth. I returned to my
own village, with an intention to fell my houfe, in
order to enable me to recover my wife.

" My houfe was well worth fixty ounces of gold;
but as my neighbours faw that I was poor, and obliged to fell it, the firft to whom I applied offered
me thirty ounces, the fecond twenty, and the third
ten. Bad as thefe offers were, I was fo blind that
I was going to ftrike a bargain, when a prince of
Hircania came to Babylon, and ravaged all in his
way. My houfe was firft facked and then burnt.

" Having thus loft my money, my wife, and my
houfe, I retired into this country, where thou now
feeft me. I have endeavoured to gain a fubfiftence
by fifhing; but the fifh make a mock of me as
well as the men. I catch none; I die with hunger; and had it not been for thee, auguft comforter, I fhould have perifhed in the river."

The fifherman was not allowed to give this long
account without interruption; at every moment,
Zadig, moved and tranfported, faid, " What!
knoweft thou nothing of the queen's fate?" " No,
my Lord, replied the fifherman; but I know that
neither the queen nor Zadig have paid me for my
cream-cheefes; that I have loft my wife, and am
now reduced to defpair." " I flatter myfelf, faid
Zadig, that thou wilt not lofe all thy money. I
have heard of this Zadig; he is an honeft man;
and if he return to Babylon, as he expects, he will
give thee more than he owes thee: but with regard to thy wife, who is not fo honeft, I advife thee
not to feek to recover her. Believe me, go to Babylon; I fhall be there before thee, becaufe I am

on horfeback, and thou art on foot.   Apply to the
illuftrious Cador; tell him thou haft met his friend ;
wait for me at his houfe : go, perhaps thou wilt not
always be unhappy.

"O powerful Oromazes! continued he, thou
employeft me to comfort this man; whom wilt thou
employ to give me confolation ?" So faying, he gave
the fifherman half the money he had brought from
Arabia.   The fifherman, ftruck with furprife, and
ravifhed with joy, kiffed the feet of the friend of Cador, and faid, " Thou art furely an angel fent from
heaven to fave me !"

Mean while Zadig continued to make frefh in-
quiries, and to fhed tears. " What ! my lord, cried
the fifherman, art thou then fo unhappy, thou who
beftoweft favours ?" " An hundred times more unhappy than thee, replied Zadig."   " But how is it
poffible, faid the good man, that the giver can be
more wretched than the receiver ?"   " Becaufe, replied Zadig, thy greateft mifery arofe from poverty,
and mine is feated in the heart."   " Did Orcan
take thy wife from thee ?" faid the fifherman.   This
word recalled to Zadig's mind the whole of his adventures. He repeated the catalogue of his misfortunes, beginning with the queen's bitch, and ending
with his arrival at the caftle of the robber Arbogad.   " Ah! faid he to the fifherman, Orcan de-
ferves to be punifhed : but it is commonly fuch men
as thofe that are the favourites of fortune.   However, go thou to the houfe of lord Cador, and there
wait my arrival."   They then parted : the fifherman walked, thanking heaven for the happinefs of
his condition ; and Zadig rode, accufing fortune
for the hardnefs of his lot.

The

The BASILISK.

ARriving in a beautiful meadow, he there faw feveral women, who were fearching for fome-thing with great application. He took the liberty to approach one of them, and to afk if he might have the honour to affift them in their fearch. " Take care that thou doft not, replied the Syrian; what we are fearching for can be touched only by women." " Strange, faid Zadig, may I prefume to afk thee what it is that women only are permitted to touch." " It is a bafilifk, faid fhe." " A bafi-lifk, madam! and for what purpofe, pray, doft thou feek for a bafilifk?" " It is for our lord and mafter Ogul, whofe caftle thou feeft on the bank of that river, at the end of the meadow. We are his moft humble flaves. The lord Ogul is fick. His phy-fician hath ordered him to eat a bafilifk, ftewed in rofe-water; and as it is a very rare animal, and can only be taken by women, the lord Ogul hath pro-mifed to choofe for his well beloved wife the woman that fhall bring him a bafilifk; let me go on in my fearch; for thou feeft what I fhall lofe if I am prevented by my companions.

Zadig left her and the other Affyrians to fearch for their bafilifk, and continued to walk in the meadow; when coming to the brink of a fmall rivulet, he found another lady lying on the grafs, and who was not fearching for any thing. Her perfon feemed to be majeftic; but her face was covered with a veil. She was inclined to-wards the rivulet, and profound fighs proceeded from her mouth. In her hand fhe held a fmall rod with which fhe was tracing characters on the fine fand that lay between the turf and the brook.

Zadig

Zadig had the curiofity to examine what this woman was writing. He drew near; he faw the letter Z, then an A; he was aftonifhed: then appeared a D; he ftarted. But never was furprife
equal to his, when he faw the two laft letters of
his name. He ftood for fome time immoveable.
At laft breaking filence with a faultering voice,
" O generous lady! pardon a ftranger, an unfor-
" tunate man, for prefuming to afk thee by what
" furprifing adventure I here find the name of Za-
" dig traced out by thy divine hand." At this
voice, and thefe words, the lady lifted up the veil
with a trembling hand, looked at Zadig, fent forth
a cry of tendernefs, furprife, and joy, and finking
under the various emotions which at once affaulted
her foul, fell fpeechlefs into his arms. It was
Aftarte herfelf; it was the queen of Babylon; it
was fhe whom Zadig adored, and whom he had reproached himfelf for adoring; it was fhe whofe
misfortunes he had fo deeply lamented, and for
whofe fate he had been fo anxioufly concerned.
He was for a moment deprived of the ufe of his
fenfes, when he had fixed his eyes on thofe of
Aftarte, which now began to open again with a
languor mixed with confufion and tendernefs:
" O ye immortal powers! cried he, who prefide
over the fates of weak mortals, do ye indeed reftore Aftarte to me! at what a time, in what a place,
and in what a condition do I again behold her?"
He fell on his knees before Aftarte, and laid his
face in the duft of her feet. The queen of Babylon raifed him up, and made him fit by her fide
on the brink of the rivulet. She frequently wiped
her eyes, from which the tears continued to flow
afrefh: fhe twenty times refumed her difcourfe,
which her fighs as often interrupted: fhe afked by
what

what ſtrange accident they were brought together;
and ſuddenly prevented his anſwers by other queſ-
tions: ſhe waved the account of her own misfortunes, and deſired to be informed of thoſe of Zadig. At laſt, both of them having a little compoſed the tumult of their ſouls, Zadig acquainted
her in a few words by what adventure he was
brought into that meadow. " But, O unhappy
and reſpectable queen! by what means do I find
thee in this lonely place, clothed in the habit of a
ſlave, and accompanied by other female ſlaves, who
are ſearching for a baſiliſk, which, by order of the
phyſician, is to be ſtewed in roſe-water?"

" While they are ſearching for their baſiliſk, ſaid
the fair Aſtarte, I will inform thee of all I have
ſuffered, for which heaven has ſufficiently recom-
penſed me, by reſtoring thee to my ſight. Thou
knoweſt that the king, my huſband, was vexed to
ſee thee the moſt amiable of mankind; and that
for this reaſon he one night reſolved to ſtrangle
thee and poiſon me. Thou knoweſt how heaven
permitted my little mute to inform me of the orders of his ſublime majeſty. Hardly had the faithful Cador obliged thee to depart, in obedience to
my command, when he ventured to enter my a-
partment at midnight by a ſecret paſſage. He carried me off, and conducted me to the temple of
Oromazes, where the magi his brother ſhut me up
in that huge ſtatue, whoſe baſe reaches to the foundation of the temple, and whoſe top riſes to the
ſummit of the dome. I was there buried in a manner; but was ſerved by the magi, and ſupplied
with all the neceſſaries of life. At break of day
his Majeſty's apothecary entered my chamber with
a potion compoſed of a mixture of henbane, opium,
hemlock, black hellebore, and aconite; and another

ther officer went to thine with a bowftring of blue
filk. Neither of us were to be found. Cador, the
better to deceive the king, pretended to come and
accufe us both. He faid that thou hadft taken the
road to the Indies, and I that to Memphis; on
which the king's guards were immediately difpatched in purfuit of us both.

" The couriers who purfued me did not know
me. I had hardly ever fhewn my face to any but
thee, and to thee only in the prefence, and by the
order of my hufband. They conducted themfelves in the purfuit by the defcription that had
been given them of my perfon. On the frontiers
of Egypt they met with a woman of the fame ftature with me, and poffeffed perhaps of greater
charms. She was weeping and wandering. They
made no doubt but that this woman was the queen
of Babylon, and accordingly brought her to Moabdar : Their miftake at firft threw the king into a
violent paffion ; but having viewed this woman
more attentively, he found her extremely handfome,
and was comforted. She was called Miffouf. I
have fince been informed, that this name in the
Egyptian language fignifies the capricious fair one.
She was fo in reality ; but fhe had as much cunning
as caprice. She pleafed Moabdar, and gained fuch
an afcendency over him as to make him chufe her
for his wife. Her character then began to appear
in its true colours. She gave herfelf up, without
fcruple, to all the freaks of a wanton imagination.
She would have obliged the chief of the magi, who
was old and gouty, to dance before her ; and on
his refufal, fhe perfecuted him with the moft unre-
lenting cruelty. She ordered her mafter of the horfe
to make her a pye of fweetmeats. In vain did he
reprefent that he was not a paftry-cook ; he was
obliged

óbliged to make it, and loſt his place, becauſe it
was baked a little too hard. The poſt of maſter of
the horſe ſhe gave to her dwarf, and that of chan-
cellor to her page. In this manner did ſhe govern
Babylon. *Every body regretted the loſs of me.
The king, who till the moment of his reſolving to
poiſon me and ſtrangle thee, had been a tolerably
good kind of man, ſeemed now to have drowned all
his virtues in his immoderate fondneſs for this capricious fair one. He came to the temple on the
great day of the feaſt held in honour of the ſacred
fire. I ſaw him implore the gods in behalf of
Miſſouf, at the feet of the ſtatue in which I was
incloſed. I raiſed my voice, I cried out, "The
gods reject the prayers of a king who is now become a tyrant, and who attempted to murder a
reaſonable wife, in order to marry a woman remarkable for nothing but her folly and extrava-
gance." "At theſe words Moabdar was confounded, and his head became diſordered. The oracle I
had pronounced, and the tyranny of Miſſouf, conſpired to deprive him of his judgment, and in a few
days his reaſon entirely forſook him.

"His madneſs, which ſeemed to be the judgment of heaven, was the ſignal to a revolt. The
people roſe, and ran to arms ; and Babylon, which
had been ſo long immerſed in idleneſs and effemi-
nacy, became the theatre of a bloody civil war. I
was taken from the heart of my ſtatue, and placed
at the head of a party. Cador flew to Memphis
to bring thee back to Babylon. The prince of Hircania, informed of theſe fatal events, returned with
his army, and made a third party in Chaldæa. He
attacked the king, who fled before him with his
capricious Egyptian. Moabdar died pierced with
wounds. Miſſouf fell into the hands of the con-

queror. I myself had the misfortune to be taken
by a party of Hircanians, who conducted me to
their prince's tent, at the very moment that Miffouf was brought before him. Thou wilt doubtlefs
be pleafed to hear that the prince thought me
more beautiful than the Egyptian; but thou wilt
be forry to be informed that he defigned me for
his feraglio. He told me, with a blunt and refo-
lute air, that as foon as he had finifhed a military
expedition, which he was juft going to undertake,
he would come to me. Judge how great muft have
been my grief. My ties with Moabdar were already deffolved; I might have been the wife of
Zadig; and I was fallen into the hands of a barbarian. I anfwered him with all the pride which my
high rank and noble fentiment could infpire. I
had always heard it affirmed, that heaven ftamped
on perfons of my condition a mark of grandeur,
which, with a fingle word or glance, could reduce
to the lowlinefs of the moft profound refpect, thofe
rafh and forward perfons who prefume to deviate
from the rules of politenefs. I fpoke like a queen,
but was treated like a maid-fervant. The Hirca-
nian, without even deigning to fpeak to me, told
his black eunuch that I was impertinent, but that
he thought me handfome. He ordered him to take
care of me, and to put me under the regimen of
favourites, that fo my complexion being improved,
I might be the more worthy of his favours, when
he fhould be at leifure to honour me with them.
I told him, that, rather than fubmit to his defires,
I would put an end to my life. He replied with a
fmile, that women, he believed, were not fo blood-
thirfty, and that he was accuftomed to fuch violent
expreffions; and then left me with the air of a
man who had juft put another parrot into his avi-
ary.

ary. What a state for the first queen of the universe, and, what is more, for a heart devoted to
Zadig!"

At these words Zadig threw himself at her feet,
and bathed them with his tears. Astarte raised
him with great tenderness, and thus continued her
story. " I now saw myself in the power of a barbarian, and rival to the foolish woman with whom
I was confined. She gave me an account of her
adventures in Egypt. From the description she
gave of your person, from the time, from the dromedary on which you was mounted, and from every other circumstance, I inferred that Zadig was
the man who had fought for her. I doubted not
but that you was at Memphis, and therefore resolved to repair thither. Beautiful Missouf, said I,
thou art more handsome than I, and will please the
prince of Hircania much better. Assist me in con-
triving the means of my escape; thou wilt then
reign alone; thou wilt at once make me happy,
and rid thyself of a rival. Missouf concerted with
me the means of my flight; and I departed secretly
with a female Egyptian slave.

" As I approached the frontiers of Arabia, a
famous robber, named Arbogad, seized me, and
sold me to some merchants, who brought me to
this castle, where lord Ogul resides. He bought
me without knowing who I was. He is a voluptuary, ambitious of nothing but good living, and
thinks that God sent him into the world for no
other purpose than to sit at table. He is so extremely corpulent, that he is always in danger of
suffocation. His physician, who has but little credit with him when he has a good digestion, governs
him with a despotic sway when he has ate too much.
He has persuaded him that a basilisk stewed in rose-

water will effect a complete cure.   The lord Ogul
hath promifed his hand to the female flave that
brings him a bafilifk.   Thou feeft that I leave them
to vie with each other in meriting this honour;
and never was I lefs defirous of finding the ba-
fililk than fince heaven hath reftored thee to my
fight."

This account was fucceeded by a long converfation between Aftarte and Zadig, confifting of every thing that their long fuppreffed fentiments, their
great fufferings, and their mutual love, could infpire
into hearts the moft noble and tender; and the
genii who prefide over love carried their words to
the fphere of Venus.

The women returned to Ogul without having
found the bafilifk.   Zadig was introduced to this
mighty lord, and fpoke to him in the following
terms : " May immortal health defcend from heaven to blefs all thy days! I am a phyfician: at the
firft report of thy indifpofition I flew to thy caftle,
and have now brought thee a bafilifk ftewed in rofe-
water.   Not that I pretend to marry thee.   All I
afk is the liberty of a Babylonian flave, who hath
been in thy poffeffion for a few days ; and, if I fhould
not be fo happy as to cure thee, magnificent lord
Ogul, I confent to remain a flave in her place."

The propofal was accepted.   Aftarte fet out for
Babylon with Zadig's fervant, promifing, immediately upon her arrival, to fend a courier to inform
him of all that had happened.   Their parting was
as tender as their meeting.   The moment of meeting, and that of parting are the two greateft epo-
chas of life, as fayeth the great book of Zend. Zadig
loved the queen with as much ardour as he profeff-
ed ; and the queen loved Zadig more than fhe
thought proper to acknowledge.

· Mean-

Meanwhile Zadig fpoke thus to Ogul: " My lord, my bafilifk is not to be eaten; all its virtue muft enter through thy pores. I have inclofed it in a little ball, blown up and covered with a fine fkin. Thou muft ftrike this ball with all thy might, and I muft ftrike it back for a confiderable time; and by obferving this regimen for a few days, thou wilt fee the effects of my art." The firft day Ogul was out of breath, and thought he fhould have died with fatigue. The fecond, he was lefs fatigued, flept better. In eight days he recovered all the ftrength, all the health, all the agility and cheerfulnefs of his moft agreeable years. " Thou haft played at ball, and haft been temperate, faid Zadig, know that there is no fuch thing in nature as a bafilifk; that temperance and exercife are the two great prefervatives of health; and that the art of reconciling intemperance and health is as chimerical as the philofopher's ftone, judicial aftrology, or the theology of the magi."

Ogul's firft phyfician obferving how dangerous this man might prove to the medical art, formed a defign, in conjunction with the apothecary, to fend Zadig to fearch for a bafilifk in the other world. Thus, after having fuffered fuch a long train of calamities on account of his good actions, he was now upon the point of lofing his life for curing a gluttonous lord. He was invited to an excellent dinner, and was to have been poifoned in the fecond courfe; but, during the firft, he happily received a courier from the fair Aftarte. " When one is beloved by a beautiful woman, fays the great Zoroafter, he hath always the good fortune to extricate himfelf out of every kind of difficulty and danger."

The COMBATS.

THE queen was received at Babylon with all those tranfports of joy which are ever felt on the return of a beautiful princefs who hath been involved in calamities. Babylon was now in greater tranquillity. The prince of Hircania had been killed in battle. The victorious Babylonians declared that the queen fhould marry the man whom they fhould chufe for their fovereign. They were refolved that the firft place in the world, that of being hufband to Aftarte and king of Babylon, fhould not depend on cabals and intrigues. They fwore to acknowledge for king the man who, upon trial, fhould be found to be poffeffed of the greateft valour and the greateft wifdom. Accordingly, at the diftance of a few leagues from the city, a fpacious place was marked out for the lift, furrounded with magnificent amphitheatres. Thither the combatants were to repair in complete armour. Each of them had a feparate apartment behind the amphitheatres, where they were neither to be feen nor known by any one. Each was to encounter four knights; and thofe that were fo happy as to conquer four, were then to engage with one another; fo that he who remained the laft mafter of the field, would be proclaimed conqueror at the games. Four days after, he was to return with the fame arms, and to explain the ænigmas propofed by the magi. If he did not explain the ænigmas, he was not king; and the running at the lances was to begin afrefh, till a man fhould be found who was conqueror in both thefe combats; for they were abfolutely determined to have a king poffeffed of the greateft wifdom and the moft invincible courage. The queen was all the while to be ftrictly guarded:

fhe

she was only allowed to be present at the games, and even there she was to be covered with a veil; but was not permitted to speak to any of the competitors, that so they might neither receive favour, nor suffer injustice.

These particulars Astarte communicated to her lover, hoping, that, in order to obtain her, he would shew himself possessed of greater courage and wisdom than any other person. Zadig set out on his journey, beseeching Venus to fortify his courage and enlighten his understanding. He arrived on the banks of the Euphrates on the eve of this great day. He caused his device to be inscribed among those of the combatants, concealing his face and his name, as the law ordained; and then went to repose himself in the apartment that fell to him by lot. His friend Cador, who, after the fruitless search he had made for him in Egypt, was now returned to Babylon, sent to his tent a complete suit of armour, which was a present from the queen; as also from himself, one of the finest horses in Persia. Zadig presently perceived that these presents were sent by Astarte; and from thence his courage derived fresh strength, and his love the most animating hopes.

Next day, the queen being seated under a canopy of jewels, and the amphitheatres filled with all the gentlemen and ladies of rank in Babylon, the combatants appeared in the circus. Each of them came and laid his device at the feet of the grand magi. They drew their devices by lot; and that of Zadig was the last. The first who advanced was a certain lord, named Itobad, very rich and very vain, but possessed of little courage, of less address, and hardly of any judgment at all. His servants had persuaded him that such a man as he ought to be king; he had said in reply, "Such a man

as I ought to reign ;" and thus they had armed him
cap-a-pee.   He wore an armour of gold enamelled
with green, a plume of green feathers, and a lance
adorned with green ribbands.   It was inftantly perceived by the manner in which Itobad managed
his horfe, that it was not for fuch a man as him,
that heaven referved the fcepter of Babylon.   The
firft knight that ran againft him threw him out of
his faddle ; the fecond laid him flat on his horfe's
buttocks, with his legs in the air, and his arms extended.   Itobad recovered himfelf, but with fo bad
a grace, that the whole amphitheatre burft out a-
laughing.   The third knight difdained to make ufe
of his lance ; but, making a pafs at him, took him
by the right leg, and wheeling him half-round, laid
him proftrate on the fand.   The fquires of the
games ran to him laughing, and replaced him in
his faddle.   The fourth combatant took him by
the left leg, and tumbled him down on the other
fide.   He was conducted back with fcornful fhouts
to his tent, where, according to the law, he was to
pafs the night ; and as he limped along, with great
difficulty, he faid ; " What an adventure for fuch
a man as I !"

The other knights acquitted themfelves with
greater ability and fuccefs.   Some of them conquered two combatants ; a few of them vanquifhed
three ; but none but prince Otamus conquered
four.   At laft Zadig fought in his turn.   He fucceffively threw four knights off their faddles, with
all the grace imaginable.   It then remained to be
feen who fhould be conqueror, Otamus or Zadig.
The arms of the firft were gold and blue, with a
plume of the fame colour ; thofe of the laft were
white.   The wifhes of all the fpectators were divided
between the knight in blue and the knight in white.

The

The queen, whofe heart was in a violent palpitation, offered prayers to heaven for the fuccefs of the
white colour.

The two champions made their paffes and vaults
with fo much agility, they mutually gave and received fuch dexterous blows with their lances, and
fat fo firmly in their faddles, that every body but
the queen wifhed there might be two kings in Babylon. At length, their horfes being tired, and
their lances broken, Zadig had recourfe to this
ftratagem : He paffes behind the blue prince;
fprings upon the buttocks of his horfe ; feizes him
by the middle; throws him on the earth ; places
himfelf in the faddle ; and wheels around Otamus
as he lay extended on the ground. All the amphitheatre cried out, " Victory to the white knight !"
Otamus rifes in a violent paffion, and draws his
fword; Zadig leaps from his horfe with his fabre
in his hand. Both of them are now on the ground,
engaged in a new combat, where ftrength and agility triumph by turns. The plumes of their helmets, the ftuds of their bracelets, and the rings of
their armour, are driven to a great diftance by the
violence of a thoufand furious blows. They ftrike
with the point and the edge; to the right, to the
left ; on the head, on the breaft ; they retreat; they
advance ; they meafure fwords ; they clofe ; they
feize each other ; they bend like ferpents ; they
attack like lions; and the fire every moment flafhes
from their blows. At laft Zadig, having recovered
his fpirits, ftops ; makes a feint; leaps upon Otamus; throws him on the ground and difarms him;
and Otamus cries out ; " It is thou alone, O white
knight, that oughteft to reign over Babylon!" The
queen was now at the height of her joy. The

knight, in blue armour, and the knight in white, were conducted each to his own apartment, as well as all the others, according to the intention of the law. Mutes came to wait upon them, and to serve them at table. It may be easily supposed that the queen's little mute waited upon Zadig. They were then left to themselves, to enjoy the sweets of repose till next morning, at which time the conqueror was to bring his device to the grand magi, to compare it with that which he had left, and make himself known.

Zadig, though deeply in love, was so much fatigued that he could not help sleeping. Itobad, who lay near him, never closed his eyes. He arose in the night, entered his apartment, took the white arms and the device of Zadig, and put his green armour in their place. At break of day, he went boldly to the grand magi, to declare that so great a man as he was conqueror. This was little expected; however, he was proclaimed while Zadig was still asleep. Astarte, surprised and filled with despair, returned to Babylon. The amphitheatre was almost empty, when Zadig awoke; he sought for his arms, but could find none but the green armour. With this he was obliged to cover himself, having nothing else near him. Astonished and enraged, he put it on in a furious passion, and advanced in this equipage.

The people that still remained in the amphitheatre and the circus received him with hoots and hisses. They surrounded him, and insulted him to his face. Never did man suffer such cruel mortifications. He lost his patience; with his sabre he dispersed such of the populace as dared to affront him; but he knew not what course to take. He could not see the queen; he could not claim the white armour

armour fhe had fent him. without expofing her; and thus, while fhe was plunged in grief, he was filled with fury and diftraction. He walked on the banks of the Euphrates, fully perfuaded that his ftar had deftined him to inevitable mifery; and revolving in his mind all his misfortunes, from the adventure of the woman who hated one-eyed men, to that of his armour; " This (faid he,) is the confequence of my having flept too long. Had I flept lefs, I fhould now have been king of Babylon, and in poffeffion of Aftarte. Knowledge, virtue, and courage, have hitherto ferved only to make me miferable." He then let fall fome fecret murmurings againft Providence, and was tempted to believe that the world was governed by a cruel deftiny, which oppreffed the good, and profpered knights in green armour. One of his greateft mortifications was his being obliged to wear that green armour which had expofed him to fuch contumelious treatment. A merchant happening to pafs by, he fold it to him for a trifle, and bought a gown and a long bonnet. In this garb he proceeded along the banks of the Euphrates, filled with defpair, and fecretly accufing Providence, which thus continued to perfecute him with unremitting feverity.

The HERMIT.

WHILE he was thus fauntering, he met a hermit, whofe white and venerable beard hung down to his girdle. He held a book in his hand, which he read with great attention. Zadig ftopt, and made him a profound obeifance. The hermit returned the compliment with fuch a noble

and

and engaging air, that Zadig had the curiosity to
enter into conversation with him. He asked him
what book it was that he had been reading? "It
is the book of destinies (said the hermit;) wouldst
thou choose to look into it?" He put the book into
the hands of Zadig, who, thoroughly versed as he
was in several languages, could not decypher a
single character of it. This only redoubled his
curiosity. "Thou seemest (said this good father,)
to be in great distress." "Alas! (replied Zadig,)
I have but too much reason." "If thou wilt permit me to accompany thee (resumed the old man,)
perhaps I may be of some service to thee. I have
often poured the balm of consolation into the bleeding heart of the unhappy." Zadig felt himself inspired with respect for the air, the beard, and the
book of the hermit. He found, in the course of
the conversation, that he was possessed of superior
degrees of knowledge. The hermit talked of fate,
of justice, of morals, of the chief good, of human
weakness, and of virtue and vice, with such a spirit-
ed and moving eloquence, that Zadig felt himself
drawn toward him by an irresistible charm. He
earnestly entreated the favour of his company till
their return to Babylon. "I ask the same favour
of thee (said the old man;) swear to me by Oromazes, that whatever I do, thou wilt not leave me
for some days." Zadig swore, and they set out
together.

In the evening, the two travellers arrived at a
a superb castle. The hermit entreated a hospitable
reception for himself and the young man who accompanied him. The porter, whom one might
have easily mistaken for a great lord, introduced
them with a kind of disdainful civility. He presented them to a principal domestic, who shewed
them

them his mafter's magnificent apartments. They
were admitted to the lower end of the table, without being honoured with the leaft mark of regard
by the lord of the caftle; but they were ferved, like
the reft, with delicacy and profufion. They were
then prefented with water to wafh their hands, in a
golden bafon adorned with emeralds and rubies.
At laft they were conducted to bed in a beautiful
apartment; and, in the morning, a domeftic
brought each of them a piece of gold, after which
they took their leave and departed.

"The mafter of the houfe (faid Zadig, as they
were proceeding on the journey,) appears to be a
generous man, though fomewhat too proud: he
nobly performs the duties of hofpitality." At that
inftant he obferved, that a kind of large pocket,
which the hermit had, was filled and diftended:
and upon looking more narrowly, he found that it
contained the golden bafon adorned with precious
ftones, which the hermit had ftolen. He durft
not then take any notice of it; but he was filled
with a ftrange furprife.

About noon, the hermit came to the door of
a paultry houfe, inhabited by a rich mifer, and
begged the favour of an hofpitable reception for
a few hours. An old fervant, in a tattered garb,
received them with a blunt and rude air, and led
them into the ftable, where he gave them fome rot-
ten olives, mouldy bread, and four beer. The
hermit ate and drank with as much feeming fatif-
faction as he had done the evening before; and
then addreffing himfelf to the old fervant, who
watched them both, to prevent their ftealing any
thing, and rudely preffed them to depart, he gave
him the two pieces of gold he had received in the
morning, and thanked him for his great civility:
"Pray

" Pray (added he,) allow me to fpeak to thy mafter." The fervant, filled with aftonifhment, introduced the two travellers. " Magnificent lord!
(faid the hermit.) I cannot but return thee my moft
humble thanks for the noble manner in which thou
haft entertained us. Be pleafed to accept of this
golden bafon as a fmall mark of my gratitude."
The mifer ftarted, and was ready to fall backwards;
but the hermit, without giving him time to recover
from his furprife, inftantly departed with his young
fellow-traveller. " Father (faid Zadig,) what is
the meaning of all this? thou feemeft to me to be
entirely different from other men; thou ftealeft a
golden bafon adorned with precious ftones, from a
lord who received thee magnificently, and giveft it
to a mifer who treats thee with indignity." " Son
(replied the old man.) this magnificent lord, who
receives ftrangers only from vanity and oftentation,
will hereby be rendered more wife; and the mifer
will learn to practife the duties of hofpitality. Be
furprifed at nothing, but follow me." Zadig knew
not as yet whether he was in company with the
moft foolifh or the moft prudent of mankind; but
the hermit fpoke with fuch an afcendancy, that
Zadig, who was moreover bound by his oath, could
not refufe to follow him.

In the evening, they arrived at a houfe built with
equal elegance and fimplicity, where nothing favoured either of prodigality or avarice. The
mafter of it was a philofopher, who had retired
from the world, and who cultivated in peace the
ftudy of virtue and wifdom, without any of that
rigid and morofe feverity, fo commonly to be
found in men of his character. He had chofen to
build this country-houfe in which he received ftrangers with a generofity free from oftentation. He

went himfelf to meet the two travellers, whom he led into a commodious apartment, where he defired them to repofe themfelves a little. Soon after he came and invited them to a decent and well ordered repaſt, during which he fpoke with great judgment of the laſt revolutions in Babylon. He feemed to be ftrongly attached to the queen, and wiſhed that Zadig had appeared in the lifts to difpute the crown: " But the people (added he,) do not deferve to have fuch a king as Zadig." Zadig bluſhed, and felt his griefs redoubled. They agreed, in the courfe of the converfation, that the things of this world did not always anfwer the wiſhes of the wife. The hermit ftill maintained that the ways of Providence were infcrutable; and that men were in the wrong to judge of a whole, of which they underſtood but the fmalleſt part.

They talked of the paſfions ; " Ah (faid Zadig,) how fatal are their effects !" "They are the winds (replied the hermit,) that fwell the fails of the ſhip: it is true, they fometimes fink her, but without them ſhe could not fail at all. The bile makes us fick and cholerick ; but without the bile we could not live. Every thing in this world is dangerous, and yet every thing in it is neceffary."

The converfation turned on pleafure ; and the hermit proved that it was a prefent beſtowed by the deity: " For (faid he,) man cannot give himfelf either fenfations or ideas : he receives all; and pain and pleafure proceed from a foreign caufe as well as his being."

Zadig was furprifed to fee a man, who had been guilty of fuch extravagant actions, capable of reaſoning with fo much judgment and propriety. At laſt, after a converfation equally entertaining and inſtructive, the hoſt led back his two gueſts to
their

their apartment, blessing heaven for having sent him two men possessed of so much wisdom and virtue. He offered them money, with such an easy and noble air as could not possibly give any offence. The hermit refused it, and said that he must now take his leave of him, as he proposed to set out for Babylon before it was light. Their parting was tender; Zadig especially felt himself filled with esteem and affection for a man of such an amiable character.

When he and the hermit were alone in their apartment, they spent a long time in praising their host. At break of day, the old man awakened his companion. " We must now depart (said he;) but while all the family are still asleep, I will leave this man a mark of my esteem and affection." So saying, he took a candle and set fire to the house. Zadig, struck with horror, cried aloud, and endeavoured to hinder him from committing such a barbarous action; but the hermit drew him away by a superior force, and the house was soon in flames. The hermit, who, with his companion, was already at a considerable distance, looked back to the conflagration with great tranquillity. " Thanks be to God (said he,) the house of my dear host is entirely destroyed! Happy man!" At these words Zadig was at once tempted to burst out a-laughing, to reproach the reverend father, to beat him, and to run away. But he did none of all these; for still subdued by the powerful ascendency of the hermit, he followed him, in spite of himself, to the next stage.

This was at the house of a charitable and virtuous widow, who had a nephew fourteen years of age, a handsome and promising youth, and her only hope. She performed the honours of her house as well as she could. Next day, she ordered her

nephew

nephew to accompany the ſtrangers to a bridge,
which being lately broken down, was become extremely dangerous in paſſing. The young man
walked before them with great alacrity. As they
were croſſing the bridge, " Come, (ſaid the hermit
to the youth,) I muſt ſhew my gratitude to thy
aunt." He then took him by the hair, and plunged
him into the river. The boy ſunk, appeared again
on the ſurface of the water, and was ſwallowed up
by the current. " O monſter! O thou moſt wicked of mankind!" cried Zadig. " Thou promiſedſt
to behave with greater patience (ſaid the hermit,
interrupting him.) Know, that under the ruins of
that houſe which Providence hath ſet on fire, the
maſter hath found an immenſe treaſure : know,
that this young man, whoſe life Providence hath
ſhortened, would have aſſaſſinated his aunt in the
ſpace of a year, and thee in that of two." " Who
told thee ſo, barbarian? (cried Zadig ;) and tho'
thou hadſt read this event in thy book of deſtinies,
art thou permitted to drown a youth who never
did thee any harm?"
 While the Babylonian was thus exclaiming, he
obſerved that the old man had no longer a beard,
and that his countenance aſſumed the features and
complexion of youth. The hermit's habit diſappeared, and four beautiful wings covered a majeſ-
tic body reſplendent with light. " O ſent of heaven! O divine angel! (cried Zadig, humbly pro-
ſtrating himſelf on the ground,) haſt thou then de-
ſcended from the Empyrean, to teach a weak mortal to ſubmit to the eternal decrees of Providence ?
" Men, (ſaid the angel Jeſrad,) judge of all without
knowing any thing ; and, of all men, thou beſt de-
ſerveſt to be enlightened." Zadig begged to be
permitted to ſpeak : " I diſtruſt myſelf (ſaid he,)

but may I prefume to afk the favour of thee to
clear up one doubt that ftill remains in my mind ;
would it not have been better to have corrected
this youth, and made him virtuous, than to have
drowned him ?" Had he been virtuous (replied
Jefrad,) and enjoyed a longer life, it would have
been his fate to be affaffinated himfelf, together
with the wife he would have married, and the
child he would have had by her." " But why (faid
Zadig,) is it neceffary that there fhould be crimes
and misfortunes, and that thefe misfortunes fhould
fall on the good ?" " The wicked (replied Jefrad,)
are always unhappy : they ferve to prove and try
the fmall number of the juft that are fcattered thro'
the earth ; and there is no evil that is not produc-
tive of fome good." " But (faid Zadig,) fuppofe
there were nothing but good and no evil at all."
" Then (replied Jefrad,) this earth would be another
earth : the chain of events would be ranged in another order and directed by wifdom ; but this other
order, which would be perfect, can exift only in
the eternal abode of the Supreme Being, to which
no evil can approach. The Deity hath created
millions of worlds, among which there is not one
that refembles another. This immenfe variety is
the effect of his immenfe power. There are not
two leaves among the trees of the earth, nor two
globes in the unlimited expanfe of heaven, that are
exactly fimilar ; and all that thou feeft on the little
atom in which thou art born, ought to be in its
proper time and place, according to the immutable
decrees of him who comprehends all. Men think
that this child who hath juft perifhed is fallen into
the water by chance ; and that it is by the fame
chance that this houfe is burnt : but there is no
fuch thing as chance ; all is either a trial, or a punifhment,

nifhment, or a reward, or a forefight. Remember the fifherman, who thought himfelf the moft wretch-ed of mankind. Oromazes fent thee to change his fate. Ceafe then, frail mortal, to difpute againft what thou oughteft to adore." " But," (faid Za-dig) ———— As he pronounced the word " But," the angel took his flight towards the tenth fphere. Zadig on his knees adored Providence, and fub-mitted. The angel cried to him from on high, " Direct thy courfe towards Babylon."

The AENIGMAS.

ZADIG, entranced as it were, and like a man about whofe head the thunder had burft, walked at random. He entered Babylon on the very day when thofe who had fought at the tour-naments were affembled in the grand veftibule of the palace, to explain the ænigmas, and to anfwer the queftions of the grand magi. All the knights were already arrived, except the knight in green armour. As foon as Zadig appeared in the city, the people crowded round him; every eye was fixed on him, every mouth bleffed him, and every heart wifhed him the empire. The envious man faw him pafs; he frowned and turned afide; the people conducted him to the place where the af-fembly was held. The queen, who was informed of his arrival, became a prey to the moft violent a-gitations of hope and fear. She was filled with anxiety and apprehenfion. She could not compre-hend why Zadig was without arms, nor why Itobad wore the white armour. A confufed murmur a-rofe at the fight of Zadig. They were equally furprifed and charmed to fee him; but none but the knights who had fought were permitted to appear in the affembly.

"I have fought as well as the other knights (faid Zadig,) but another here wears my arms; and while I wait for the honour of proving the truth of my affertion, I demand the liberty of prefenting myfelf to explain the ænigmas." The quefiion was put to the vote, and his reputation for probity was ftill fo deeply impreffed in their minds, that they admitted him without fcruple.

The firft queftion propofed by the grand magi was, " What, of all things in the world, is the longeft and the fhorteft, the fwifteft, and the floweft, the moft divifible and the moft extended, the moft neglected and the moft regretted, without which nothing can be done, which devours all that is little, and enlivens all that is great?"

Itobad was to fpeak. He replied, that fo great a man as he did not underftand ænigmas; and that it was fufficient for him to have conquered by his ftrength and valour. Some faid that the meaning of the ænigma was Fortune; fome, the Earth; and others, the Light. Zadig faid that it was Time: " Nothing (added he) is longer, fince it is the meafure of eternity; nothing is fhorter, fince it is infufficient for the accomplifhment of our projects; nothing more flow to him that expects, nothing more rapid to him that enjoys; in greatnefs it extends to infinity, in fmallnefs it is infinitely divifible; all men neglect it, all regret the lofs of it; nothing can be done without it; it configns to oblivion whatever is unworthy of being tranfmitted to pofterity, and it immortalizes fuch actions as are truly great." The affembly acknowledged that Zadig was in the right.

The

The next queftion was: " What is the thing which we receive without thanks, which we enjoy without knowing how, which we give to others when we know not where we are, and which we lofe without perceiving it?"

Every one gave his own explanation. Zadig alone gueffed that it was Life, and explained all the other ænigmas with the fame facility. Itobad always faid that nothing was more eafy, and that he could have anfwered them with the fame readinefs, had he chofen to have given himfelf the trouble. Queftions were then propofed on juftice, on the fovereign good, and on the art of government.— Zadig's anfwers were judged to be the moft folid. " What a pity is it (faid they,) that fuch a great genius fhould be fo bad a knight!"

" Illuftrious lords (faid Zadig,) I have had the honour of conquering in the tournaments. It is to me that the white armour belongs. Lord Itobad took poffeffion of it during my fleep. He probably thought that it would fit him better than the green. I am now ready to prove in your prefence, with my gown and fword, againft all that beautiful white armour which he took from me, that it is I who have had the honour of conquering the brave Otamus."

Itobad accepted the challenge with the greateft confidence. He never doubted, but that, armed as he was, with a helmet, a cuirafs, and braffarts, he would obtain an eafy victory over a champion in a cap and a night-gown. Zadig drew his fword, faluting the queen, who looked at him with a mixture of fear and joy. Itobad drew his without faluting any one. He rufhed upon Zadig, like a man who had nothing to fear; he was ready to cleave him in two. Zadig knew how to ward off his blows,

by

by oppofing the ftrongeft part of his fword to the
weakeft of that of his adverfary, in fuch a manner
that Itobad's fword was broken. Upon which Zadig, feizing his enemy by the waift, threw him on
the ground ; and fixing the point of his fword at
the extremity of his breaft-plate; " Suffer thyfelf to be difarmed, (faid he,) or thou art a
dead man." Itobad, always furprifed at the dif-
graces that happened to fuch a man as he, was obliged to yield to Zadig, who took from him with
great compofure, his magnificent helmet, his fuperb
cuirafs, his fine braffarts, his fhining cuifhes ; cloathed himfelf with them, and in this drefs ran to throw
himfelf at the feet of Aftarte. Cador eafily proved
that the armour belonged to Zadig. He was acknowledged king by the unanimous confent of the
whole nation, and efpecially by that of Aftarte,
who, after fo many calamities, now tafted the exquifite pleafure of feeing her lover worthy, in the
eyes of all the world, to be her hufband. Itobad
went home to be called lord in his own houfe.—
Zadig was king, and was happy ; he recollected
what the angel Jefrad had faid to him ; he even
remembered the grain of fand that became a diamond. The queen and Zadig adored Providence.
He left the capricious beauty Miffouf to run thro'
the world. He fent in fearch of the robber Arbogad, to whom he gave an honourable poft in his
army, promifing to advance him to the firft digni-
ties, if he behaved like a true warrior ; and threatening to hang him, if he followed the profeffion of
a robber.

Setoc, with the fair Almona, was called from the
heart of Arabia, and placed at the head of the commerce of Babylon. Cador was preferred and diftinguifhed according to his great fervices. He
was

was the friend of the king; and the king was then the only monarch on earth that had a friend. The little mute was not forgotten. A fine houfe was given to the fifherman; and Orcan was condemned to pay him a large fum of money, and to reftore him his wife; but the fifherman, who was now become wife, took only the money.

But neither could the beautiful Semira be comforted, for having believed that Zadig would be blind of an eye; nor did Azora ceafe to lament her having attempted to cut off his nofe: their griefs, however, he foftened by his prefents. The envious man died of rage and fhame. The empire enjoyed peace, glory, and plenty. This was the happieft age of the earth; it was governed by love and juftice. The people bleffed Zadig, and Zadig bleffed heaven.

THE

The WORLD as it GOES,

The Vision of BABOUC.*

Written by himself.

AMONG the genii, who preside over the empires of the earth, Ithuriel held one of the first ranks, and had the department of Upper Asia. He one morning descended into the abode of Babouc, the Scythian, who dwelt on the banks of the Oxus, and said to him; "Babouc, the follies and vices of the Persians have drawn upon them our indignation; yesterday was held an assembly of the genii of Upper Asia, to consider whether we would chastise Persepolis, or destroy it entirely. Go to that city; examine every thing; return and give me a faithful account; and, according to thy report, I will then determine whether to correct or extirpate the inhabitants." "But, my lord, (said Babouc with great humility,) I have never been in Persia, nor do I know a single person in that country." " So much the better (said the angel,) thou wilt be the more impartial; thou hast received from heaven the spirit of discernment, to which I now add the power of inspiring confidence. Go, see, hear,

---

* This appears to be a satire on the city of Paris.

hear, obferve, and fear nothing ; thou fhalt every where meet with a favourable reception.

Babouc mounted his camel, and fet out with his fervants. After having travelled fome days, he met, near the plains of Senaar, the Perfian army, which was going to attack the forces of India. He firft addreffed himfelf to a foldier, whom he found at a diftance from the main army; and afked him what was the occafion of the war. " By all the gods, (faid the foldier,) I know nothing of the matter. It is none of my bufinefs ; my trade is to kill and be killed, to get a livelihood. It is of no confequence to me whom I ferve. To morrow, perhaps, I may go over to the Indian camp ; for it is faid that they give their foldiers nearly half a copper drachma a day more than we have in this curfed fervice of Perfia : if thou defireft to know why we fight, fpeak to my captain."

Babouc, having given the foldier a fmall prefent, entered the camp. He foon became acquainted with the captain, and afked him the fubject of the war. " How canft thou imagine that I fhould know it ? (faid the captain,) or of what importance is it to me ? I live about two hundred leagues from Perfepolis ; I hear that war is declared ; I inftantly leave my family, and, having nothing elfe to do, go, according to our cuftom, to raife my fortune, or to fall by a glorious death." " But are not thy companions (faid Babouc,) a little better in- formed than thee ?" " No, (faid the officer,) there are none but our principal fatrapes that know the true caufe of our cutting one another's throats."

Babouc, ftruck with aftonifhment, introduced himfelf to the generals, and foon became familiarly acquainted with them. At laft one of them faid ; " The

†   N   " The

" The caufe of this war, which for twenty years
paft hath defolated Afia, fprang originally from a
quarrel between a eunuch belonging to one of the
concubines of the great king of Perfia, and the
clerk of a factory belonging to the great king of
India. The difpute was about a claim, which a-
mounted nearly to the thirtieth part of a daric. Our
firft minifter and that of India maintained the rights
of their mafters with becoming dignity: the difpute grew warm: both parties fent into the field
an army of a million of foldiers. This army muft
be every year recruited with upwards of four hundred thoufand men. Maffacres, burning of houfes,
ruin and devaftation, are daily multiplied; the
univerfe fuffers; and their mutual animofity ftill
continues. The firft minifters of the two nations
frequently proteft, that they have nothing in view
but the happinefs of mankind; and every protefta-
tion is attended with the deftruction of a town, or
the defolation of a province*.

Next day, on a report being fpread that peace
was going to be concluded, the Perfian and Indian
generals made hafte to come to an engagment.
The battle was long and bloody. Babouc beheld
every crime, and every abomination: he was witnefs to the arts and ftratagems of the principal fatrapes, who did all that lay in their power to expofe their general to the difgrace of a defeat. He
faw officers killed by their own troops, and foldiers
ftabbing their already expiring comrades, in order
to ftrip them of a few bloody garments, torn and
co-

* Such indeed are the trifling caufes, which often produce
horror, mifery, and devaftation.

covered with dirt. He entered the hofpitals, to which they were conveying the wounded, moft of whom died through the inhuman negligence of thofe who were well paid by the king of Perfia to affift thefe unhappy men. " Are thefe men, (cried Babouc,) or are they wild beafts? Ah! I plainly fee that Perfepolis will be deftroyed."

Full of this thought, he went over to the camp of the Indians, where, according to the prediction of the genii, he was as well received as in that of the Perfians; but he faw there the very fame crimes which had already filled him with horror. " Oh! (faid he to himfelf,) if the angel Ithuriel fhould exterminate the Perfians, the angel of India muft certainly deftroy the Indians." But being afterwards more particularly informed of all that paffed in both armies, he heard of fuch acts of generofity, humanity, and greatnefs of foul, as at once furprifed and charmed him : " Unaccountable mortals! as ye are, (cried he,) how can you thus unite fo much bafenefs and fo much grandeur, fo many virtues and fo many vices!"

Meanwhile the peace was proclaimed; and the generals of the two armies, neither of whom had gained a complete victory, but who, for their own private intereft, had fhed the blood of fo many of their fellow-creatures, went to folicit their courts for rewards. The peace was celebrated in public writings, which announced the return of virtue and happinefs to the earth. " God be praifed, (faid Babouc,) Perfepolis will now be the abode of fpotlefs innocence, and will not be deftroyed, as the cruel genii intended. Let us hafte without delay to this capital of Afia."

N 2   He

*   *   *   *   *   *   *

He entered that immenfe city by the ancient
gate, which was entirely barbarous, and offended
the eye by its difagreeable rufticity. All that part
of the town favoured of the time when it was built;
for, notwithftanding the obftinacy of men, in praifing ancient at the expence of modern times, it muft
be owned that the firft effays in every art are rude
and unfinifhed.

Babouc mingled in a crowd of people, compofed
of the moft nafty and deformed of both fexes, who
were thronging with a ftupid air into a large and
gloomy inclofure. By the conftant hum; by the
geftures of the people; by the money which fome
perfons gave to others for the liberty of fitting
down, he imagined that he was in a market, where
chairs were fold: but obferving feveral women fall
down on their knees, with an appearance of looking
directly before them, while in reality they were
leering at the men by their fides, he was foon convinced that he was in a temple. Shrill, hoarfe,
favage, and difcordant voices, made the vault re-
echo with ill-articulated founds, that produced the
fame effect as the braying of wild affes, when, in
the plains of Pictavia, they anfwer the cornet that
calls them together. He ftopped his ears; but he
was ready to fhut his eyes and hold his nofe, when
he faw feveral labourers enter into the temple with
crows and fpades, who removed a large ftone, and
threw up the earth on both fides, from whence ex-
haled a peftilential vapour: at laft fome others approached, depofited a dead body in the opening,
and replaced the ftone upon it. "What! (cried
Babouc,) do thefe people bury their dead in the
place where they adore the Deity? What! are their
temples

temples paved with carcafes? I am no longer furprifed at thofe peftilential difeafes * that frequently
depopulate Perfepolis.   The putrefaction of the
dead, and the infected breath of fuch numbers of
the living, affembled and crowded together in the
fame place, are fufficient to poifon the whole ter-
reftrial globe.   Oh! what an abominable city is
Perfepolis! The angels probably intend to deftroy
it, in order to build a more beautiful one in its
place, and to people it with inhabitants who are
more virtuous and better. fingers.   Providence
may have its reafons for fo doing; to its difpofal
let us leave all future events."

*   *   *   *   *   *

Meanwhile the fun approached his meridian
height.   Babouc was to dine at the other end of
the city with a lady, for whom her hufband, an officer in the army, had given him fome letters : but
he firft took feveral turns in Perfepolis ; where he
faw other temples, better built and more richly a-
dorned, filled with a polite audience, and refounding
with harmonious mufic; he beheld public fountains,
which, tho' ill-placed, ftruck the eye by their beauty ; fquares where the beft kings that had governed

---

* Indeed one would imagine that the European churches, efpecially in this kingdom, had been contrived in order to difguft
the people, and deter them from public worfhip.   The chilling
dampnefs which reigns in every church, efpecially in the winter, is not more pernicious to the health, than the earthy cada-
verous fmell is to the fenfe ; and the eye is entertained with a
variety of funeral epitaphs and ornaments, which cannot fail to
excite fuperftitious horror in minds naturally fufceptible of
gloomy impreffions.

I

ed Perfia feemed to breathe in bronze, and others
where he heard the people crying out; "When
fhall we fee our beloved mafter?" He admired
the magnificent bridges built over the river; the fuperb and commodious quays; the palaces raifed on
both fides; and an immenfe houfe, where thoufands
of old foldiers, covered with fcars and crowned
with victory, offered their daily praifes to the god
of armies *. At laft he entered the houfe of the
lady, who, with a fet of fafhionable people, waited
his company to dinner. The houfe was neat and
elegant; the repaft delicious; the lady young, beautiful, witty, and engaging; and the company worthy of her; and Babouc every moment faid to himfelf, "The angel Ithuriel has little regard for the
world, or he would never think of deftroying fuch
a charming city."

*　　*　　*　　*　　*　　*

In the mean time he obferved that the lady, who
had begun by tenderly afking news about her hufband, fpoke ftill more tenderly to a young magi, towards the conclufion of the repaft. He faw a magiftrate, who, in prefence of his wife, paid his court
with great vivacity to a widow, while that indulgent
widow had one arm around the magiftrate's neck,
and held out her other hand to a young citizen, remarkable for his modefty and graceful appearance.
The magiftrate's wife rofe firft from table, to go to
converfe

---

* We perceive our author has an eye to the celebrated fountain on the *Pont Neuf*, the Place des Victoires, the two great
bridges over the Seine, with the ftone quays on each fide, the
palace of the Louvre, and the hofpital for invalids.

converfe in an adjoining clofet with her director, who came too late, and for whom they had waited dinner; and the director, a man of great eloquence, fpoke to her with fuch vehemency and holy zeal, that when fhe returned, her eyes were humid, her cheeks inflamed, her gait irregular, and her voice trembling.

Babouc then began to fear that the genius Ithuriel had but too much reafon. The talent he poffeffed of gaining confidence let him that fame day into all the fecrets of the lady. She confeffed to him her affection for the young magi, affured him that in all the houfes in Perfepolis, he would meet with much the fame behaviour as he had found in her's. Babouc concluded that fuch a fociety could not poffibly fubfift; that jealoufy, difcord, and vengeance, muft defolate every houfe; that tears and blood muft be daily·fhed; that the hufbands muft certainly kill the gallants of the wives, or be killed by them; and, in fine, that Ithuriel would do well to deftroy immediately a city abandoned to continual difafters.

$$* \quad * \quad * \quad * \quad * \quad *$$

Such were the gloomy ideas that poffeffed his mind, when a grave man in a black gown appeared at the gate, and humbly begged to fpeak to the young magiftrate. This ftripling, without rifing or taking the leaft notice of the old gentleman, gave him fome papers, with a haughty and carelefs air, and then difmiffed him. Babouc afked who this man was. The miftrefs of the houfe faid to him in a low voice, " He is one of the beft advocates in the city, and hath ftudied the law thefe fifty years. The other, who is but twenty-five years of age, and has only been a fatrape of the law for two days,
hath

hath ordered him to make an extract of a procefs,
he is going to determine, though he has not as yet
examined it." " This giddy youth acts wifely,
faid Babouc, in afking counfel of an old man. But
why is not the old man himfelf the judge ?" " Thou
art furely in jeft, faid they ; thofe who have grown
old in laborious and inferior pofts are never raifed
to places of dignity. This young man has a great
poft, becaufe his father is rich ; and the right of difpenfing juftice is purchafed here like a farm." " O
manners ! O unhappy city ! cried Babouc, this is
the height of anarchy and confufion. Thofe who
have thus purchafed the right of judging will doubtlefs fell their judgments ; nothing do I fee here but
an abyfs of iniquity."

While he was thus expreffing his grief and furprife, a young warrior, who that very day had returned from the army, faid to him why wouldeft
thou not have feats in the courts of juftice to be
purchafed ? I myfelf purchafed the right of braving
death at the head of two thoufand men, who are
under my command : it has this year coft me forty
thoufand darics of gold to lie on the earth thirty
nights fucceffively in a red drefs, and at laft to receive two wounds with an arrow, of which I ftill
feel the fmart. If I ruin myfelf to ferve the emperor of Perfia, whom I never faw, the fatrape of the
law may well pay fomething for enjoying the pleafure of giving audience to pleaders." Babouc was
filled with indignation, and could not help condemning a country, where the higheft pofts in the army
and the law were expofed to fale. He at once concluded, that the inhabitants muft be entirely ignorant of the art of war, and the laws of equity ; and
that though Ithuriel fhould not deftroy them, they
                                                    muft

must soon be ruined by their detestable adminiftration.

He was ftill further confirmed in his bad opinion
by the arrival of a fat man, who, after faluting all
the company with great familiarity, went up to the
young officer, and faid, " I can only lend thee fifty
thoufand darics of gold ; for indeed the taxes
of the empire have this year brought me in but three
hundred thoufand." Babouc enquired into the character of this man, who complained of having gained fo little, and was informed, that in Perfepolis
there were forty plebeian kings, who held the empire of Perfia by leafe, and paid a fmall tribute to
the monarch *.

*   *   *   *   *   *

After dinner he went into one of the moft fuperb
temples in the city, and feated himfelf amidft a
crowd of men and women, who were come thither
to pafs away the time. A magi appeared in a machine elevated above the heads of the people, and
talked a long time of vice and virtue. He divided
into feveral parts what needed no divifion at all :
he proved methodically what was fufficently clear,
and he taught what every body knew ; he threw
himfelf into a paffion with great compofure, and
went away fweating, and out of breath. The affembly then awoke, and imagined they had been
prefent at a very inftructive difcourfe. Babouc
faid, " This man has done his beft to tire two or
Vol. I.   O   ‡   three

* Thefe are the farmers-general of France, who were fuffered
to amafs vaft fortunes by fleecing the people, in confideration
of fupplying the government.

three hundred of his fellow-citizens; but his intention was good; and there is nothing in this that should occafion the deftruction of Perfepolis.'?

Upon leaving the affembly, he was conducted to a public entertainment, which was exhibited every day in the year. It was in a kind of great hall, at the end of which appeared a palace. The moft beautiful women in Perfepolis, and the moft confiderable fatrapes were ranged in order, and formed fo fine a fpectacle, that Babouc at firft believed that this was all the entertainment. Two or three perfons, who feemed to be kings and queens, foon appeared in the veftibule of their palace. Their language was very different from that of the people; it was meafured, harmonious, and fublime. No body flept. The audience kept a profound filence which was only interrupted by expreffions of fenfibility and admiration. The duty of kings, the love of virtue, and the dangers arifing from unbridled paffions, were all defcribed by fuch lively and affecting ftrokes, that Babouc fhed tears. He doubted not but that thefe heroes and heroines, thefe kings and queens whom he had juft heard, were the preachers of the empire; he even purpofed to engage Ithuriel to come and hear them; confident that fuch a fpectacle would for ever reconcile him to the city *.

As foon as the entertainment was finifhed, he refolved to vifit the principal queen, who had recommended fuch pure and noble morals in the palace. He defired to be introduced to her majefty, and was led up a narrow ftaircafe to an ill-furnifhed apartment in the fecond ftory, where he found a woman in a mean drefs, who faid to him with a noble and pathetic air, " This employment does not afford
me

me a fufficient maintenance; one of the princes
whom thou fawest has got me with child; I fhall
foon be brought to bed; I want money, and without money there is no lying in." Babouc gave her
an hundred darics of gold, faying, "Had there
been no other evil in the city but this, Ithuriel would
have been to blame for being fo much offended."

From thence he went to fpend the evening at the
houfe of a tradefman who dealt in magnificent
trifles. He was conducted thither by a man of fenfe,
with whom he had contracted an acquaintance.
He bought whatever pleafed his fancy; and the toyman with great politnefs fold him every thing for
more than it was worth. On his return home his
friend fhewed him how much he had been cheated.
Babouc fet down the name of the tradefman in his
pocket-book, in order to point him out to Ithuriel
as the object of peculiar vengeance on the day
when the city fhould be punifhed. As he was
writing, he heard fomebody knock at the door:
this was the toyman himfelf, who came to reftore
him his purfe, which he had left by miftake on the
counter. "How canft thou, cried Babouc, be fo
generous and faithful, when thou haft had the affurance to fell me thefe trifles for four times their
value?" "There is not a tradefman, replied the
merchant, of ever fo little note in the city, that
would not have returned thee thy purfe; but whoever faid that I fold thee thefe trifles for four times
their value, is greatly miftaken: I fold them for
ten times their value; and this is fo true, that wert
thou to fell them again in a month hence, thou
wouldft not get even this tenth part. But nothing
is more juft, it is the variable fancies of men that
fet a value on thefe baubles; it is this fancy that

O 2　　　　　maintains

maintains an hundred workmen whom I employ ; it is this that gives me a fine houfe and a hand-fome chariot and horfes ; it is this, in fine, that ex-cites induftry, encourages tafte, promotes circula-tion, and produces abundance.

"I fell the fame trifles to the neigbouring na-tion at a much higher rate than I have fold them to thee, and by thefe means I am ufeful to the empire." Babouc, after having reflected a moment, erafed the tradefman's name from his tablets.

*   *   *   *   *   *

Babouc, not knowing as yet what to think of Perfepolis, refolved to vifit the magi and the men of letters ; for, as the one ftudied wifdom, and the other religion, he hoped that they in conjunction would obtain mercy for the reft of the people. Ac-cordingly, he went next morning into a college of magi. The archimandrite confeffed to him, that he had an hundred thoufand crowns a-year for having taken the vow of poverty, and that he enjoy-ed a very extenfive empire in virtue of his vow of humility ; after which he left him with an inferior brother, who did him the honours of the place.

While the brother was fhewing him the mag-nificence of this houfe of penitence, a report was fpread abroad that Babouc was come to reform all thefe houfes. He immediately received petitions from each of them, the fubftance of which was, " Preferve us and deftroy all the reft." On hearing their apologies all thefe focieties were abfolutely ne-ceffary : on hearing their mutual accufations they all deferved to be abolifhed. He was fuprifed to find that all the members of thefe focieties were fo
extremely

extremely defirous of edifying the world, that they wifhed to have it entirely under their dominion.

Soon after appeared a little man, who was a de-mimagi, and who faid to him, " I plainly fee that the work is going to be accomplifhed : for Zerduft is returned to earth ; and the little girls prophecy, pinching themfelves before, and whipping them-felves behind. We therefore implore thy protection againft the great lama." " What! faid Babouc, a-gainft the royal pontiff, who refides at Tibet?" " Yes, againft him himfelf." " What! you are then ma-king war upon him, and raifing armies !" " No, but he fays that man is a free agent, and we deny it. We have wrote feveral pamphlets againft him, which he never read ; hardly has he heard our name mentioned ; he hath only condemned us in the fame manner as a man orders the trees in his garden to be cleared from caterpillars." Babouc was in-cenfed at the folly of thefe men who made pro-feffion of wifdom ; and at the intrigues of thofe who had renounced the world ; and at the ambi-tion, pride, and avarice of fuch as taught humility and a difinterefted fpirit ; from all which he con-cluded that Ithuriel had good reafon to deftroy the whole race.

*   *   *   *   *   *

On his return home, he fent for fome new books to alleviate his grief, and, in order to exhilerate his fpirits, invited fome men of letters to dine with him ; when, like wafps attracted by a pot of honey, there came twice as many as he defired. Thefe parafites were equally eager to eat and to fpeak ; they praifed two forts of perfons, the dead and themfelves ; but none of their co-temporaries, except

cept the mafter of the houfe. If any of them happened to drop a fmart and witty expreffion, the reft
caft down their eyes and bit their lips, out of mere
vexation that it had not been faid by themfelves.
They had lefs diffimulation than the magi, becaufe
they had not fuch grand objeſts of ambition. Each
of them behaved at once with all the meannefs of
a valet, and all the dignity of a great man. They
faid to each other's face the moft infulting things,
which they took for ftrokes of wit. They had fome
knowledge of the defign of Babouc's commiffion ;
one of them entreated him in a low voice to
extirpate an author who had not praifed him
fufficiently about five years before ; another re-
quefted the ruin of a citizen who had never laughed at his comedies ; and a third demanded the deftruction of the academy, becaufe he had not been
able to get admitted into it. The repaft being
ended, each of them departed by himfelf ; for in
the whole crowd there were not two men that
could endure the company or converfation of each
other, except at the houfes of the rich, who invited
them to their tables. Babouc thought that it would
be no great lofs to the public if all thefe vermin
were deftroyed in the general cataftrophe.

* * * * * *

Having now got rid of thefe men of letters, he
began to read fome new books, where he difcovered the true fpirit by which his guefts had been ac-
tuated. He obferved with particular indignation
thofe flanderous gazettes, thofe archives of bad
tafte, dictated by envy, bafenefs, and hunger ; thofe
ungenerous fatires, where the vulture is treated
with lenity, and the dove torn in pieces ; and thofe

dry

dry and infipid romances, filled with characters of women to whom the author was an utter ftranger.

All thefe deteftable writings he committed to the flames, and went to pafs the evening in walking. In this excurfion he was introduced to an old man poffeffed of great learning, who had not come to increafe the number of his parafites. This man of letters always fled from crowds ; he underftood human nature, availed himfelf of his knowledge, and imparted it to others with great difcretion.---- Babouc told him how much he was grieved at what he had feen and read.

"Thou haft read very defpicable performances, faid the man of letters ; but in all times, in all countries, and in all kinds of literature, the bad fwarm and the good are rare. Thou haft received into thy houfe the very dregs of pedantry ; for, in all profeffions, thofe who are leaft worthy of appearing, are always fure to prefent themfelves with the greateft impudence. The truly wife live among themfelves in retirement and tranquillity ; and we have ftill fome men and fome books worthy of thy attention." While he was thus fpeaking, they were joined by another man of letters ; and the converfation became fo entertaining and inftructive, fo elevated above vulgar prejudices, and fo conformable to virtue, that Babouc acknowledged he had never heard the like. " Thefe are men, faid he to himfelf, whom the angel Ithuriel will not prefume to touch, or he muft be a mercilefs being indeed.

Though reconciled to men of letters, he was ftill enraged againft the reft of the nation. " Thou art a ftranger, faid the judicious perfon who was talking to him ; abufes prefent themfelves to thy eyes in crowds, while the good, which lies concealed,

ed, and which is even fometimes the refult of thefe
very abufes, efcapes thy obfervation." He then
learned, that among men of letters there were
fome who were free from envy; and that even a-
mong the magi themfelves there were fome men of
virtue. In fine, he concluded that thefe great-bo-
dies, which, by their mutual fhocks, feemed to
threaten their common ruin, were at bottom very
falutary inftitutions; that each fociety of magi
was a check upon its rivals; and that though thefe
rivals might differ in fome fpeculative points, they
all taught the fame morals, inftructed the people,
and lived in fubjection to the laws, not unlike to
thofe preceptors who watch over the heir of a family, while the mafter of the houfe watches over
them. He converfed with feveral of thefe magi,
and found them poffeffed of exalted fouls. He likewife learned that even among the fools who pretended to make war on the great lama, there had
been fome men of diftinguifhed merit; and, from
all thefe particulars, he conjectured that it might
be with the manners of Perfepolis as it was with
the buildings; fome of which moved his pity,
while others filled him with admiration.

*   *   *   *   *   *

He faid to the man of letters, " I plainly fee
that thefe magi, whom I at firft imagined to be
fo dangerous, are, in reality, extremely ufeful; e-
fpecially when a wife government hinders them
from rendering themfelves too neceffary; but thou
wilt at leaft acknowledge, that your young magiftrates who purchafe the office of a judge as foon
as they can mount a horfe, muft difplay in their
tribunals the moft ridiculous impertinence, and the
moft

most iniquitous perverfenefs. It would doubtlefs be better to give thefe places gratuitoufly to thofe old civilians who have fpent their lives in the ftudy of the law."

The man of letters replied, "Thou haft feen our army before thy arrival at Perfepolis; thou knoweft that our young officers fight with great bravery, though they buy their pofts; perhaps thou wilt find that our young magiftrates do not give wrong decifions, though they purchafe the right of difpenfing juftice."

He led him next day to the grand tribunal, where an affair of great importance was to be decided. The caufe was known to all the world. All the old advocates that fpoke on the fubjeét were wavering and unfettled in their opinions: they quoted an hundred laws, none of which were applicable to the queftion. They confidered the matter in a hundred different lights, but never in its true point of view. The judges were more quick in their decifion than the advocates in raifing doubts. They were unanimous in their fentiments; they decided juftly, becaufe they followed the light of reafon. The others reafoned falfely, becaufe they only confulted their books.

Babouc concluded that the beft things frequently arofe from abufes. He faw the fame day, that the riches of the receivers of the public revenue, at which he had been fo much offended, were capable of producing an excellent effeét; for the emperor having occafion for money, he found in an hour by their means what he could not have procured in fix months by the ordinary methods. He faw that thofe great clouds, fwelled with the dews of the earth, reftored in plentiful fhowers what they had thence derived. Befides, the children of thefe

new gentlemen, who were frequently better educated than thofe of the moft ancient families, were
fometimes more ufeful members of fociety ; for he
whofe father hath been a good accomptant may
eafily become a good judge, a brave warrior, and
an able ftatefman.

*   *   *   *   *   *

Babouc was infenfibly brought to excufe the a-
varice of the farmer of the revenues, who in reality was not more avaricious than other men, and
befides was extremely neceffary. He overlooked
the folly of thofe who ruined themfelves, in order
to obtain a poft in the law or army ; a folly that
produces great magiftrates and heroes. He for-
gave the envy of men of letters, among whom
there were fome that enlightened the world ; and
he was reconciled to the ambitious and intriguing
magi, who were poffeffed of more great virtues
than little vices. But he had ftill many caufes of
complaint. The gallantries of the ladies efpecially, and the fatal effects which thefe muft neceffarily produce, filled him with fear and terror.

As he was defirous of prying into the characters of men of every condition, he went to wait
on a minifter of ftate ; but trembled all the way,
left fome wife fhould be affaffinated by her hufband
in his prefence. Having arrived at the ftatefman's,
he was obliged to remain two hours in the anti-chamber before his name was fent in, and two
hours more after that was done. In this inter-
val, he refolved to recommend to the angel
Ithuriel both the minifter and his infolent por-
ters. The anti-chamber was filled with ladies
of every rank, magi of all colours, judges, merchants,

chants, officers, and pedants; and all of them complained of the minifter. The mifer and the ufurer faid, " Doubtlefs this man plunders the provinces." The capricious reproached him with ficklenefs; the voluptuary faid, " He thinks of nothing but his pleafure." The factious hoped to fee him foon ruined by a cabal; and the women flattered themfelves that they fhould foon have a younger minifter.

Babouc heard their converfation, and could not help faying, " This is furely a happy man; he hath all his enemies in his anti-chamber; he crufhes with his power thofe that envy his grandeur; he beholds thofe who deteft him grovelling at his feet." At length he was admitted into the prefence-chamber, where he faw a little old man bending under the weight of years and bufinefs, but ftill lively and full of fpirits.

The minifter was pleafed with Babouc, and to Babouc he appeared to be a man of great merit. The converfation became interefting. The minifter confeffed that he was very unhappy; that he paffed for rich, while in reality he was poor; that he was believed to be all-powerful, and yet was conftantly contradicted; that he had obliged none but a parcel of ungrateful wretches; and that, in the courfe of forty years labour, he had hardly enjoyed a moment's reft. Babouc was moved with his misfortunes; and thought that if this man had been guilty of fome faults, and Ithuriel had a mind to punifh him, he ought not to cut him off, but to leave him in pof-feffion of his place.

* * * * * *

While Babouc was talking to the minifter, the

beautiful lady with whom he had dined, entered haftily, her eyes and her forehead difcovering the fymptoms of grief and indignation. She burft into reproaches againft the ftatefman; fhe fhed tears; fhe complained bitterly that her hufband had been refufed a place to which his birth allowed him to afpire, and which he had fully merited by his wounds and his fervice; fhe expreffed herfelf with fuch force; fhe uttered her complaints with fuch a graceful air; fhe overthrew objections with fo much addrefs, and enforced her arguments with fo much eloquence, that fhe did not leave the chamber till fhe had made her hufband's fortune.

Babouc gave her his hand, and faid, " Is it poffible, madam, that thou canft take fo much pains to ferve a man whom thou doft not love, and from whom thou haft every thing to fear ?" " A man whom I do not love! cried fhe; know, Sir, that my hufband is the beft friend I have in the world; that there is nothing I would not facrifice for him, except my lover; and that he would do any thing for me, except that of leaving his miftrefs. I muft introduce you to her acquaintance; fhe is a charming woman, fprightly, and fweet-tempered; we fup together this very night, with my hufband and my little magi; come and fhare our joy.

The lady conducted Babouc to her own houfe. The hufband, who was at laft arrived, overwhelmed with grief, received his wife with tranfports of joy and gratitude. He embraced by turns his wife, his miftrefs, the little magi, and Babouc. Wit, harmony, cheerfulnefs, and all the graces, embellifhed the repaft. " Know, faid the lady with whom he fupped, that thofe who are fometimes called difhoneft women have almoft always the merit of very honeft men; and to convince thee

of

of this, I invite thee to dine with me to-morrow at the beautiful Theona's. There are some old vestals that tear her character in pieces; but she does more good than all of them together. She would not commit the least act of injustice to gain the greatest advantage; she gives the most generous advice to her lover; she consults only his glory; and he would blush before her, should he let slip any opportunity of doing good; for nothing can more effectually excite a man to the performance of virtuous actions, than to have for the witnefs and judge of his conduct a mistrefs whose esteem he wishes to deserve."

Babouc did not fail to keep the appointment. He saw a house where all the pleasures seemed to reign, with Theona at the head of them, who well knew how to preserve the most perfect order. Her easy wit made all around her happy; she pleased almost without intending to do so; she was as amiable as beneficent; and, what enhanced the merit of all her good qualities, she was a beauty.

Babouc, though a Scythian, and sent by a genii, found, that should he continue much longer in Persepolis, he would forget Ithuriel for Theona. He began to grow fond of a city, the inhabitants of which were polite, affable, and beneficent, tho' fickle, slanderous, and vain. He was much afraid that Persepolis would be condemned. He was even afraid to give in his account.

This, however, he did in the following manner: he caused a little statue, composed of all kinds of metals, of earth, and stones the most precious and the most vile, to be cast by one of the best founders in the city, and carried it to Ithuriel. "Wilt thou break, said he, this pretty statue, because it is not wholly composed of gold and diamonds?" Ithuriel

thuriel immediately underftood his meaning, and
refolved to think no more of punifhing Perfepolis,
but to leave " The world as it goes."   " For, faid
he, if all is not well, all is paffable."   Thus Perfepolis was fuffered to remain ; nor did Babouc complain like Jonas, who was fo highly incenfed at the
prefervation of Nineveh. But when a man has
been three days in a whale's belly, he cannot be
fuppofed to be in fo good a humour as when he
has been at an opera or a comedy, and hath fupped with good company.

MICROMEGAS.

MICROMEGAS;

A

COMIC ROMANCE,

BEING

A SEVERE SATIRE

UPON THE

PHILOSOPHY, IGNORANCE, and SELF-
CONCEIT of MANKIND.

MICROMEGAS†.

CHAP. I.

A Voyage to the Planet SATURN, by an Inhabitant of the Star SIRIUS.

IN one of the planets that revolve round the ſtar known by the name of Sirius, was a certain young gentleman of promiſing parts, whom I had the honour to be acquainted with, in his laſt voyage to this our little ant-hill. His name was Micromegas, an appellation admirably ſuited to all great men, and his ſtature amounted to eight leagues in height, that is, four and twenty thouſand geometrical paces, five feet in each.

Some of your mathematicians, a ſet of people always uſeful to the public, will, perhaps, inſtantly ſeize the pen, and calculate, that Mr Micromegas, inhabitant of the country of Sirius, being from head to foot four and twenty thouſand paces in length, making one hundred and twenty thouſand royal feet ; that we, denizens of this earth, being at a medium little more than five feet high, and

---

* A name compounded of two Greek words, ſignifying *little* and *great*.

our globe nine thousand leagues in circumference.;
these things being premised, I say, they will conclude, that the periphery of the globe which produced him, must be exactly one and twenty millions six hundred thousand times greater than that
of this our tiny ball. Nothing in nature is more
simple and common. The dominions of some so-
vereigns of Germany or Italy, which may be com-
passed in half an hour, when compared with the
empires of Ottoman, Muscovy, or China, are no
other than faint instances of the prodigious difference which nature hath made in the scale of beings.
The stature of his excellency being of these extraordinary dimensions, all our painters and statuaries
will easily agree, that the round of his belly might
amount to fifty thousand royal feet : a very agreeable and just proportion.

His nose being equal in length to one third of
his face, and his jolly countenance engrossing one
seventh part of his height, it must be owned that
the nose of this same Sirian, was six thousand three
hundred and thirty-three royal feet to a hair ; which
was to be demonstrated.—With regard to his understanding, it is one of the best cultivated I have
known ; he is perfectly well acquainted with abundance of things, some of which are of his own in-
vention : for, when his age did not exceed two
hundred and fifty years, he, according to the custom of his country, studied at the most celebrated
university of the whole planet, and by the force of
his genius, found out upwards of fifty propositions
of Euclid, having the advantage by more than eighteen, of Blaise Paschal, who (as we are told by his
own sister) demonstrated two and thirty for his
amusement, and then left off, choosing rather to be
n indifferent philosopher, than a great mathematician.

tician.—About the four hundred and fiftieth year
of his age, or latter end of his childhood, he diffect-
ed a great number of fmall infects not more than
one hundred feet in diameter, which are not per-
ceivable by ordinary microfcopes, of which he compofed a very curious treatife, which involved him in
fome trouble: the mufti of the nation, though very
old and very ignorant, made fhift to difcover in his
book certain lemmas that were fufpicious, unfeem-
ly, rafh, heretick and unfound; and profecuted
him with great animofity; for, the fubject of the
author's inquiry was, whether in the world of Sirius, there was any difference between the fubftan-
tial forms of a flea and a fnail.

Micromegas defended his philofophy with fuch
fpirit as made all the female fex his profelytes; and
the procefs lafted two hundred and twenty years; at
the end of which, in confequence of the mufti's
intereft, the book was condemned by judges who
had never read it, and the author expelled from
court, for the term of eight hundred years.

Not much afflicted at his banifhment from a
court that teemed with nothing but turmoils and
trifles, he made a very humurous fong upon
the mufti, who gave himfelf no trouble about the
matter, and fet out on his travels from planet to
planet, in order (as the faying is) to improve his
mind and finifh his education. Thofe who never
travel but in a poft chaife or berlin, will, doubtlefs,
be aftonifhed at the equipages ufed above: for we
that ftrut upon this little mole-hill, are at a lofs to
conceive any thing that furpaffes our own cuftoms.
But our traveller was a wonderful adept in the laws
of gravitation, together with the whole force of at-
traction and repulfion; and made fuch feafonable
ufe of his knowledge, that fometimes, by the help

of a fun-beam, and fometimes by the convenience of a comet, he and his retinue glided from fphere to fphere, as a bird hops from one bough to another. He in a very little time, pofted through the milky way; and I am obliged to own, he faw not a twinkle of thofe ftars fuppofed to adorn that fair empyrean, which the illuftrious doctor Derham brags to have obferved through his telefcope. Not that I pretend to fay the doctor was miftaken. God forbid! but Micromegas was upon the fpot, an exceeding good obferver, and I have no mind to contradict any man. Be that as it will, after many windings and turnings, he arrived at the planet Saturn; and, accuftomed as he was to the fight of novelties, he could not for his life reprefs that fupercilious and conceited fmile which often efcapes the wifeft philofopher, when he perceived the fmallnefs of that globe, and the diminutive fize of its inhabitants: for really Saturn is but about nine hundred times larger than this our earth, and the people of that country mere dwarfs, about a thoufand fathoms high. In fhort, he at firft derided thofe poor pigmies, juft as an Italian fidler laughs at the mufic of Lully, at his firft arrival in Paris: but as this Sirian was a perfon of good fenfe, he foon perceived that a thinking being may not be altogether ridiculous, even though he is not quite fix thoufand feet high; and therefore he became familiar with them, after they had ceafed to wonder at his extraordinary appearance. In particular, he contracted an intimate friendfhip with the fecretary of the academy of Saturn, a man of good underftanding, who, though in truth he had invented nothing of his own, gave a very good account of the inventions of others, and enjoyed, in peace, the reputation of a little poet and great calculator.

And

And here, for the edification of the reader, I will repeat a very fingular converfation that one day paffed between Mr. fecretary and Micromegas.

CHAP. II.

The converfation between MICROMEGAS and the inhabitant of SATURN.

HIS excellency having laid himfelf down, and the fecretary approached his nofe, "It muft be confeffed," faid Micromegas, "that nature is full of variety."—"Yes," replied the Saturnian, na- "ture is like a parterre whofe flowers—" "Pfhaw!" cried the other, "a truce with your parter- res."—"It is," refumed the fecretary, "like an affembly of fair and brown women whofe dreffes--" "What a plague have I to do with your bru- nettes?" faid our traveller. "Then it is like a gallery of pictures, the ftrokes of which---" "Not at all," anfwered Micromegas, "I tell you once for all, nature is like nature, and comparifons are odious." "Well, to pleafe you," faid the fecre- tary--"I won't be pleafed," replied the Sirian, "I want to be inftructed: begin therefore, without further preamble, and tell me how many fenfes the people of this world enjoy."---We have feventy and two," faid the academician, "but, we are daily complaining of the fmall number; as our imagina- nation tranfcends our wants; for, with thefe feventy two fenfes, our five moons and ring, we find our- felves very much reftricted; and notwithftanding our curiofity, and the no fmall number of thofe paf- fions that refult from thefe few fenfes, we have ftill time enough to be tired of idlenefs." "I fincere-

ly

ly believe what you fay," cried Micromegas, " for,
though we Sirians have near a thoufand different
fenfes, there ftill remains a certain vague defire; an
unaccountable inquietude inceſſantly advertifing us
of our own unimportance, and giving us to underftand, that there are other beings who are much
our fuperiors in point of perfection. I have travelled a little, and feen mortals both above and below myfelf in the fcale of being : but I have
met with none who had not more defire than neceſſity and more want than gratification ; perhaps,
I fhall one day arrive in fome country, where nought
is wanting ; but, hitherto I have had no certain information of fuch an happy land." The Saturnian
and his gueft exhaufted themfelves in conjectures
upon this fubject, and after abundance of argumen-
tation equally ingenious and uncertain, being fain
to return to matter of fact, " To what age do you
commonly live?" faid the Sirian.   " Lack-a-day ! a
mere trifle," replied the little gentleman.   " It is
the very fame cafe with us," refumed the other,
" the fhortneſs of life is our daily complaint, fo
that this muft be an univerfal law in nature."
" Alas !" cried the Saturnian, " few, very few on
this globe, outlive five hundred great revolutions of
the fun ; (thefe, according to our way of reckoning, amount to about fifteen thoufand years.) So,
you fee, we in a manner begin to die the very moment we are born : our exiftence is no more than
a point, our duration an inftant, and our globe an
atom.   Scarce do we begin to learn a little, when
death intervenes, before we can profit by experience : for my own part, I am deterred from laying
fchemes, when I confider myfelf as a fingle drop in
the midft of an immenfe ocean. I am particularly
                                               afham-

afhamed, in your prefence, of the ridiculous figure
I make among my fellow-creatures."

To this declaration, Micromegas replied, " If
you were not a philofopher, I fhould be afraid of
mortifying your pride, by telling you that the term
of our lives, is feven hundred times longer than the
date of your exiftence : but, you are very fenfible,
that when the texture of the body is refolved, in
order to reanimate nature in another form, which
is the confequence of what we call death : when
that moment of change arrives, there is not the
leaft difference betwixt having lived a whole eternity, or a fingle day. I have been in fome countries where the people live a thoufand times longer
than with us, and yet they murmured at the fhort-
nefs of their time : but one will find every where,
fome few perfons of good fenfe, who know how to
make the beft of their portion, and thank the author of nature for his bounty. There is a profufion
of variety fcattered through the univerfe, and yet
there is an admirable vein of uniformity that runs
thro the whole: for example, all thinking beings are
different among themfelves, though at bottom they
refemble one another, in the powers and paffions
of the foul : matter, though interminable, hath different properties in every fphere. How many principal attributes do you reckon in the matter of this
world ?" " If you mean thofe properties," faid
the Saturnian, " without which we believe this our
globe could not fubfift, we reckon in all three hundred, fuch as extent, impenetrability, motion, gravitation, divifibility, et cætera."—" That fmall
number," replied the traveller, " probably anfwers
the views of the creator, on this your narrow fphere.
I adore his wifdom in all his works. I fee infinite
variety,

variety, but every where proportion. Your globe is fmall; fo are the inhabitants: you have few fenfations; becaufe your matter is endued with few properties: thefe are the works of unerring providence. Of what colour does your fun appear when accurately examined?" "Of a yellowifh white," anfwered the Saturnian; "and in feparating one of his rays, we find it contains feven colours." "Our fun," faith the Sirian, "is of a reddifh hue, and we have no lefs than thirty-nine original colours. Among all the funs I have feen, there is no fort of refemblance; and in this fphere of your's, there is not one face like another."

After divers queftions of this nature, he afked how many fubftances, effentially different, they counted in the world of Saturn; and underftood that they numbered but thirty; fuch as God; fpace; matter; beings endued with fenfe and extenfion; beings that have extenfion, fenfe, and reflection; thinking beings who have no extenfion; thofe that are penetrable; thofe that are impenetrable, and the reft. But this Saturnian philofopher was prodigioufly aftonifhed, when the Sirian told him, they had no lefs then three hundred, and that he himfelf had difcovered three thoufand more in the courfe of his travels. In fhort, after having communicated to each other what they knew, and even what they did not know, and argued during a complete revolution of the fun, they refolved to fet out together on a fmall philofophical tour.

CHAP.

CHAP. III.

The Voyage of those Two INHABITANTS of the
other World.

OUR two philofophers were juft ready to embark for the atmofphere of Saturn, with a
jolly provifion of mathematical inftruments, when
the Saturnian's miftrefs, having got an inkling of
their defign, came all in tears to make her remonftrances. She was a little handfome brunette, not
above fix hundred and threefcore fathom high ; but
her agreeable attractions made amends for the
fmallnefs of her ftature. " Ah! cruel man," cried
fhe; "after a refiftance of fifteen hundred years,
when at length I furrendered, and fcarce have paffed two hundred more in thy embrace, to leave me
thus, before the honey moon is over, and go a
rambling with a giant of another world! go, go;
thou art a mere virtuofo, devoid of tendernefs and
love! if thou wert a true Saturnian, thou wouldft
be faithful and invariable. Ah! whither art thou
going? what is thy defign? our five moons are not
fo inconftant, nor our ring fo changeable as thee!
but take this along with you, henceforth I ne'er
fhall love another man." The little gentleman
embraced and wept over her, notwithftanding his
philofophy; and the lady, after having fwooned
with great decency, went to confole herfelf with
the converfation of a certain beau.

Meanwhile, our two virtuofi fet out, and at one
jump leaped upon the ring, which they found pretty
flat, according to the ingenious guefs of an illuftrious inhabitant of this our little earth: from thence
they eafily flipped from moon to moon; and a co-

met chancing to pafs, they fprung upon it with all
their fervants and apparatus. Thus carried about
one hundred and fifty million of leagues, they met
with the fatellites of Jupiter, and arrived upon the
body of the planet itfelf, where they continued a
whole year; during which they learned fome very
curious fecrets, which would actually be fent to the
prefs, were it not for fear of the gentlemen inquifitors, who have found among them fome corolla-
ries very hard of digeftion. Neverthelefs, I have
read the manufcript in the library of the illuftrious
archbifhop of.... who has granted me permiffion to
perufe his books with that generofity and goodnefs
which can never be enough commended: wherefore I promife he fhall have a long article in the
next edition of Moreri, where I fhall not forget the
young gentlemen his fons, who give us fuch pleafing hopes of feeing perpetuated the race of their
illuftrious father. But to return to our travellers.
When they took leave of Jupiter, they traverfed a
fpace of about one hundred millions of leagues, and
coafting along the planet Mars, which is well
known to be five times fmaller than our little earth,
they defcryed two moons fubfervient to that orb,
which have efcaped the obfervation of all our aftro-
nomers. I know father Caftel will write, and that
pleafantly enough, againft the exiftence of thefe
two moons; but I entirely refer myfelf to thofe who
reafon by analogy: thofe worthy philofophers are
very fenfible that Mars, which is at fuch a diftance
from the fun, muft be in a very uncomfortable fituation, without the benefit of a couple of moons: be
that as it may, our gentlemen found the planet fo
fmall, that they were afraid they fhould not find
room to take a little repofe; fo that they purfued
their journey like two travellers who defpife the
paultry

paultry accommodation of a village, and pufh forward to the next market town. But the Sirian and his companion foon repented of their delicacy; for, they journeyed a long time, without finding a refting place, till at length they difcerned a fmall fpeck, which was the Earth. Coming from Jupiter, they could not but be moved with compaffion at fight of this miferable fpot, upon which, however, they refolved to land, left they fhould be a fecond time difappointed. They accordingly moved towards the tail of the comet, where, finding an Aurora Borealis ready to fet fail, they embarked, and arrived on the northern coaft of the Baltic on the fifth day of July, new ftile, in the year 1737.

C H A P. IV.

What befel them upon this our GLOBE.

HAVING taken fome repofe, and being defirous of reconnoitring the narrow field in which they were, they traverfed it at once from north to fouth. Every ftep of the Sirian and his attendants meafured about thirty thoufand royal feet: whereas, the dwarf of Saturn, whofe ftature did not exceed a thoufand fathoms, followed at a diftance quite out of breath; becaufe, for every fingle ftride of his companion, he was obliged to make twelve good fteps at leaft. The reader may figure to himfelf, (if we are allowed to make fuch comparifons,) a very little rough fpaniel dodging after a captain of the Pruffian grenadiers.

As thofe ftrangers walked at a good pace, they compaffed the globe in fix and thirty hours; the fun, it is true, or rather the earth, defcribes the fame

space in the course of one day; but it must be observed that it is much more easy to turn upon an
axis than to walk a-foot. Behold them then returned to the spot from whence they had set out,
after having discovered that almost imperceptible
sea, which is called the Mediterranean; and the
other narrow pond that surrounds this mole-hill,
under the denomination of the great ocean; in
wading through which, the dwarf had never wet
his mid-leg, while the other scarce moistened his
heel. In going and coming through both hemispheres, they did all that lay in their power to discover whether or not the globe was inhabited.
They stooped, they lay down, they groped in every corner; but their eyes and hands were not at
all proportioned to the small beings that crawl upon
this earth; and, therefore, they could not find the
smallest reason to suspect that we and our fellow citizens of this globe had the honour to exist.

The dwarf, who sometimes judged too hastily,
concluded at once that there was no living creature upon earth; and his chief reason was, that he
had seen nobody. But, Micromegas, in a polite
manner, made him sensible of the unjust conclusion; " For, (said he,) with your diminutive eyes
you cannot see certain stars of the fiftieth magnitude, which I distinctly perceive; and do you take
it for granted that no such stars exist?" " But I
have groped with great care," replied the dwarf.
" Then your sense of feeling must be bad," resumed the other. " But this globe, (said the dwarf,)
is ill contrived; and so irregular in its form as to
be quite ridiculous. The whole together looks
like a chaos. Do but observe these little rivulets;
not one of them runs in a strait line: and these
ponds which are neither round, square, nor oval,
nor

nor indeed of any regular figure; together with
thofe little fharp pebbles, (meaning the mountains,)
that roughen the whole furface of the globe, and
have tore all the fkin from my feet. Befides, pray
take notice of the fhape of the whole, how it flat-
tens at the poles, and turns round the fun in an
awkward oblique manner, fo as that the polar
circles cannot poffibly be cultivated. Truly, what
makes me believe there is no inhabitant on this
fphere, is a full perfuafion that no fenfible being
would live in fuch a difagreeable place." " What
then ? (faid Micromegas,) perhaps the beings that
inhabit it come not under that denomination ; but,
in all appearance, it was not made for nothing.
Every thing here feems to you irregular ; becaufe
you fetch all your comparifons from Jupiter or Saturn. Perhaps this is the very reafon of the feeming confufion which you condemn ; have not I told
you, that in the courfe of my travels I have always
met with variety ?" The Saturnian replied to all
thefe arguments ; and perhaps the difpute would
have known no end, if Micromegas in the heat of
the conteft had not luckily broke the ftring of his
diamond necklace ; fo that the jewels fell to the
ground, confifting of pretty fmall unequal karats,
the largeft of which weighed four hundred pounds,
and the fmalleft fifty. The dwarf, in helping to
pick them up, perceived, as they approached his
eye, that every fingle diamond was cut in fuch a manner as to anfwer the purpofe of an excellent microfcope. He therefore took up a fmall one, about one
hundred and fixty feet in diameter, and applied it
to his eye, while Micromegas chofe another of two
thoufand five hundred ; though they were of excellent powers, the obfervers could perceive nothing by
their affiftance, fo that they were altered and ad-
justed ;

justed : at length, the inhabitant of Saturn discern-
ed something almost imperceptible moving between
two waves in the Baltic : this was no other than a
whale, which, in a dexterous manner, he caught
with his little finger, and, placing it on the nail of
his thumb, shewed it to the Syrian, who laughed
heartily at the excessive smallness peculiar to the
inhabitants of this our globe. The Saturnian, by
this time convinced that our world was inhabited,
began to imagine we had no other animals than
whales ; and being a mighty arguer, he forthwith set
about investigating the origin and motion of this
small atom, curious to know whether or not it was
furnished with ideas, judgment, and free will. Micromegas was very much perplexed upon this subject, he examined the animal with the most patient attention, and the result of his inquiry was, that
he could see no reason to believe a soul was lodged
in such a body. The two travellers were actually
inclined to think there was no such thing as mind
in this our habitation, when, by the help of their
microscope, they perceived something as large as a
whale floating upon the surface of the sea. It is
well known, that at this period a flight of philosophers were upon their return from the polar circle,
where they had been making observations, for
which nobody has hitherto been the wiser *. The
ga-

---

* Caffini, who had measured a degree of the meridian in France,
published in 1718 his book upon the size and figure of the
earth, in which he concludes it is lengthened at the poles, in
contradiction to the theory of Newton and Huygens ; the French
king ordered a company of academicians to measure a degree
of the equator, and another to take the dimensions of a degree at
the polar circle, in order to determine this dispute. Messrs.
Goden, Bouguer, and de la Condamine, were sent to Peru ;
while

gazettes record, that their veffel ran afhore on the
coaft of Bothnia, and that they with great difficulty
faved their lives; but in this world one can never
dive to the bottom of things: for my own part, I
will ingenuoufly recount the tranfaction juft as it
happened, without any addition of my own; and
this is no fmall effort in a modern hiftorian.

CHAP. V.

MIcromegas ftretched out his hand gently towards the place where the object appeared,
and advanced two fingers, which he inftantly pulled back, for fear of being difappointed, then opening foftly and fhutting them all at once, he very
dexteroufly feized the fhip that contained thofe
gentlemen, and placed it on his nail, avoiding too
much preffure, which might have crufhed the whole
in pieces. "This," faid the Saturnian dwarf,
" is a creature very different from the former:"
upon which, the Sirian placing the fuppofed animal
in the hollow of his hand, the paffengers and crew,
who believed themfelves thrown by a hurricane
upon fome rock, began to put themfelves in motion.
The failors having hoifted out fome cafks of wine,
jump-

while Maupertuis, Clairaut, Camus, Monnier, and Outhier, fet
out for Lapland. The obfervations of both companies, reinfor-
ced by thofe of Don Jorge Juan, and Antonio d'Ulloa, two Spa-
nifh philofophers employed by his Catholick Majefty, confirmed
the theory of Sir Ifaac Newton, that the earth was an oblate
fpheroid, flattened at the poles. A curious account of the
voyage to Lapland, and of the obfervations there made, is to be
found in the works of Maupertuis, publifhed at Lyons in the
year 1756.

jumped after them into the hand of Micromegas:
the mathematicians having fecured their quadrants,
fectors, and Lapland miftreffes, went over-board at
a different place, and made fuch a buftle in their
defcent, that the Sirian at length felt his fingers
tickled by fomething that feemed to move. An
iron crow chanced to penetrate about a foot deep
into his fore finger; and from this prick he
concluded that fomething had iffued from the little
animal he held in his hand; but at firft he fufpected nothing more: for the microfcope, that fcarce
rendered a whale and a fhip vifible, had no effect
upon an object fo imperceptible as man.---I do not
intend to fhock the vanity of any perfon whatever;
but here I am obliged to beg your people of importance, to confider, that fuppofing the ftature of a
man to be about five feet, we mortals make juft
fuch a figure upon the earth, as an animal the
fixty thoufandth part of a foot in height, would
exhibit upon a bowl ten feet in circumference.
When you reflect upon a being who could hold
this whole earth in the palm of his hand, and is
endued with organs proportioned to thofe we poffefs, you will eafily conceive that there muft be a
great variety of created fubftances;———and pray,
what muft fuch beings think of thofe battles by
which a conqueror gains a fmall village, to lofe it
again in the fequel? I do not at all doubt, but if
fome captain of grenadiers fhould chance to read
this work, he would add two large feet at leaft to
the caps of his company: but I affure him his labour will be in vain; for, do what he will, he and
his foldiers will never be other than infinitely diminutive and inconfiderable. What wonderful addrefs muft have been inherent in our Sirian philofopher, that enabled him to perceive thofe atoms of
which

which we have been fpeaking. When Leuwenhoek and Hartfoecker obferved the firft rudiments of which we are formed, they did not make fuch an aftonifhing difcovery. What pleafure, therefore, was the portion of Micromegas, in obferving the motion of thofe little machines, in examining all their pranks, and purfuing them in all their opera- tions! with what joy did he put his microfcope in- to his companion's hand ; and with what tranfport did they both at once exclaim, " l fee them dif- tinctly,—don't you perceive them carrying burdens, lying down and rifing up again ?" So faying, their hands fhook with eagernefs to fee, and apprehenfi- on to lofe fuch uncommon objects.—The Saturnian, making a fudden tranfition, from the moft cautious diftruft, to the moft exceffive credulity, imagined he faw them in the very work of propagation, and cried aloud, " I have furprifed nature in the very fact." Neverthelefs, he was deceived by appear- ances : a cafe too common, whether we do or do not make ufe of microfcopes.

CHAP. VI.

What happened in their intercourfe with Men.

MICROMEGAS being a much better obferv- er than his dwarf, perceived diftinctly that thofe atoms fpoke ; and made the remark to his companion, who was fo much afhamed of being miftaken in the article of generation, that he would not believe fuch a puny fpecies could poffibly com- municate their ideas : for, though he had the gift of tongues, as well as his companion, he could not hear thofe particles fpeak ; and therefore fuppofed they had no language : befides, how fhould fuch

S † im-

imperceptible beings have the organs of speech?
and what in the name of God can they say to one
another? in order to speak, they must have something like thought, and if they think, they must surely have something equivalent to a foul: now, to attribute any thing like a foul to fuch an infect fpecies, appears a mere abfurdity.---" But juft now," replied the
Sirian, " you believed they made love to each o-
ther; and do you think this could be done without
thinking, without ufing fome fort of language, or
at leaft fome way of making themfelves underftood?
or do you fuppofe it is more difficult to advance an
argument than to produce a child? for my own
part, I look upon both thefe faculties as alike my-
fterious." " I will no longer venture to believe or
deny," anfwered the dwarf: " in fhort I have no
opinion at all. Let us endeavour to examine thefe
infects, and we will reafon upon them afterwards.---"
" With all my heart," faid Micromegas, who taking out a pair of fciffars, which he kept for paring
his nails, cut off a paring from his thumb nail, of
which he immediately formed a large kind of
fpeaking trumpet, like a vaft tunnel, and clapped
the pipe to his ear: as the circumference of this
machine included the fhip and all the crew, the moft
feeble voice was conveyed along the circular fibres
of the nail; fo that, thanks to his induftry, the
philofopher could diftinctly hear the buzzing of our
infects that were below; in a few hours he diftinguifhed articulate founds, and at laft plainly
underftood the French language. The dwarf heard
the fame, though with more difficulty.

The aftonifhment of our travellers increafed every
inftant. They heard a neft of mites talk in a pretty
fenfible ftrain: and that Lufus Naturæ feemed to
them inexplicable. You need not doubt but the
Sirian

Sirian and his dwarf glowed with impatience to enter into converſation with ſuch atoms. Micromegas being afraid that his voice, like thunder, would deafen and confound the mites, without being underſtood by them, ſaw the neceſſity of diminiſhing the ſound; each, therefore, put into his mouth a ſort of ſmall tooth-pick, the ſlender end of which reached to the veſſel. The Sirian ſetting the dwarf upon his knees, and the ſhip and crew upon his nail, held down his head and ſpoke ſoftly.——In fine, having taken theſe and a great many more pre-cautions, he addreſſed himſelf to them in theſe words.

" O ye inviſible inſects, whom the hand of the Creator hath deigned to produce in the abyſs of in-finite littleneſs, I give praiſe to his goodneſs, in that he hath been pleaſed to diſcloſe unto me thoſe ſecrets that ſeemed to be impenetrable; perhaps the court of Sirius will not diſdain to behold you with admi-ration : for my own part, I deſpiſe no creature, and therefore offer you my protection."

If ever there was ſuch a thing as aſtoniſhment, it ſeized upon the people who heard this addreſs, and who could not conceive from whence it proceeded. The chaplain of the ſhip repeated exorciſms, the ſailors ſwore, and the philoſophers formed a ſyſtem ; but, notwithſtanding all their ſyſtems, they could not divine who the perſon was that ſpoke to them. Then the dwarf of Saturn, whoſe voice was ſofter than that of Micromegas, gave them briefly to un-derſtand what ſpecies of beings they had to do with. He related the particulars of their voyage from Saturn, made them acquainted with the rank and quality of Monſieur Micromegas ; and after having pitied their ſmallneſs, aſked if they had al-ways been in that miſerable ſtate, ſo near a-kin to annihilation ; and what their buſineſs was upon

that

that globe which feemed to be the property of whales; he alfo defired to know if they were happy in their fituation, if they propagated their fpecies, if they were infpired with fouls? and put a hundred queftions of the like nature.

A certain mathematician on board, more coura-geous than the reft, and fhocked to hear his foul called in queftion, planted his quadrant, and having taken two obfervatioas of this interlocutor, " You believe then, Mr. what d'ye callum," faid he, " that becaufe you meafure from head to foot a thoufand fathoms"——" A thoufand fathoms!" cried the dwarf, " good heaven! how fhould he know the height of my ftature? a thoufand fathoms! my very dimenfions to an hair. What, meafured by a mite! this atom, forfooth, is a geometrician, and knows exactly how tall I am; while I, who can fcarce perceive him through a microfcope, am utterly ig-norant of his extent! " Yes, I have taken your mea-fure," anfwered the philofopher, " and I will now do the fame by your tall companion." The pro-pofal was embraced; his excellency laid himfelf a-long: for, had he ftood upright, his head would have reached too far above the clouds. Our ma-thematicians planted a tall tree in a certain part of himwhich doctor Swift would have mentioned with-out hefitation, but which I forbear to call by its name, out of my inviolable refpect for the ladies; then, by a feries of triangles joined together, they difcovered, that the object of their obfervation was a ftrapping youth, exactly one hundred and twen-ty thoufand royal feet in length.

In confequence of this calculation, Micromegas uttered thefe words: " I am now more than ever convinced that we ought to judge of nothing by its external magnitude. O God! who haft beftowed

ſtowed underſtanding upon ſuch ſeemingly contemptible ſubſtances, thou canſt with equal eaſe
produce that which is infinitely ſmall, as that which
is incredibly great : and if it be poſſible, that among
thy works there are beings ſtill more diminutive
than theſe, they may neverthelcſs, be endued
with underſtanding ſuperior to the intelligence of
thoſe ſtupendous animals I have ſeen in heaven, a
ſingle foot of whom is larger than this whole globe
on which I have alighted." One of the philoſophers
bid him be aſſured, that there were intelligent beings
much ſmaller than man, and recounted not only
Virgil's whole fable of the bees, but alſo deſcribed
all that Swammerdam hath diſcovered, and Reau-
mur diſſected. In a word, he informed him that
there are animals which bear the ſame proportion
to bees, which bees bear to man ; the ſame as the
Sirian himſelf was to thoſe vaſt beings whom he
had mentioned ; and as thoſe huge animals were to
other ſubſtances, before whom they would appear
like ſo many particles of duſt. Here the converſation
became very intereſting, and Micromegas proceeded
in theſe words.

CHAP. VII.

A converſation that paſſed between our travellers
and the men they had encountered.

"O YE intelligent atoms, in whom the Supreme Being hath been picaſed to maniſeſt
his omniſcience and power, without all doubt your
joys on this earth muſt be pure and exquiſite : for
being unincumbered with matter, and, to all appearance, little elſe than ſoul, you muſt ſpend your
lives

lives in the delights of love and reflection, which
are the true enjoyments of a perfect spirit. True
happiness I have no where found; but certainly
here it dwells." At this harangue, all the philosophers shook their heads, and one among the rest,
more candid than his brethren, frankly owned,
that, excepting a very small number of inhabitants,
who were very little esteemed by their fellows, all
the rest were a parcel of knaves, fools, and miserable wretches. " We have matter enough," said
he, " to do abundance of mischief, if mischief
comes of matter; and too much understanding, if
evil flows from understanding; you must know,
for example, that this very moment, while I am
speaking, there are one hundred thousand animals
of our own species, covered with hats, slaying an
equal number of fellow-creatures who wear tur-
bans; at least, they are either slaying or slain; and
this hath been nearly the case all over the earth
from time immemorial." The Sirian shuddering
at this information, begged to know the cause of
those horrible quarrels among such a puny race;
and was given to understand, that the subject of
the dispute was some pitiful mole-hill no bigger
than his heel: not that any one of those millions
who cut one another's throats pretends to have
the least claim to the smallest particle of that clod;
the question is to know, whether it shall belong to
a certain person who is known by the name of Sultan, or to another whom (for what reason I know
not) they dignify with the appellation of Cæsar.
Neither one nor t'other has ever seen, or ever will
see, the pitiful corner in question; and scarce one
of those wretches who sacrifice one another hath
ever beheld the animal on whose account they are
mutually sacrificed!

" Ah

" Ah miscreants ! (cried the indignant Sirian)
such excess of desperate rage is beyond conception.,
I have a good mind to take two or three steps, and,
trample the whole nest of such ridiculous assassins
under my feet." " Don't give yourself the trouble,
(replied the philosopher), they are industrious e-
nough in procuring their own destruction; at the
end of ten years the hundredth part of those
wretches will be no more : for, you must know,,
that though they should not draw a sword in the
cause they have espoused, famine, fatigue, and intemperance, would sweep almost all of them from
the face of the earth. Besides, the punishment
should not be inflicted upon them, but upon those
sedentary and slothful barbarians, who, from their
close-stools, give orders for murthering a million of
men, and then solemnly thank God for their suc-
cess."

Our traveller, moved with compassion for the
little human race, in which he discovered such a-
stonishing contrasts, " Since you are of the small
number of the wise, (said he) and in all likelihood
do not engage yourselves in the trade of murder
for hire, be so good as to tell me your occupa-
tion." " We anatomize flies, (replied the philosopher) we measure lines, we make calculations,
we agree upon two or three points which we understand, and dispute upon two or three thousand
that are beyond our comprehension." Then the
strangers being seized with the whim of interro-
gating those thinking atoms, upon the subjects a-
bout which they were agreed, " How far (said the
Sirian) do you reckon the distance between the
great star of the constellation Gemini, and that
called Caniculus?" To this question all of them
answered with one voice, " Thirty-two degrees
and

and an half." "And what is the diftance from
hence to the moon ?" "Sixty femidiameters of the
earth." He then thought to puzzle them by afking the weight of the air; but they anfwered diftinctly, that common air is about nine hundred
times fpecifically lighter than an equal column of
the lighteft water, and nineteen hundred times
lighter than current gold. The little dwarf of Saturn, aftonifhed at their anfwers, was now tempted
to believe thofe very people forcerers, whom, but
a quarter of an hour before, he would not allow to
be infpired with fouls.

"Well, (faid Micromegas,) fince you know fo
well what is without you, doubtlefs you are ftill
more perfectly acquainted with that which is within; tell me what is the foul, and how your ideas
are framed?" Here the philofophers fpoke all together as before; but each was of a different opinion: the eldeft quoted Ariftotle; another pronounced the name of Defcartes; a third mentioned
Mallebranche; a fourth Leibnitz; and a fifth
Locke: an old peripatician lifting up his voice, exclaimed with an air of confidence, "The foul is
perfection and reafon, having power to be fuch as
it is:" as Ariftotle exprefsly declares, page 633,
of the Louvre edition.

Ἐντελἐχεια τις ἴςι, καί λόγος τῦ δυνάμιν ἔχοντος τοιȣδι ἴιται.

"I am not very well verfed in Greek," faid the
giant: "Nor I neither," replied the philofophical
mite. "Why then do you quote that fame Arif-
ftotle in Greek?" refumed the Sirian: "Becaufe,
(anfwered the other,) it is but reafonable we fhould
quote what we do not comprehend in a language
we do not underftand."

Here the Cartefian interpofing, "The foul (faid
he,)

he,) is a pure fpirit or intelligence, which hath received in the mother's womb all the metaphyfical ideas; but, upon leaving that prifon, is obliged to go to fchool, and learn anew that knowledge which it hath loft, and will never more attain." " So it was neceffary (replied the animal of eight leagues,) that thy foul fhould be learned in thy mother's womb, in order to be fo ignorant when thou haft got a beard upon thy chin : but, what doft thou underftand by fpirit? " To what purpofe do you afk me that queftion? (faid the philofopher,) I have no idea of it : indeed it is fuppofed to be immaterial." " At leaft, thou knoweft what matter is?" refumed the Sirian. " Perfectly well, (anfwered the other.) For example, that ftone is grey, is of a certain figure, has three dimenfions, fpecifick weight, and divifibility." " Right, (faid the giant,) I want to know what that object is, which, according to thy obfervation, hath a grey colour, weight, and divifibility." "Thou feeft a few qualities, but doft thou know the nature of the thing itfelf?" " Not I truly," anfwered the Cartefian. Upon which the other told him he did not know what matter was. Then addreffing himfelf to another fage who ftood upon his thumb, he afked what is the foul? and what are her functions? " Nothing at all, (replied this difciple of Mallebranche;) God hath made every thing for my convenience ; in him I fee every thing, by him I act; he is the univerfal Agent, and I never meddle in his work." " That is being a non-entity indeed," faid the Sirian fage ; who, turning to a follower of Leibnitz, " Hark ye, friend, what is thy opinion of the foul?" " In my opinion, anfwered this metaphyfician) the foul is the hand that points at the hour, while my body does the office of a clock ; or, if you pleafe, the foul is the clock, and the body is the pointer; or again, my soul is the mirrour of the universe, and my body the frame. All this is clear and uncontrovertible.

A little partizan of Locke, who chanced to be present, being afked his opinion on the fame fubject, "I do not know (faid he) by what power I think; but well I know, that I fhould never have thought without the affiftance of my fenfes : that there are immaterial and intelligent fubftances, I do not at all doubt; but that it is impoffible for God to communicate the faculty of thinking to matter, I doubt very much. I revere the eternal Power, to which it would ill become me to prefcribe bounds : I affirm nothing, and am contented to believe that many more things are poffible than are ufually thought fo." The Sirian fmiled at this declaration, and did not look upon the author as the leaft fagacious of the company : and as for the dwarf of Saturn, he would have embraced this adherent of Locke, had it not been for the extreme difproportion in their different fizes. But unluckily there was another animalcule in a fquare cap, who, taking the word from all his philofophical brethren, affirmed that he knew the whole fecret which was contained in the abridgement of St Thomas : he furveyed the two celeftial ftrangers from top to toe, and maintained to their faces that their perfons, their fafhions, their funs and their ftars, were created folely for the ufe of man. At this wild affertion our two travellers let themfelves tumble topfy turvy, feized with a fit of that inextinguifhable laughter, which (according to Homer) is the portion of the immortal gods ; their bellies quivered, their fhoulders rofe and fell, and, during thefe convulfions, the veffel fell from the Sirian's nail into the

the Saturnian's pocket, where thefe worthy people
fearched for it a long time with great diligence.—
At length, having found the fhip, and fet every
thing to rights again, the Sirian refuming the difcourfe with thofe diminutive mites, promifed to
compofe for them a choice book of philofophy,
which would teach them abundance of 'admirable
fciences, and demonftrate the very effence of things.
Accordingly, before his departure, he made them
a prefent of the book, which was brought to the
academy of fciences at Paris; but when the old
fecretary came to open it, he faw nothing but blank
paper, upon which " Ay, ay, (faid he) this is juft
what I fufpected."

T 2   LE

LE TAUREAU BLANC:

OR,

THE WHITE BULL.

FROM THE FRENCH.

Tranſlated from the SYRIAC,

By M. DE VOLTAIRE.

WHITE BULL.

CHAP. I.

How the Princefs Amafidia meets a Bull.

THE young Princefs Amafidia, daughter of Amafi, King of Tanis in Egypt, took a walk upon the high-way of Pelufium with the ladies of her train. She was funk in a deep melancholy; the tears gufhed from her beautiful eyes. The caufe of her grief is known, as well as the fears fhe entertained, left that grief fhould difpleafe the king her father. The old man Mambres, ancient magician and eunuch of the Pharaohs, was befide her, and feldom left her. He was prefent at her birth; he had educated her, and taught her all that a fair princefs was allowed to know of the fciences of Egypt. The mind of Amafidia equalled her beauty; her fenfibility and tendernefs did not yield to the charms of her perfon; and it was this fenfibility which coft her fo many tears.

The Princefs was four and twenty years old; the magician Mambres about thirteen hundred. It was he, as every one knows, who had that famous

difpute

difpute with Mofes, in which the victory was fo long doubtful betwixt thefe two profound philofophers. If Mambres yielded, it was owing to the vifible protection of the celeftial powers who favoured his rival: it required gods to overcome Mambres.

Amafis made him fuperintendant of his daughter's houfhold, and he acquitted himfelf in this office with his ufual prudence. His compaffion was excited by the fighs of the beautiful Amafidia.

" O my lover," cried fhe fometimes to herfelf, " my young, my dear lover, O greateft of conquerors, moft accomplifhed, moft beautiful of men! Almoft feven years haft thou difappeared from the world: What god has fnatched thee from thy tender Amafidia? Thou art not dead. The wife Egyptian prophets confefs this. But thou art dead to me, I am alone in the world; to me it is a defart. By what extraordinary prodigy haft thou abandoned thy throne and thy miftrefs? Thy throne, which was the firft in the world;---however, that is a matter of fmall confequence:---but to abandon me who adores thee, O! my dear Na---."

She was going on---" Tremble to pronounce that fatal name," (faid Mambres, the ancient eunuch and magician of the Pharaohs,) " you would perhaps be difcovered by fome of the ladies of your court; they are all very much devoted to you, and all fair ladies certainly make it a merit to ferve the noble paffions of fair princeffes. But there may be one amongft them indifcreet, and even treacherous. You know that your father, although he loves you, has fworn to put you to death, fhould you pronounce the terrible name always ready to efcape your lips. This law is fevere; but you have not been educated in Egyptian wifdom to be ignorant of the government of the tongue: remember that Harpocrates, one of our greateft gods, has always his finger upon his mouth."

The beautiful Amafidia wept, and was filent.

As fhe penfively advanced towards the banks of the Nile, fhe perceived at a diftance under a thicket, watered by the river, an old woman in a tattered grey garment, feated on a hillock; fhe had befide her a fhe-afs, a dog, a he-goat: oppofite to her was a ferpent, which was not like the common ferpents; for its eyes were mild, its phyfiognomy noble and engaging, its fkin fhone with the livelieft and fweeteft colours. A huge fifh, half immerfed in the river, was not the leaft aftonifhing figure in the groupe. And on a neighbouring tree were perched a raven and a pigeon. All thefe creatures feemed to carry on a very animated converfation.

" Alas !" faid the princefs in a low tone, thefe animals undoubtedly fpeak of their loves, and it is not fo much as allowed me to mention the name of mine."

The old woman held in her hand a flender fteel chain, a hundred fathoms long, to which was made faft a bull who fed in the meadow. This bull was white, perfectly well made, plump, and at the fame time agile, which is a thing feldom to be found. He was the moft beautiful that was ever feen of his kind. Neither the bull of Pafiphae, nor that in whofe fhape Jupiter appeared when he carried off Europa, could be compared to this noble animal. The charming young heifer into which Ifis was changed would have fcarce been worthy of him.

As foon as he faw the princefs, he ran towards her with the fwiftnefs of a young Arabian horfe, who flies over the plains and rivers of the ancient Saana, to approach the lovely mare who reigns in his heart, and makes him prick up his ears. The old woman ufed her utmoft efforts to reftrain him. The ferpent wanted to terrify him by its hiffing. The dog followed him, and bit his beautiful limbs. The fhe-afs croffed his way, and kicked him to make him return. The great fifh remounted the Nile, and darting himfelf out of the water, threat-ened to devour him : The he-goat remained im-moveable, and ftruck with fear. The raven flut-tered round his head as if he wanted to tear out his eyes. The pigeon alone accompanied him from curiofity, and applauded him by a fweet mur-mur.

So extraordinary a fight threw Mambres into ferious reflections. In the meanwhile, the white bull, dragging after him his chain and the old wo-man, had already reached the princefs, who was ftruck with aftonifhment and fear. He throws himfelf at her feet, he kiffes them, he fheds tears, he looks upon her with eyes, in which there was an uncommon mixture of grief and joy. He da-red not to low, left he fhould terrify the beautiful Amafidia. He could not fpeak. A weak ufe of the voice, granted by Heaven to certain animals, was denied him ; but all his actions were eloquent. The princefs was delighted with him ; fhe found that a trifling amufement could fufpend for fome moments even the moft pungent grief. " Here, faid fhe, is a moft amiable animal ; I could wifh much to have him in my ftable."

At thefe words the bull bent himfelf on his four
knees

knees and kiffed the ground. " He underftands me, cried the princefs; he fhews me that he wants to be mine. Ah, heavenly magician; ah, divine eunuch, give me this confolation. Purchafe this beautiful cherubim *. Settle the price with the old woman, to whom he no doubt belongs. This animal muft be mine: do not refufe me this innocent comfort." All the ladies joined their requefts to the entreaties of the princefs. Mambres yielded to them, and went to fpeak to the old woman.

CHAP. II.

How the wife Mambres, formerly Magician of Pharaoh, knew again the old Woman, and was known by her.

" MADAM," faid he to her, " you know that ladies, and particularly princeffes, have need of amufement. The daughter of the king is diftractedly fond of your bull, I beg that you will fell him to us; you fhall be paid in ready money."

" Sir," anfwered the old woman, " this precious animal does not belong to me. I am charged, together with all the beafts which you fee, to keep him with care, to watch all his motions, and to give an exact account of them. God forbid that I fhould ever have any inclination to fell this invaluable animal."

Mambres, upon this difcourfe, began to have a

U 2   con-

---

* Cherubim fignifies, in Chaldean, a Bull.

confused remembrance of something which he could not yet properly distinguish. He eyed the old woman in the grey cloak with greater attention.—" Respectable lady," said he to her, " I either mistake, or I have seen you formerly."----" I make no mistake," replied the old woman, " I have seen you seven hundred years ago, in a journey which I made from Syria into Egypt some months after the destruction of Troy, when Hiram the second reigned at Tyre, and Nephel-Keres in ancient Egypt."—" Ah! madam," cried the old man, " you are the remarkable witch of Endor."--"--And you, Sir," said the forceress, embracing him, " are the great Mambres of Egypt."—

" O unforeseen meeting! memorable day! eternal decrees! said Mambres; it certainly is not without permission of the universal providence that we meet again in this meadow upon the banks of the Nile, near the noble city of Tanis. What, is it you who are so famous upon the banks of your little Jordan, and the first person in the world for raising apparitions?"

" What, is it you, Sir, who are so famous for changing rods into a serpent, the day into darkness, and rivers into blood?" " Yes, madam, but my great age has, in part, deprived me of my knowledge and power. I am ignorant from whence you have this beautiful bull, and who these animals are, that, together with you, watch around him." The old woman recollecting herself, raised her eyes to heaven, then replied :

" My dear Mambres, we are of the same profession; but it is expressly forbidden me to tell you who this bull is. I can satisfy you with regard to the other animals. You will easily know them by
the

the marks which characterife them. The ferpent is that which perfuaded Eve to eat an apple, and to make her hufband partake of it. The afs, that which fpoke to your cotemporary Balaam in a hollow way. The fifh, which always carries its head above water, is that which fwallowed Jonas a few years ago. The dog is he who followed the angel Raphael and the young Tobit in their journey to Ragufa in Media, in the time of the great Salmanazar. This goat is he who expiates all the fins of your nation. The raven and the pigeon, thofe which were in the ark of Noah:---great event! univerfal cataftrophe! of which almoft all the world is ftill ignorant. You are now informed;---but of the bull you can know nothing."

Mambres, having liftened with refpect, faid, " The Eternal, O illuftrious witch! reveals and conceals what he thinks proper. All the animals, who, together with you, are entrufted with the cuftody of the white bull, are only known to your generous and agreeable nation, which is itfelf unknown to almoft all the world. The miracles which you and your's, I and mine, have performed, fhall one day be a great fubject of doubt and fcandal to falfe philofophers. But happily thefe miracles fhall find belief with the real fages who fhall prove fubmiffive to the enlightened in one corner of the world; and this is all that is neceffary."

As he fpoke thefe words, the princefs pulled him by the fleeve, and faid to him, " Mambres, will you not buy my bull?" The magician, plunged into a deep reverie, made no reply, and Amafidia poured forth her tears.

She then addreffed herfelf to the old woman,
" My

"My good woman," said she, "I conjure you, by all you hold most dear in the world, by your father, by your mother, by your nurse, who are certainly still alive, to sell me not only your bull, but likewise your pigeon, which seems very much attached to him.

"As for the other animals, I do not want them; but I shall catch the vapours if you do not sell me this charming bull, who will be all the happiness of my life."

The old woman respectfully kissed the fringe of her gauze robe, and replied, "Princess, my bull is not to be sold; your illustrious magician is acquainted with this. All that I can do for your service is, to permit him to feed every day near your palace. You may caress him, give him biscuits, and make him dance about at your pleasure; but he must always be under the eyes of all these animals who accompany me, and who are charged with the keeping of him. If he does not endeavour to escape from them, they will prove peaceable; but if he attempts once more to break his chain, as he did upon seeing you, wo be unto him; for I would not answer for his life: this large fish, which you see, will certainly swallow him, and keep him longer than *three* days in his belly; or this serpent, who appears to you so mild, will give him a mortal sting."

The white bull, who understood perfectly the old woman's conversation, but was unable to speak, humbly accepted all the proposals; he laid himself down at her feet; he lowed softly; and looking tenderly at Amasidia, seemed to say to her, "Come and see me sometimes upon the grass." The serpent now took up the conversation: "Princess," cefs," faid he, " I advife you to act implicitly as mademoifelle of Endor has told you." The the afs likewife put in her word, and was of the opinion of the ferpent.

Amafidia was afflicted that this ferpent and this afs fhould fpeak fo well; while a beautiful bull, who had fuch noble and tender fentiments, was unable to exprefs them. "Alas," faid fhe in a low voice, "nothing is more common at court: one fees there every day fine lords who cannot converfe, and contemptible wretches who fpeak with affurance."

"This ferpent," faid Mambres, "is not a contemptible wretch; he is perhaps the perfonage of the greateft importance."

The day now declined, and the princefs was obliged to return home, after having promifed to come back next day at the fame hour. Her ladies of the palace were aftonifhed, and underftood nothing of what they had feen or heard. Mambres made reflections. The princefs recollecting that the ferpent called the old woman Mifs, concluded at random that fhe was a virgin, and felt fome affliction that fhe was ftill one herfelf; refpectable affliction! which fhe concealed with as much care as the name of her lover.

CHAP. III.

How the beautiful Amafidia had a fecret Converfation with a beautiful Serpent.

THE beautiful princefs recommended fecrecy to her ladies with regard to what they had feen.

seen. They all promised it, and kept it for a whole day.

We may believe that Amasidia slept little this night; an inexplicable charm continually recalled the idea of her beautiful bull. As soon therefore as she was at freedom with her wise Mambres, she said to him: " O, sage! this animal turns my head." ----" He employs mine very much," said Mambres. " I see plainly that this cherubim is very much superior to those of his species. I see that there is a great mystery, and I suspect a fatal event. Your father Amasis is suspicious and violent; and this affair requires that you conduct yourself with the greatest precaution."

" Ah!" said the princess, " I have too much curiosity to be prudent. It is the only sentiment which can unite in my heart with that which preys upon me on account of the lover I have lost. Can I not know who this white bull is that gives me such strange disquiet?"

Mambres replied, " I have already confessed to you, madam, that my knowledge declines in proportion as my age advances; but I mistake much if the serpent is not informed of what you are so very desirous of knowing. He does not want sense; he expresses himself with propriety; he has been long accustomed to interfere in the affairs of the ladies."   " Ah! undoubtedly," said Amasidia, " this is the beautiful serpent of Egypt, who, by fixing his tail into his mouth, is the emblem of eternity; who enlightens the world when he opens his eyes, and darkens it when he shuts them."— " No, madam."----" It is then the serpent of Esculapius----" Still less."---It is perhaps Jupiter under the figure of a serpent."----" Not at all."----" Ah, now I see, I see; it is the rod which you----formerly

merly changed into a ferpent."---" No, madam, it
is not, but all thefe ferpents are of the fame family;
the prefent has a very high charaƈter in his own
country; he paffes there for the moft extraordinary
ferpent that was ever feen. Addrefs yourfelf to
him. However, I warn you it is a dangerous undertaking. Were I in your place, I would hardly
trouble myfelf either with the bull, the fhe-afs, the
ferpent, the fifh, the raven, or the pigeon,---but
paffion hurries you on; and all I can do is to pity
you, and tremble."

The princefs conjured him to procure her a tete
a tete with the ferpent. Mambres, who was obliging, confented, and making profound refleƈtions,
he went and communicated to the witch in fo in-
finuating a manner the whim of the princefs, that
the old woman told him Amafidia might lay her
commands upon her; that the ferpent was per-
feƈtly well bred, and fo polite to the ladies, that he
wifhed for nothing more than to oblige them, and
would not fail the princefs's affignation.

The ancient magician returned to inform the
princefs of this good news; but he ftill dreaded
fome misfortune, and made refleƈtions.---" You
defire to fpeak with the ferpent, madam; this you
may accomplifh whenever your highnefs thinks
proper. But remember you muft flatter him; for
every animal has a great deal of felf-love, and he
in particular. It is faid he was formerly driven out
of heaven for exceffive pride."---" I have never
heard of it," replied the princefs.---" I believe it,"
faid the old man. He then informed her of all the
reports which had been fpread about this famous
ferpent. " But, madam, whatever fingular adventures may have happened to him, you never can
extort thefe fecrets from him but by flattery: hav-

ing formerly deceived women, it is reasonable that
a woman in her turn should deceive him."—" I
will do my utmoſt," ſaid the princeſs ; and departed with her maids of honour. The old woman
was feeding the bull at a conſiderable diſtance.

Mambres left Amaſidia to herſelf, and went and
diſcourſed with the witch. One lady of honour
chatted with the ſhe-aſs, the others amuſed themſelves with the goat, the dog, the raven, and the
pigeon. As for the large fiſh that frightened every
body, he plunged himſelf into the Nile by order
of the old woman.

The ſerpent then attended the beautiful Amaſidia into the grove, where they had the following
converſation.

Serpent.

" You cannot imagine, madam, how much I am
flattered with the honour which your highneſs
deigns to confer upon me."

Princeſs.

" Your great reputation, Sir, the beauty of
your countenance, and the brilliancy of your eyes,
have readily determined me to ſeek for this converſation ; I know by public report (if it is not
falſe) that you were formerly a very great lord in
the empyrean heaven."

Serpent.

" It is true, madam, I had there a very diſtin-
guiſhed place. It is pretended I am a diſgraced
favourite. This is a report which at once went
abroad in India *. The Brachmans were the firſt
who

---

* The Brachmans were in faſt the firſt who imagined a revolt

who gave a hiſtory of my adventures. And I doubt not but one day or other the poets of the north will make them the ſubjeᵲ of an extravagant epick poem ; for in truth it is all that can be made of them. Yet I am not ſo much fallen, but that I have left in this globe a very extenſive dominion. I might venture to aſſert that the whole earth belongs to me."

Princeſs.

" I believe it ; for they tell me that your powers of perſuaſion are irreſiſtible, and to pleaſe is to reign."

Serpent.

" I feel, madam, while I behold and liſten to you, that you have over me the ſame power which you aſcribe to me over ſo many others."

Princeſs.

" You are, and I believe it, an amiable con-queror : it is ſaid that your conqueſts among the fair-ſex have been numerous, and that you began with our common mother, whoſe name I have forgot."

Serpent.

" They do me injuſtice. She honoured me with her confidence, and I gave her the beſt advice. I deſired that ſhe and her huſband ſhould eat hear-tily of the fruit of the tree of knowledge. I ima-gined in doing this that I ſhould pleaſe the Ruler of all things. It ſeemed to me, that a tree ſo ne-ceſſary to the human race was not planted to be entirely uſeleſs. Would the ſupreme Being have

X 2   wiſhed

volt in heaven, and this fable long after ſerved as the ground-work for the hiſtory of the wars of the giants, and ſome other hiſtories.

wifhed to have been ferved by fools and idiots ? Is
not the mind formed for the acquifition of knowledge and for improvement ? Is not the knowledge
of good and evil neceffary for doing the one and
avoiding the other ? I certainly merited their
thanks."

Princefs.

" Yet, they tell me that you have fuffered for
it. Probably it is fince this period that fo many
minifters have been punifhed for giving good advice, and fo many real philofophers and men of
genius perfecuted for their writings that were ufeful to mankind."

Serpent.

" It is my enemies who have told you thefe ftories : they cry that I am out of favour at court.—
But a proof that my influence there has not declined, is their own confeffion that I entered into the
council when it was in agitation to try the good
man Job : and I was again called upon when the
refolution was taken to deceive a certain petty
king called Ahab*. I alone was charged with this
honourable commiffion."

Princefs.

" Ah, Sir ! I do not believe that you are formed to deceive. But fince you are always in the mi-
niftry,

* Firft book of Kings, chap. xxii. ver. 20, 21, 22.—" And
the Lord faid, Who fhall perfuade Ahab king of Ifrael, that
he may go up and fall at Ramoth Gilead ?—And there came
forth a fpirit and ftood before the Lord, and faid, I will perfuade him : and the Lord faid unto him, How? and he faid, I
will go forth and be a lying fpirit in the mouths of all his prophets. And he faid, Thou fhalt perfuade him, and prevail alfo : go forth, and do fo."

niftry, may I beg a favour of you ? I hope fo amiable a lord will not deny me."

Serpent.

" Madam, your requefts are laws ; name your commands."

Princefs.

" I intreat you will tell me who this white bull is, for whom I feel fuch extraordinary fentiments, that they both affect and alarm me. I am told that you would deign to inform me."

Serpent.

" Madam, curiofity is neceffary to human nature, and efpecially to your amiable fex. Without it they would live in the moft fhameful ignorance. I have always fatisfied, as far as lay in my power, the curiofity of the ladies. I am accufed indeed of ufing this complaifance only to vex the Ruler of the world. I fwear to you, that I could propofe nothing more agreeable to myfelf than to obey you ; but the old woman muft have informed you that the revealing of this fecret will be attended with fome danger to you."

Princefs.

" Ah ! it is that which makes me ftill more curious."

Serpent.

" In this I difcover the fex to whom I have formerly done fervice."

Princefs.

" If you poffefs any feeling, if rational beings fhould mutually affift each other ; if you have compaffion for an unfortunate creature, do not refufe my requeft."

Serpent.

Serpent.

" You affect me, I must satisfy you, but do not interrupt me."

Princess.

" I promise you I will not."

Serpent.

" There was a young king, beautiful, charming, in love, beloved. . . ."

Princess.

" A young king! beautiful, charming, in love, beloved! and by whom? and who was this king? How old was he? what is become of him? where is his kingdom? what is his name?"

Serpent.

" See, I have scarce begun, and you have already interrupted me : take care ; if you have not more command over yourself, you are undone."

Princess.

" Ah, pardon me, Sir ; I will not repeat my indiscretion : go on, I beseech you."

- Serpent.

" This great king, the most valiant of men, victorious wherever he carried his arms, often dreamed when asleep, and forgot his dreams when a-wake ; he wanted his magicians to remember and inform him what he had dreamed, otherwise he declared he would hang them, for that nothing was more equitable. It is now near seven years since he dreamed a fine dream, which he entirely forgot when he awoke ; and a young Jew, full of experience, having revealed it to him, this amiable
able

able king was immediately changed into an ox for . . . ."

Princefs.

" Ah! it is my dear Nabu . . . ." She could not finifh, fhe fainted away. Mambres, who liften-ed at a diftance, faw her fall, and believed her dead.

CHAP. IV.

How they wanted to facrifice the Bull, and exorcife the Princefs.

MAMBRES runs to her weeping. The fer-pent is affected ; he, alas, cannot weep; but he hiffes in a mournful tone, he cries out " *She is dead.*" The afs repeats, " *She is dead :*" the raven tells it over again. All the other animals appear-ed afflicted, except the fifh of Jonas, which has always been mercilefs. The lady of honour, the ladies of the court, arrive and tear their hair. The white bull, who fed at a diftance, and heard their cries, runs to the grove, dragging the old woman after him, while his loud bellowings made the neighbouring echoes refound. To no purpofe did the ladies pour upon the expiring Amafidia their bottles of rofe-water, of pink, of myrtle, of benja-min, of balm of Gilead, of amomum, of gilly flow-er, of nutmeg, of ambergreafe. She had not as yet given the fmalleft figns of life.---But as foon as fhe perceived that the beautiful white bull was be-fide her, fhe came to herfelf, more blooming, more beautiful and lively than ever. A thoufand times did fhe kifs this charming animal, who languifh-ingly leaned his head on her fnowy bofom. She called

called him " My mafter, my king, my dear, my
life." She throws her fair arms around his neck,
which was whiter than the fnow; the light ftraw
does not adhere more clofely to the amber, the vine
to the elm, nor the ivy to the oak. The fweet
murmur of her fighs was heard, her eyes were feen
now fparkling with a tender flame, and now obfcu-
red by thofe precious tears which love makes us
fhed.

We may eafily judge into what aftonifhment the
lady of honour and ladies of her train were
thrown. As foon as they entered the palace, they
related to their lovers this extraordinary adventure,
and every one with different circumftances, which
increafed its fingularity, and which always contri-
butes to the variety of all hiftories.

No fooner was Amafis, king of Tanis, informed
of thefe events, than his royal breaft was inflamed
with juft indignation. Such was the wrath of
Minos, when he underftood that his daughter Pafiphae lavifhed her tender favours upon the father of
the Minotaur. Thus raged Juno, when fhe beheld
Jupiter careffing the beautiful cow Io, daughter of
the river Inachus. Amafis fhut up the fair Amafidia in her chamber, and placed upon her a guard
of black eunuchs; then he affembled his privy
council.

The grand magician prefided there, but had no
longer the fame influence as formerly. All the
minifters of ftate concluded that this white bull
was a forcerer. It was quite the contrary; he
was bewitched : but in delicate affairs they are
always miftaken at court.

It was carried by a great majority that the princefs fhould be exorcifed, and the old woman and
the bull facrificed.

The

The wife Mambres contradicted not the opinion of the king and council. The right of exorcifing belonged to him; he could delay it under fome plaufible pretence. The god Apis was lately dead at Memphis. A god ox dies juft like another ox. And it was not allowed to exorcife any perfon in Egypt till a new ox was found to replace the deceafed.

It was decreed in the council, to wait the nomination which fhould be made of a new god at Memphis.

The good old man, Mambres, perceived to what danger his dear princefs was expofed. He knew who her lover was. The fyllables NABU·.... which had efcaped her, laid open the whole myftery to the eyes of this fage.

The dynafty of Memphis belonged at that time to the Babylonians; they preferved this remainder of the conquefts they had gained under the greateft king of the world, to whom Amafis was a mortal enemy. Mambres had occafion for all his wifdom to conduct himfelf properly in the midft of fo many difficulties. If the king Amafis fhould difcover the lover of his daughter, her death was inevitable, he had fworn it. The great, the young, the beautiful king of whom fhe was enamoured, had dethroned the king her father, and Amafis had only recovered his kingdom about feven years. From that time it was not known what was become of the adorable monarch, the conqueror and idol of the nations, the tender and generous lover of the charming Amafidia; but facrificing the bull would infallibly occafion the death of the beautiful Amafidia.

What could Mambres do in fuch critical circumftances? He went after the council broke up to find his dear fofter daughter; "My dear child," he fays, "I will ferve you; but I repeat it, they will behead you if ever you pronounce the name of your lover."

"Ah! what fignifies *my neck*," replied the beautiful Amafidia, "if I cannot embrace that of Nabuco... My father is a cruel man; he not only refufes to give me a charming prince whom I adore, but he declared war againft him; and when he was conquered by my lover, he has found the fecret of changing him into an ox. Did one ever fee more frightful malice? If my father was not my father, I do not know what I fhould do to him."

"It was not your father who played him this cruel trick," faid the wife Mambres; it was a native of Paleftine, one of our ancient enemies, an inhabitant of a little country, comprehended in that crowd of kingdoms which your lover fubdued, in order to polifh and refine them.

"Such metamorphofes muft not furprife you; you know that formerly I performed more extraordinary. Nothing was at that time more common than thofe changes which at prefent aftonifh philofophers. True hiftory, which we have read together, informs us, that Lycaon, king of Arcadia, was changed into a wolf; the beautiful Califta, his daughter, into a bear; Io, the daughter of Inachus, our venerable Ifis, into a cow; Daphnis into a laurel; Sirinx into a flute; the fair Edith, wife of Lot, the beft and moft affectionate father that ever was in the world, is fhe not become, in our neighbourhood, a pillar of falt very fharp tafted, which has preferved all the marks of her fex and periodi-
cal

cal returns*, as the great men atteſt who have
ſeen it: I was witneſs to this change in my youth.
I ſaw ſeven powerful cities in the moſt dry and
parched ſituation in the world, all at once tranſ-
formed into a beautiful lake. In the early part
of my life the whole world was full of metamor-
phoſes.

"In fine, madam, if examples can ſooth your
grief, remember that Venus changed Ceraſtes into
an ox." "I do not know," ſaid the princeſs,
"that examples comfort us: If my lover was
dead, could I comfort myſelf by the idea that all
men die?" "Your pain may at leaſt be alleviated,"
replied the ſage; "and ſince your lover has become an ox, it is poſſible from an ox he may become a man. As for me, I deſerve to be changed
into a tyger or a crocodile, if I did not employ the
little power I have in the ſervice of a princeſs
worthy of the adoration of the world, for the beautiful Amaſidia whom I have nurſed upon my
knees, and whom fatal deſtiny expoſes to ſuch rude
trials."

CHAP. V.

How the wiſe Mambres conducted himſelf wiſely.

THE divine Mambres having ſaid every thing
he could to comfort the princeſs, but without
having comforted her, ran to the old woman----

"My

* Tertullian, in his poem of Sodom ſays, "Dicitur vi-
rens alio ſub corpore ſexus, manificos, ſolito diſpungere ſangui-
ne menſes." St. Irenæus, book 4to, per naturalia quæ ſunt
conſuetudine fœminæ oſtendens."

" My companion," faid he to her, " ours is a
charming profeffion, but it is very dangerous. You
run the rifk of being hanged, and your ox of
being burnt, drowned, or devoured.   I don't know
what they will do with your other animals ; for
prophet as I am, I know very little ; but do you
carefully conceal the ferpent and the fifh.   Let
not the one fhew his head above water, nor the
other go out of his hole.   I will place the ox in
one of my ftables in the country ; you fhall be
there with him, fince you fay that it is not allowed
you to abandon him.   The good fcape-goat may
upon the occafion ferve as an expiation ; we will
fend him into the defart loaded with the fins of all
the reft ; he is accuftomed to this ceremony, which
does him no harm ; and every one knows that all is
expiated by means of a he-goat who walks about
for his amufement.   I only beg of you to lend me
immediately Tobit's dog, who is a very fwift grey-
hound ; Balaam's afs, who runs better than a dromedary ; the raven and the pigeon of the ark, who
fly with amazing fwiftnefs.   I want to fend them on
an embaffy to Memphis, in an affair of great confequence."

The old woman replied to the magician, " You
may difpofe as you pleafe of Tobit's dog, of Balaam's afs, of the raven and the pigeon of the ark, and
of the fcape-goat ; but my ox cannot enter into a
ftable.   It is faid, Daniel, chap. v. That he muft be
always made faft to an iron chain, be always wet
with the dew of heaven, and eat the grafs of the
field, and his portion be with the wild beafts.

" He is trufted to me, and I muft obey. What
would Daniel, Ezekiel, and Jeremiah, think of me,
if I trufted my ox to any other than to myfelf ? I
fee you know the fecret of this extraordinary animal,

mal, but I have not to reproach myfelf with having revealed it to you. I am going to conduct him far from this polluted land, towards the lake Sirbon, where he will be fheltered from the cruelties of the king of Tanis. My fifh and my ferpent will defend me; I fear nobody when I ferve my mafter."

" My good woman," anfwered the wife Mambres, " let the will of God be done! provided I can find your white bull again, the lake Sirbon, the lake Maris, or the lake of Sodom, are to me perfectly indifferent. I want to do nothing but good to him and to you. But why have you fpoken to me of Daniel, Ezekiel, and Jeremiah?" " Ah! Sir," anfwered the old woman, " you know as well as I what concern they have in this important affair. But I have no time to lofe. I don't defire to be hanged; I want not that my bull fhould be burned, drowned, or devoured; I go to the lake Sirbon by Canepus, with my ferpent and my fifh. Adieu."

The bull followed her penfively, after having teftified his gratitude to the beneficent Mambres.

The wife Mambres was greatly troubled; he faw that Amafis king of Tanis, diftracted by the foolifh paffion of his daughter for this animal, and believing her bewitched, would purfue every where the unfortunate bull; who would infallibly be burnt as a forcerer in the public place of Tanis, or given to the fifh of Jonas, or be roafted and ferved up to table.—Mambres wanted at all events to fave the princefs from this cruel difafter.

He wrote a letter to the high prieft of Memphis, his friend, in facred characters, upon the paper of Egypt, which was not yet in ufe. Here are the identical words of his letter:

" Light

" Light of the world, lieutenant of Isis, Osiris, and Horus, chief of the circumcised, you whose altar is justly raised above all thrones! I am informed that your god the ox Apis is dead. I have one at your service. Come quickly with your priests to acknowledge, to worship him, and to conduct him into the stable of your temple. May Isis, Osiris, and Horus, keep you in their holy and worthy protection, and likewise you the priests of Memphis in their holy care.

Your affectionate friend,
Mambres."

He made four copies of this letter for fear of accidents, and enclosed them in cases of the hardest ebony. Then calling to him his four couriers, whom he had destined for this employment, (these were the ass, the dog, the raven, and the pigeon,) he said to the ass, " I know with what fidelity you served Balaam my brother, serve me with the same. There is not an unicorn who equals you in swiftness. Go, my dear friend, and deliver this letter to the person himself to whom it is directed, and return."

The ass answered, " Sir, as I served Balaam, I will serve you; I will go, and I will return." The sage put the box of ebony into her mouth, and she departed, swift as lightning.

Then he called Tobit's dog. " Faithful dog," said Mambres, " more speedy in thy course than the nimble-footed Achilles, I know what you performed for Tobit son of Tobit, when you and the angel Raphael accompanied him from Nineveh to Ragusa in Media, and from Ragusa to Nineveh; and that he brought back to his father ten* talents, which
the

* About 20 thousand crowns of France, present currency.

the flave Tobit the father had lent to the flave Ga-
bellus; for the flaves at that time were very rich.
Carry this letter as it is directed, which is much
more valuable than ten talents of filver." The dog
then replied, " Sir, if I formerly followed the
meffenger Raphael, I can with equal eafe execute
your commiffion." Mambres put the letter into
his mouth.

He next fpoke in the fame manner to the pigeon, who replied, " Sir, if I brought back a
bough into the ark, I will likewife bring you back
an anfwer." She took the letter in her bill, and
the three meffengers were out of fight in a moment.

Then Mambres addreffed the raven: " I know
that you fed the great prophet Elias * when he was
concealed near the torrent of Carith, fo much celebrated in the world. You brought him every
day good bread and fat pullets; I only afk of you
to carry this letter to Memphis."

The raven anfwered in thefe words: " It is true,
Sir, that I carried every day a dinner to the greatpro-
phet Elias the Thifbite; I faw him mount in a chariot of fire drawn by fiery horfes; altho' this is not
the ufual method of travelling: but I always took
care to eat half the dinner myfelf. I am very well
pleafed to carry your letter, provided you make me
certain of two good meals every day, and that I
am paid money in advance for my commiffion."

Mambres, angry, replied, " Gluttonous and malicious creature, I am not aftonifhed that Apollo
has made you black as a mole, from being white
as a fwan, as you was formerly, before you betrayed in the plains of Theffaly the beautiful Coronis,
the

* IIId. book of Kings, chap. 17.

the unfortunate mother of Æfculapius. Tell me,
did you eat ribs of beef and pullets every day when
you was ten whole months in the ark?"—" Sir,"
faid the raven, " we had there very good cheer;
they ferved up roaft meat twice a-day to all the
fowls of my fpecies who live upon nothing but
flefh, fuch as the vultures, kites, eagles, buzzards,
fparrow-hawks, owls, tarfels, falcons, great owls,
and an innumerable crowd of birds of prey. They
furnifhed with the moft plentiful profufion the
tables of the lions, leopards, tigers, panthers, hy-
ænas, wolves, bears, foxes, polecats, and all forts of
carnivorous quadrupeds. There were in the ark
eight perfons of diftinction, (and the only ones who
were then in the world,) continually employed in the
care of our table and our wardrobe; Noah and his
wife, who were about fix hundred years old, their
three fons, and their three wives. It was charming
to fee with what care, what dexterity, what cleanli-
nefs, our eight domeftics ferved four thoufand of
the moft ravenous guefts, without reckoning the
amazing trouble which about ten or twelve thoufand other animals required, from the elephant and
the gyraffe to the filk-worm and fly. What afto-
nifhes me is, that our purveyor Noah is unknown
to all the nations of whom he is the ftem, but I
don't much mind it. I had already been prefent
at a fimilar * entertainment with Xefuftres king of
Thrace; fuch things as thefe happen from time
to time for the inftruction of the ravens. In a
word,

---

* Berofus, a Chaldean author, relates an affair that the fame
adventure happened to Xefuftres king of Thrace: it was ftill
more wonderful, for his ark was about 5 ftadii long, and 2
broad. There is a great difpute amongft the learned, whether
king Xefuftres or Noah was the moft ancient.

word, I want to have good cheer, and to be paid in ready money."

The wife Mambres took care not to give his letter to such a discontented and babbling animal; and they separated very much dissatisfied with each other.

But it is necessary to know what became of the white bull, and not to lose the traces of the old woman and the serpent. Mambres ordered his intelligent and faithful domestics to follow them; and as for himself, he advanced in a litter by the side of the Nile, always making reflections.

"How is it possible," said he to himself, "that a serpent should be master of almost all the world, as he boasts, and as so many learned men acknowledge, and that he nevertheless obeys an old woman? How is it, that he is sometimes called to the council of the Most High while he creeps upon earth? In what manner can he enter by his power alone into the bodies of men, and that so many men pretend to dislodge him by means of words? In short, why does he pass with a small neighbouring people for having ruined the human race? and how is it that the human race are entirely ignorant of this? I am old, I have studied all my life, but I see a crowd of inconsistencies which I cannot reconcile; I cannot account for what has happened to myself, neither for the great things which I long ago performed, nor those of which I have been witness. Every thing well considered, I begin to think that this world subsists by contradictions, *rerum concordia discors*, as my master Zoroaster formerly said in his language."

While he was plunged in this obscure metaphysical reasoning, such are all metaphysics, a boatman singing a jovial song, made fast a small boat by the side of the river, and three grave personages, half clothed in dirty tattered garments, landed from it, but preserved, under the garb of poverty, the most majestic and august air. These were *Daniel, Ezekiel, and Jeremiah.*

***

CHAP. VI.

How Mambres met three Prophets, and gave them a good Dinner.

THESE three great men who had the prophetic light in their countenance, knew the wise Mambres to be one of their brethren, by some marks of the same light which he had still remaining, and prostrated themselves before his litter. Mambres likewise knew them to be prophets, more by their dress, than by those gleams of fire which proceeded from their august heads ; he conjectured that they came to learn news of the white bull ; and conducting himself with his usual propriety, he alighted from his carriage, and advanced a few steps towards them, with a politeness mixed with dignity. He raised them up, caused tents to be erected, and prepared a dinner, of which he judged that the prophets had very great need.

He invited the old woman to it, who was only about five hundred paces from them, who accepted the invitation, and arrived, leading her white bull.

Two soups were served up, one *de Bisque*, and the other *a la Reine.* The first course consisted of a carp's tongue pye, livers of eel-pouts, and pikes; fowls dressed with pistachios, pigeons with truffles

and

and olives; two young turkeys with gravy of cray fish, mushrooms, and morels; and a chipotata. The second course was composed of pheasants, partridges, quails, and ortolans, with four sallads; the epargne was in the higheft taste; nothing could be more delicious than the fide dishes; nothing more brilliant and more ingenious than the defert. But the wife Mambres took great care to have no boiled beef, nor fhort ribs, nor tongue, nor palate of an ox, nor cows udder, left the unfortunate monarch near at hand fhould think that they infulted him.

This great and unfortunate prince was feeding near the tent; and never did he feel in a more cruel manner the fatal revolution which had deprived him of his throne for feven long years. "Alas!" faid he to himfelf, "this Daniel who has changed me into a bull, and this forcerefs my keeper, make the best cheer in the world; while I, the fovereign of Afia, am reduced to the neceffity of eating grafs, and drinking water."

When they had drank heartily of the wine of Engaddi, of Tadmor, and of Schiras, the prophets and witch converfed with more franknefs than at the firft courfe. "I muft acknowledge," faid Daniel, "that I did not live fo well in the lion's den." "What, Sir," faid Mambres, "did they put you into a den of lions? how came you not to be devoured?"

"Sir," faid Daniel, "you know that lions never eat prophets."—"As for me," faid Jeremiah, "I have paffed my whole life ftarving of hunger. This is the only day I have ever ate a good meal; and were I to fpend my life over again, and had it in my power to choofe my condition, I muft own

Z 2   I

I would much rather be comptroller-general or bishop of Babylon, than prophet at Jerusalem."

Ezekiel cried (chap. iv.) " I was once ordered to sleep three hundred four score and ten days upon my left side, and to eat all that time bread of barley, millet, vetches, beans, and wheat, covered in the most delicious manner. All that I was able to obtain was to cover it with cows dung. I must own that the cookery of Seigneur Mambres is much more delicate; however the prophetic trade has its advantages, and the proof is, that there are thousands who follow it."

After they had spoken thus freely, Mambres entered upon business; he asked the three pilgrims the reason of their journey into the dominions of the king of Tanis. Daniel replied, " That the kingdom of Babylon had been all in a flame since Nabucodnoser had disappeared; that according to the custom of the court, they had persecuted all the prophets, who passed their lives in sometimes seeing kings humbled at their feet, and sometimes receiving a hundred lashes from them; that at length they had been obliged to take refuge in E-gypt for fear of being starved.—Ezekiel and Jeremiah likewise spoke a long time in so very fine terms that it was almost impossible to understand them. As for the witch, she had always a strict eye over her charge: the fish of Jonas continued in the Nile opposite to the tent, and the serpent sported upon the grass. After drinking coffee, they took a walk by the side of the Nile; and the white bull, perceiving the three prophets, his enemies, bellowed most dreadfully, ran furiously at them, gored them with his horns; and as prophets never have any thing but skin upon their bones, he would certainly have run them through; but the Ruler

of

of the world who fees all and remedies all, changed them immediately into magpies ; and they continued to chatter as before. The fame thing happened fince to the Pierides ; fo much has fable always imitated hiftory.

This incident promoted new reflections in the
mind of the wife Mambres. " Here," faid he,
" are three great prophets changed into magpies ;
this ought to teach us never to fpeak too much, and
always to obferve a fuitable difcretion :" he concluded that wifdom was better than eloquence, and
thought profoundly as ufual, when a great and terrible fpectacle prefented itfelf to his eyes.

C H A P. VII.

How King Amafis wanted to give the White Bull
to be devoured by the Fifh of Jonas, and did
not do it.

CLOUDS of duft floated from fouth to north ;
the noife of drums, fifes, pfalteries, harps,
and fackbuts was heard, feveral fquadrons and
battalions advanced, and Amafis king of Tanis
was at their head upon an Arabian horfe, capari-
foned with fcarlet trappings embroidered with gold,
while the heralds proclaimed that they fhould feize
the white bull, bind him, and throw him into the
Nile, to be devoured by the fifh of Jonas ; " for
the king our lord, who is juft, wants to revenge
himfelf upon the white bull, who has bewitched
his daughter."

The good old man Mambres made more reflections than ever. He faw very plainly that the malicious

licious raven had told all to the king, and that the
princefs ran a great rifk of being beheaded. "My
dear friend," faid he to the ferpent, "go quickly
and comfort the fair Amafidia, my fofter daughter; bid her fear nothing whatever may happen,
and tell her ftories to alleviate her inquietude; for
ftories always amufe the ladies, and it is only by
them that one can fucceed in the world."

Mambres next proftrated himfelf before Amafis
king of Tanis, and thus addreffed him; "O king,
live for ever, the white bull fhould certainly be facrificed, for your majefty is always in the right;
but the Ruler of the world has faid, this bull muft
not be fwallowed up by the fifh of Jonas till Memphis fhall have found a god to fupply the place of
him who is dead; then thou fhalt be revenged, and
thy daughter exorcifed, for fhe is poffeffed. Your
piety is too great not to obey the commands of the
Ruler of the univerfe."

Amafis king of Tanis remained fome time pen-
five. "The god Apis," faid he at laft, "is dead!
God reft his foul! when do you think another ox
will be found to reign over the fruitful Egypt?"

"Sire," replied Mambres, "I afk but eight
days." "I grant them to you," replied the king,
who was very religious, "and I will remain here the
eight days; after which I will facrifice the feducer
of my daughter." Amafis immediately ordered
his tents, his cooks, his muficians, and remained
here eight days, as it is related in Manethon.

The old woman was in defpair that the bull fhe
had in charge had but eight days to live. She raifed phantoms every night, in order to diffuade the
king from his cruel refolution; but Amafis forgot in the morning the phantoms he had feen in
the

the night; similar to Nebuchadnezar, who had always forgot his dreams.

C H A P. VIII.

How the Serpent told Stories to the Princess to comfort her.

MEAN while the serpent told stories to the fair Amasidia to sooth her. He related to her how he had formerly cured a whole nation of the bite of certain little serpents, only by shewing himself at the end of a staff. He informed her of the conquests of a hero who made a charming contrast with Amphion, architect of Thebes in Bœotia. Amphion assembled hewn stones by the sound of his violin; to build a city he had only to play a rigodoon and a minuet; but the other hero destroyed them by the sound of rams horns; he caused to hang thirty-one powerful kings in a country of four leagues in length and four in breadth; he made stones rain down from heaven upon a battalion of routed Amorites; and having thus exterminated them, he stopped the sun and moon at noon day between Gibeon and Askalon, in the road to Bethoron, to exterminate them still more, after the example of Bacchus, who had stopt the sun and the moon in his journey to the Indies.

The prudence which every serpent ought to have, did not allow him to tell the fair Amasidia of the powerful Jepthah, son of ——, who beheaded his daughter, because he had gained a battle. This would have struck too much terror into the mind of the fair princess; but he related to her the adventures of the great Sampson, who killed a thoufand

sand Philiftines with the jaw-bone of an afs, who
tied together three hundred foxes by the tail, and
who fell into the fnares of a lady, lefs beautiful,
lefs tender, and lefs faithful than the charming A-
mafidia.

He related to her the unfortunate loves of Se-
chem and the lovely Dinah, who was fix years old;
and the more fortunate amours of Ruth and Boaz;
thofe of Judah with his daughter-in-law Thamar;
thofe even of Lott, with his two daughters, who
did not chufe that the human race fhould be ex-
tinguifhed; thofe of Abraham and Jacob with their
fervant maids; thofe of Ruben with his mother;
thofe of David and Bathfheba; thofe of the great
king Solomon; in fhort, every thing which could
diffipate the grief of a fair princefs.

CHAP. IX.

How the Serpent did not comfort the Princefs.

" ALL thefe ftories tire me," faid Amafidia,
for fhe had underftanding and tafte,
" they are good for nothing but to be comment-
ed upon amongft the Irifh by that madman Ab-
badie, or amongft the Welfh * by that prattler
d'Houteville. Stories which might have amufed
the great, great, great grandmother of the great,
great, great grandmother of my grandmother,
appear infipid to me who have been educated by
the wife Mambres, and who have read *human underftanding* by the Egyptian philofopher named
Locke, and the *Matron of Ephefus*; I chufe that
a ftory

---

* The French.

a ſtory ſhould be founded on probability, and not always reſembling a dream ; I deſire to find nothing in it trivial or extravagant ; and I want, above all, that under the appearance of fable there may appear ſome latent truth, obvious to the diſcerning eye, though it eſcape the obſervation of the vulgar.

"I am weary of a ſun and of a moon, which an old beldame diſpoſes at her pleaſure, of mountains which dance, of rivers which return to their ſources, and of dead men who riſe again ; but I am above meaſure diſguſted when ſuch inſipid ſtories are written in a bombaſt and unintelligible manner. A lady who expects to ſee her lover ſwallowed up by a great fiſh, and who is apprehenſive of being beheaded by her own father, has need of amuſement ; but ſuit my amuſement to my taſte."

"You impoſe a very difficult taſk upon me," replied the ſerpent. "I could have formerly made you paſs a few hours agreeably enough, but for ſome time paſt I have loſt both my imagination and memory. Alas ! what is become of that time when I amuſed the ladies ? Let me try, however, if I can recollect one moral tale for your entertainment.

"Five and twenty thouſand years ago king Gnaof and queen Patra reigned in Thebes with its hundred gates. King Gnaof was very handſome, and queen Patra ſtill more beautiful ; but his attempts to have children were unſucceſsful. The king Gnaof propoſed a reward for the perſon who ſhould diſcover the beſt method of perpetuating the royal race.

"The faculty of medicine, and the academy of ſurgery, wrote excellent treatiſes upon this queſtion.

Not one of them fucceeded. The queen was fent to drink mineral waters ; fhe fafted and prayed ; fhe made magnificent prefents to the temple of Jupiter Ammon, from whence comes the fal armoniac ; but all was to no purpofe. At length a young prieft of five and twenty prefented himfelf to the king : " Sire, faid he, I imagine that I am in poffeffion of the charm which will produce the effect your majefty fo earneftly defires. I muft whifper fomething in private to madam, your fpoufe, and if fhe does not become fruitful, I confent to be hanged." " I accept the propofal," faid king Gnaof. " They left the queen and the prieft but a quarter of an hour together ; the queen became pregnant, and the king wanted to hang the prieft."

" My God !" faid the princefs, " but I fee where this leads : this ftory is too common, and I muft likewife tell you that it offends my modefty. Relate fome very true and moral ftory, which I have never yet heard, to complete the improvement of my underftanding and my heart, as the Egyptian profeffor Lenro fays."

" Here then, madam," faid the beautiful ferpent, " is one moft inconteftibly authentic.

" There were three prophets all equally ambitious and difcontented with their condition : they had in common the folly to wifh to be kings : for there is only one ftep from the rank of a prophet to that of a monarch, and man always afpires to the higheft ftep in the ladder of fortune. In other refpects, their inclinations and their pleafures were totally different. The firft preached admirably to his affembled brethren, who applauded him by clapping their hands ; the fecond was diftractdiftraftedly fond of mufic; and the third was a paffionate lover of the fair fex.

" The angel Ithuriel prefented himfelf one day to them when they were at table difcourfing on the fweets of royalty. " The Ruler of the world, faid the angel to them, fends me to you to reward your virtue; not only fhall you be kings, but you fhall conftantly fatisfy your ruling paffions. You, firft prophet, I make king of Egypt, and you fhall continually prefide in your council, who fhall applaud your eloquence and your wifdom; and you, fecond prophet, I make king over Perfia, and you fhall continually hear moft heavenly mufic; and you, third prophet, I make king of India, and I give you a charming miftrefs who fhall never forfake you.

" He, to whofe lot Egypt fell, began his reign by affembling his council, which was compofed only of two hundred fages. He made them a long and eloquent fpeech, which was very much applauded, and the monarch enjoyed the pleafing fatisfaction of intoxicating himfelf with praifes uncorrupted by flattery.

" The council for foreign affairs fucceeded to the privy council; this was much more numerous. And a new fpeech received ftill greater encomiums; and it was the fame in the other councils. There was not a moment of intermiffion in the pleafures and glory of the prophet king of Egypt. The fame of his eloquence filled the world.

" The prophet king of Perfia began his reign by an Italian opera, whofe chorufes were fung by fifteen hundred eunuchs; their voices penetrated his foul even to the very marrow of the bones, where it refides. To this opera fucceeded another, and to the fecond a third without interruption.

" The

" The king of India fhut himfelf up with his miftrefs, and enjoyed perfect pleafure with her. He confidered the neceffity of always careffing her as the higheft felicity, and pitied the wretched fi-tuation of his two brethren, of whom one was obliged always to convene his council, and the other to be continually at an opera.

" It happened at the end of a few days, that each of thefe kings beheld from his window wood-cutters who came from an ale-houfe, and were go-ing to work in a neighbouring foreft; they walk-ed arm in arm with their fweet-hearts, with whom they were happy, and changed them at pleafure.--- The kings begged of the angel Ithuriel that he would intercede with the Ruler of the world, and make *them* wood-cutters."

" I do not know whether the Ruler of the world granted their requeft," interrupted the ten-der Amafidia, " and I do not care much about it; but I know very well that I fhould afk for no-thing of any one, were I in private with my lover, with my dear NABUCODNOSER."

The vaults of the palace refounded this mighty name; at firft Amafidia had only pronounced Na---afterwards Nabu—then Nabuco—at length paffion hurried her on, and fhe pronounced entire the fa-tal name, notwithftanding the oath fhe had fworn to the king her father. All the ladies of the court repeated NABUCODNOSER, and the malicious raven did not fail to carry the tidings to the king. The countenance of Amafis, king of Tanis, funk, becaufe his heart was troubled. And thus it was that the ferpent, the wifeft, and moft fubtile of animals, always beguiled the women, thinking to do them fervice.

Amafis, in a fury, fent twelve alguazils for his daugh-

daughter; thefe men are always ready to execute barbarous orders, becaufe they are paid for it.

CHAP. X.

How they wanted to behead the Princefs, and did not behead her.

NO fooner had the princefs entered the camp of the king, than he faid to her; " My daughter, you know that all princeffes who difobey their fathers are put to death ; without which it would be impoffible that a kingdom could be well governed. I charged you never to mention the name of your lover Nabucodnofer, my mortal enemy, who dethroned me about feven years ago, and difappeared. In his place you have chofen a white bull, and you have cried NABUCODNOSER. It is juft that I behead you."

The princefs replied, " My father, thy will be done! but grant me fome time to bewail my virginity." " That is reafonable," faid king Amafis ; " and it is a rule eftablifhed amongft the moft judicious princes. I give you a whole day to bewail your virginity, fince you fay that you have it. Tomorrow, which is the eighth day of my encampment, I will caufe the white bull to be fwallowed up by the fifh, and I will behead you precifely at nine o'clock in the morning."

The beautiful Amafidia then went forth to bewail all that remained to her of her virginity by the fide of the Nile, accompanied with the ladies of her train.

The

The wise Mambres pondered befide her, and reckoned the hours and the moments. " Well! my dear Mambres," faid fhe to him, " you have changed the waters of the Nile into blood, according to cuftom, and cannot you change the heart of Amafis, king of Tanis, my father? Will you fuffer him to behead me to-morrow at nine o'clock in the morning?"——" That depends," replied the reflecting Mambres, " upon the fpeed and diligence of my couriers."

The next day, as foon as the fhadows of the obelifks and pyramids marked upon the ground the ninth hour of the day, the white bull was bound to be thrown to the fifh of Jonas; and they brought to the king his large fabre. " Alas! alas!" faid Nabucodnofer to himfelf, " I a king have been an ox for near feven years; and fcarcely have I found the miftrefs I had loft when I am condemned to be devoured by a fifh."

Never had the wife Mambres made fuch profound reflections; and he was quite abforbed in his melancholy thoughts when he faw at a diftance all he expected. An innumerable crowd drew nigh. Three figures of Ifis, Ofiris, and Horus, joined together, advanced, drawn in a carriage of gold and precious ftones by a hundred fenators of Memphis, preceded by a hundred girls playing upon the facred fiftrums. Four thoufand priefts, with their heads fhaved, were each mounted upon a hippopotamus.

At further diftance appeared with the fame pomp the fheep of Tpebes, the dog of Babaftes, the cat of Phœbe, the crocodile of Arfinoe, the goat of Mendez, and all the inferior gods of Egypt, who came to pay homage to the great ox, to the mighty Apis.

Apis, as powerful as Ifis, Ofiris, and Horus, united together.

In the midft of the demigods, forty priefts carried an enormous bafket filled with facred onions: thefe were, it is true, gods, but they refembled onions very much.

On both fides of this file of gods, followed by an innumerable crowd of people, marched forty thoufand warriors, with helmets on their heads, fcymetars upon their left thighs, quivers at their fhoulders, and bows in their hands.

All the priefts finging in chorus, with a harmony which ravifhed the foul, and which melted it,

" Alas! alas! our ox is dead——
" We'll have a finer in his ftead."

And at every paufe was heard the found of the fiftrums, of cymbals, of tabors, of pfalteries, of bagpipes, harps, and fackbuts.

Amafis, king of Tanis, aftonifhed at this fpectacle beheaded not his daughter; he fheathed his fcymetar.

C H A P. XI.

How the Princefs married her Ox.

" GREAT king," faid Mambres to him, " the order of things is changed; your majefty muft fet the example. O king! quickly unbind the white bull, and be the firft to adore him."

Amafis obeyed, and proftrated himfelf with all his people. The high prieft of Memphis prefented to the new god Apis the firft handful of hay; the princefs Amafidia tied to his beautiful horns feftoons

ftoons of rofes, anemonies, ranunculufes, tulips,
pinks, and hyacinths. She took the liberty to kifs
him, but with a profound refpect. The priefts
ftrewed palms and flowers on the road, by which
they were to conduct him to Memphis. And the
wife Mambres, making reflections, whifpered to
his friend the ferpent : " Daniel changed this monarch into an ox, and I have changed this ox into
a god."

They returned to Memphis in the fame order,
and the king of Tanis, in fome confufion, followed
the band.   Mambres, with a ferene and compofed
air, walked by his fide. The old woman came after, much amazed ; fhe was accompanied by the
ferpent, the dog, the fhe-afs, the raven, the pigeon,
and the fcape-goat.   The great fifh mounted up
the Nile ; Daniel, Ezekiel, and Jeremiah, changed
into magpies, brought up the rear. When they
had reached the frontiers of the kingdom, which
are not far diftant, king Amafis took leave of the
ox Apis, and faid to his daughter, " My daughter,
let us return into my dominions, that I may behead you, as it has been determined in my royal
breaft, becaufe you have pronounced the name of
Nabucodnofer my enemy, who dethroned me feven
years ago. When a father has fworn to behead
his daughter, he muft either fulfil his oath, or fink
into hell for ever ; and I will not damn myfelf out
of love to you."

The fair princefs Amafidia replied to the king
Amafis : " My dear father, whom it pleafes you
go and behead, but it fhall not be me : I am now
in the territories of Ifis, Ofiris, Horus, and Apis ;
I will never forfake my beautiful white bull, and
I will continue to kifs him till I have feen his apo-
theofis in his ftable in the holy city of Memphis.
It

It is a weaknefs pardonable in a young lady of high birth."

Scarce had fhe fpoke thefe words, when the ox Apis cried out, "My dear Amafidia, I will love you whilft I live." This was the firft time that the god Apis had been heard to fpeak during forty thoufand years that he had been worfhipped. The ferpent and the fhe-afs cried out, "*the feven years are accomplifhed.*" And the three magpies repeated, "*the feven years are accomplifhed.*" All the priefts of Egypt raifed their hands to heaven. The god on a fudden was feen to lofe his two hind legs; his two fore legs were changed into two human legs; two white ftrong mufcular arms grew from his fhoulders; his taurine phyz was changed to the face of a charming hero; and he once more became the moft beautiful of mortals. "I choofe," cried he, "rather to be the lover of the beautiful Amafidia than a god. I am NABUCODNOSER, KING of KINGS."

This metamorphofis aftonifhed all the world, except the wife Mambres; but what furprifed nobody was, that Nabucodnofer immediately married the fair Amafidia in prefence of this affembly. He left his father-in-law in quiet poffeffion of the kingdom of Tanis, and made noble provifion for the fhe-afs, the ferpent, the dog, the pigeon, and even for the raven, the three magpies, and the large fifh; fhewing to all the world that he knew how to forgive as well as to conquer. The old woman had a confiderable penfion; the fcape-goat was fent for a day into the wildernefs, that all paft fins might be expiated; and had afterwards twelve fhe-goats for his reward. The wife Mambres returned to his palace, and made reflections.

Nabucodnofer, after having embraced the magician his benefactor, governed in tranquillity the kingdoms of Memphis, Babylon, Damafcus, Balbec, Tyre, Syria, Afia *minor*, Scythia, the countries of Thiras, Mofok, Tubal, Madai, Gog, Magog, Javan, Sogdiana, Aroriana, the Indies, and the Ifles; and the people of this vaft empire cried out aloud every morning, " Long live Nabucodnofer, king of kings, who is no longer an ox !" Since which time it has been a cuftom in Babylon, when the fovereign, deceived by his fatraps, his magicians, treafurers, or wives, at length acknowledges his errors, and amends his conduct, for all the people to cry out at his gate, " Long live our great king, who is no longer an ox."

THE

THE

Hiftory of the TRAVELS of

SCARMENTADO. *

Written by himfelf.

I Was born in Candia in the year 1600. My
father was governor of the city ; and I remember that a poet of middling parts, and of a moft
unmufical ear, whofe name was Iro, compofed
fome verfes in my praife, in which he made me to
defcend from Minos in a direct line ; but my father
being afterwards difgraced, he wrote fome other
verfes, in which he derived my pedigree from no
nobler an origin than the amours of Pafiphae and
her gallant. This Iro was a moft mifchievous
rogue, and one of the moft troublefome fellows in
the ifland.

My father fent me at fifteen years of age to profecute my ftudies at Rome. There I arrived in full
hopes of learning all kinds of truth ; for I had hitherto been taught quite the reverfe, according to

the

---

* The reader will at once perceive that this is a fpirited
fatire on mankind in general, and particularly on perfecution for
confcience fake.

the cuſtom of this lower world from China to the Alps. Monſignor Profondo, to whom I was re-commended, was a man of a very ſingular charac-ter, and one of the moſt terrible ſcholars in the world. He was for teaching me the categories of Ariſtotle, and was juſt on the point of placing me in the category of his minions; a fate which I narrowly eſcaped. I ſaw proceſſions, exorciſms, and ſome robberies. It was commonly ſaid, but without any foundation, that *la Signora Olimpia*, a lady of great prudence, ſold ſeveral things that ought not to be ſold. I was then of an age to re-liſh all theſe comical adventures. · A young lady of great ſweetneſs of temper, called *la Signora Fatelo*, thought proper to fall in love with me: ſhe was courted by the reverend father *Poignardini*, and by the reverend father *Aconiti*,* young monks of an order which is now extinct; and ſhe reconciled the two rivals, by granting her favours to me; but at the ſame time I ran the riſk of being excommuni-cated and poiſoned. I left Rome highly pleaſed with the architecture of St Peter.

I travelled to France: it was during the reign of Lewis the Juſt. The firſt queſtion put to me was, whether I chuſed to breakfaſt on a ſlice of the mareſchal D'Ancre †, whoſe fleſh the people had roaſted,

---

* Alluding to the infamous practice of poiſoning and aſſaſſi-nation, at that time prevalent in Rome.

† This was the famous Concini, who was murdered on the draw-bridge of the Louvre by the intrigues of De Luines, not without the knowledge of the king, Lewis XIII. His body, which had been ſecretly interred in the church of St Germain de l'Auxerrois, was next day dug up by the populace, who dragged it through the ſtreets, then burned the fleſh, and threw the bones into the river. The mareſchal's greateſt crime was his being a foreigner.

roafted, and diftributed with great liberality to fuch as chufed to tafte it?

This kingdom was continually involved in civil wars, fometimes for a place at court, fometimes for two pages of theological controverfy. This fire, which one while lay concealed under the afhes, and at another burft forth with great violence, had defolated thefe beautiful provinces for upwards of fixty years. The pretext was, the defending the liberties of the Gallican church. "Alas! faid I, thefe people are neverthelefs born with a gentle difpofition: what can have drawn them fo far from their natural character? They joke and keep holy days*. Happy the time when they fhall do nothing but joke!"

I went over to England, where the fame difputes occafioned the fame barbarities. Some pious Catholics had refolved, for the good of the church, to blow up into the air with gun-powder the king, the royal family, and the whole parliament, and thus to deliver England from all thefe heretics at once. They fhewed me the place where queen Mary of bleffed memory, the daughter of Henry VIII. had caufed more than five hundred of her fubjects to be burnt. An Irifh prieft affured me that it was a very good action; firft, becaufe thofe who were burnt were Englifhmen; and, fecondly, becaufe they did not make ufe of holy water, nor believe in St Patrick's Hole. He was greatly furprifed that queen Mary was not yet canonized; but he hoped fhe would receive that honour as foon as the cardinal nephew fhould be a little more at leifure.

From

---

* Referring to the maffacre of the Proteftants, perpetrated on the eve of St Bartholomew.

From thence I went to Holland, where I hoped to find more tranquillity among a people of a more cold and phlegmatic conſtitution. Juſt as I arrived at the Hague, the people were cutting off the head of a venerable old man. It was the bald head of the prime miniſter Barnevelt, a man who deſerved better treatment from the republic. Touched with pity at this affecting ſcene, I aſked what was his crime, and whether he had betrayed the ſtate? " He has done much worſe, replied a preacher in a black cloak ; he believed that men may be ſaved by good works as well as by faith. You muſt be ſenſible, adds he, that if ſuch opinions were to gain ground, a republic could not ſubſiſt ; and that there muſt be ſevere laws to ſuppreſs ſuch ſcandalous and horrid blaſphemies." A profound politician ſaid to me with a ſigh, " Alas ! Sir, this happy time will not laſt long ; it is only by chance that the people are ſo zealous : they are naturally inclined to the abominable doctrine of toleration, and they will certainly at laſt grant it." This reflection ſet him a-groaning. For my own part, in expectation of that fatal period, when moderation and indulgence ſhould take place, I inſtantly quitted a country where ſeverity was not ſoftened by any lenitive, and embarked for Spain.

The court was then at Seville ; the galleons were juſt arrived ; and every thing breathed plenty and gladneſs in the moſt beautiful ſeaſon of the year. I obſerved at the end of an alley of orange and citron trees, a kind of large ring, ſurrounded with ſteps covered with rich and coſtly cloth. The king, the queen, the infants, and the infantas, were ſeated under a ſuperb canopy. Oppoſite to the royal family was another throne, raiſed higher than that on which his majeſty ſat. I ſaid to one of my
fellow

fellow travellers, " Unlefs this throne be referved for God, I don't fee what purpofe it can ferve." This unguarded expreffion was overheard by a grave Spaniard, and coft me dear. Mean while, I imagined we were going to a caroufal, or a match of bull-baiting, when the grand inquifitor appeared on that elevated throne, from whence he bleffed the king and the people.

Then came an army of monks, who filed off in pairs, white, black, grey, fhod, unfhod, bearded, beardlefs, with pointed cowls, and without cowls : next followed the hangman ; and laft of all were feen, in the midft of the guards and grandees, about forty perfons clad in fackcloth, on which were painted the figures of flames and devils. Some of thefe were Jews, who could not be prevailed upon to renounce Mofes entirely; others were Chriftians, who had married women with whom they had ftood fponfors to a child ; who had not adored our Lady of Atocha, or who had refufed to part with their ready money in favour of the Hieronymite brothers. Some pretty prayers were fung with much devotion, and then the criminals were burnt at a flow fire ; a ceremony with which the royal family feemed to be greatly edified.

As I was going to bed in the evening, two members of the inquifition came to my lodging with a figure of St Hermandad. They embraced me with great tendernefs, and conducted me in folemn filence to a well-aired prifon, furnifhed with a bed of mat and a beautiful crucifix. There I remained for fix weeks ; at the end of which the reverend father, the inquifitor, fent for me. He preffed me in his arms for fome time with the moft paternal affection, and told me that he was forry to hear that I had been fo ill lodged ; but that all the apart-

apartments of the houfe were full, and hoped I
fhould be better accommodated the next time. He
then afked me with great cordiality if I knew for
what reafon I was imprifoned? I told the reverend
father that it was evidently for my fins. " Very
well, fays he, my dear child; but for what particular fin? Speak freely." I racked my brain with
conjectures, but could not poffibly guefs. He then
charitably difmiffed me.

At laft I remembered my unguarded expreffion.
I efcaped with a little bodily correction, and a fine
of thirty thoufand reals. I was led to make my
obeifance to the grand inquifitor, who was a man
of great politenefs. He afked me how I liked his
little feaft? I told him it was a moft delicious one;
and then went to prefs my companions to quit the
country, beautiful as it was. They had found
time to inform themfelves of all the great things
which the Spaniards had done for the intereft of
religion. They had read the memoirs of the famous bifhop of Chiapa, by which it appears that
they had maffacred, or burnt, or drowned, about
ten millions of infidels in America, in order to
convert them. I believe the accounts of the bifhop
are a little exaggerated; but fuppofe we reduce the
number of victims to five millions, it will ftill be a
moft glorious achievement.

The itch of travelling ftill poffeffed me. I had
propofed to finifh the tour of Europe with Turky;
and thither we now directed our courfe. I put on
a firm refolution not to give my opinion of the public feafts I might fee for the future. " Thefe
Turks, faid I to my companions, are a fet of mif-
creants that have not been baptized, and of confequence will be more cruel than the reverend fathers
the

the inquifitors. Let us obferve a profound filence while we are among the Mahometans."

Accordingly we arrived among them. I was greatly furprifed to fee more Chriftian churches in Turky than in Candia. I even faw fome nume- rous troops of monks, who were allowed to pray to the virgin Mary with great freedom, and to curfe Mahomet; fome in Greek, fome in Latin, and others in Armenian. " What good-natured people are thefe Turks," cried I. The Greek Chriftians, and the Latin Chriftians in Conftantinople were mortal enemies. Thefe flaves perfecuted each other in much the fame manner as dogs fight in the ftreets, till their mafters part them with a cud- gel. The grand vizier was at that time the protec- tor of the Greeks. The Greek partriarch accufed me of having fupped with the Latin patriarch; and I was condemned in full divan to receive an hun- dred blows on the foles of my feet, redeemable for five hundred fequins. Next day the grand vizier was ftrangled. The day following his fucceffor, who was for the Latin party, and who was not ftrangled till a month after, condemned me to fuf- fer the fame punifhment, for having fupped with the Greek patriarch. Thus was I reduced to the fad neceffity of abfenting myfelf entirely from the Greek and Latin churches. In order to confole myfelf for this lofs, I took into keeping a very handfome Circaffian. She was the moft obliging lady I ever knew in a private converfation, and the moft devout at the mofque. One night as fhe was embracing me in the fweet tranfports of love, fhe cried, " Alla, Illa, Alla ;" thefe are the facramen- tal words of the Turks. I imagined they were the expreffions of love, and therefore cried in my

VOL. I.   †   C c   turn,

turn, and with a very tender accent, " Alla, Illa, Alla." " Ah! said she, God be praised, thou art then a Turk. I told her that I was blessing God for having given me so much strength, and that I thought myself extremely happy. In the morning the iman came to circumcise me; and, as I made some difficulty to submit to the operation, the cadi of that district, a man of great loyalty, proposed to have me impaled. I saved my prepuce and my posteriors by paying a thousand sequins, and then fled directly into Persia, resolved for the future never to hear Greek or Latin mass, nor to cry " Alla Illa, Alla," in a love rencounter.

On my arrival at Ispahan, the people asked me whether I was for white or black mutton? I told them it was a matter of indifference to me, provided it was tender. It must be observed that the Persian empire was at that time split into two factions, that of the white mutton and that of the black. The two parties imagined that I made a jest of them both; so that I found myself engaged in a very troublesome affair at the gates of the city, and it cost me a great number of sequins to get rid of the white and the black mutton.

I proceeded as far as China, in company with an interpreter, who assured me that this country was the seat of gaiety and freedom. The Tartars had made themselves masters of it, after having destroyed every thing with fire and sword. The reverend fathers the Jesuits on the one hand, and the reverend fathers the Dominicans on the other, alledged that they had gained many souls to God in that country, without any one knowing aught of the matter. Never were seen such zealous converters: they alternately persecuted one another: they transmitted to Rome whole volumes of slander,

der, and treated each other as infidels and preva-
ricators for the fake of one foul. But the moft
violent difpute between them was with regard to
the manner of making a bow. The Jefuits would
have the Chinefe to falute their parents, after the
fafhion of China; and the Dominicans would have
them to do it after the fafhion of Rome. I happened unluckily to be taken by the Jefuits for a
Dominican. They reprefented me to his Tartarian
majefty as a fpy of the pope. The fupreme council charged a prime mandarin, who ordered a fer-
jeant, who commanded four fbires of the country,
to feize me and bind me with great ceremony. In
this manner I was conducted before his majefty,
after having made about an hundred and forty
genuflexions. He afked me if I was a fpy of the
pope's and if it was true that that prince was to
come in perfon to dethrone him. I told him that
the pope was a prieft of feventy years of age; that
he lived at the diftance of four thoufand leagues
from his facred Tartaro-chinefe majefty; that he
had about two thoufand foldiers, who mounted
guard with umbrellas; that he never dethroned any
body; and that his majefty might fleep in perfect
fecurity. Of all the adventures of my life this was
the leaft fatal. I was fent to Macao, and there I
took fhipping for Europe.

My fhip required to be refitted on the coaft of
Golconda. I embraced this opportunity to vifit
the court of the great Aureng-Zeb, of whom fuch
wonderful things have been told, and who was
then in Deli. I had the pleafure to fee him on the
day of that pompous ceremony in which he receives the celeftial prefent fent him by the Sherif
of Mecca: this was the befom with which they had
fweeped the holy houfe, the Caaba, and the Beth

Alla. It is a fymbol that fweeps away all the pollutions of the foul. Aureng-Zeb feemed to have no need of it: he was the moft pious man in all Indoftan. It is true, he had cut the throat of one of his brothers, and poifoned his father. Twenty Rajas, and as many Omras, had been put to death; but that was a trifle; nothing was talked of but his devotion. No king was thought comparable to him, except his facred majefty Muley Ifmael, the moft ferene emperor of Morocco, who cut off fome heads every Friday after prayers.

I fpoke not a word. My travels had taught me wifdom. I was fenfible that it did not belong to me to decide between thefe auguft fovereigns. A young Frenchman, indeed, a fellow-lodger of mine, was wanting in refpect to the emperor of the Indies, and to that of Morocco. He happened to fay very imprudently, that there were fovereigns in Europe, who governed their dominions with great equity, and even went to church without killing their fathers or brothers, or cutting off the heads of their fubjects. This impious difcourfe of my young friend our interpreter tranfmitted to Indou. Inftructed by former experience, I inftantly caufed my camels to be faddled, and fet out with my Frenchman. I was afterwards informed that that very night the officers of the great Aureng-Zeb, having come to feize me, found only the interpreter, who was executed in public; and all the courtiers declared without flattery that his punifhment was extremely juft.

I had now only Africa to vifit, in order to enjoy all the pleafures of our continent; and thither I went in reality. The fhip in which I embarked was taken by the Negro-Corfairs. The mafter of the veffel complained loudly, and afked why they thus

thus violated the laws of nations.   The captain of the Negroes replied : " You have a long nofe and we have a fhort one : your hair is ftrait and ours is curled : your fkin is afh-coloured, and ours is of the colour of ebon ; and therefore we ought, by the facred laws of nature, to be always at enmity. You buy us in the public markets on the coaft of Guiney like beafts of burden, to make us labour in I don't know what kind of drudgery, equally hard and ridiculous.   With the whip held over our heads, you make us dig in mountains for a kind of yellow earth, which in itfelf is good for nothing, and is not fo valuable as an Egyptian onion.   In like manner, wherever we meet you, and are fuperior to you in ftrength, we make you flaves, and oblige you to manure our fields ; or in cafe of refufal cut off your nofe and ears."

To fuch a learned difcourfe it was impoffible to make any anfwer.   I went to labour in the ground of an old female Negro, in order to fave my nofe and ears.   After continuing in flavery for a whole year, I was at laft ranfomed.   I had now feen all that was rare, good, or beautiful on earth.   I refolved for the future to fee nothing but my own home.   I took a wife, and was cuckolded ; and found that of all conditions of life this was the happieft.

How

How far we ought to impofe upon the
PEOPLE.

IT is a queftion of great importance, however little regarded, how far the people, i. e. nine
tenths of the human kind, ought to be treated like
apes. The deceiving party have never examined
this problem with fufficient care ; and for fear of
being miftaken in the calculation, they have heap-
ed up all the vifionary notions they could in the
heads of the party deceived.

The good people, who fometimes read Virgil, or
the Provincial Letters, do not know that there are
twenty times more copies of the Almanac of Liege
and of the " Courier boiteux" printed, than of all
the ancient and modern books together. No one,
furely, has a greater veneration than myfelf for the
illuftrious authors of thefe Almanacs and their brethren. I know, that ever fince the time of the ancient Chaldeans, there have been fixed and ftated
days for taking phyfic, paring our nails, giving
battle, and cleaving wood. I know that the beft
part of the revenue of an illuftrious academy confifts in the fale of thefe kind of Almanacs. May I
prefume to afk, with all poffible fubmiffion, and a
becoming diffidence of my own judgment, what
harm it would do to the world, were fome powerful aftrologer to affure the peafants and the good
inhabitants of little villages, that they might fafely
pare their nails when they pleafe, provided it be
done

done with a good intention? The people, I fhall be told, would not buy the Almanacs of this new aftrologer. On the contrary, I will venture to affirm, that there would be found among your great geniufes many who would make a merit in following this novelty. Should it be alledged that thefe geniufes would form factions, and kindle a civil war, I have nothing farther to fay on the fubject, but readily give up, for the fake of peace, my too dangerous opinion.

Every body knows the king of Boutan. He is one of the greateft princes in the univerfe. He tramples under his feet the thrones of the earth; and his fhoes (if he has any) are provided with fceptres inftead of buckles. He adores the devil, as is well known, and his example is followed by all his courtiers. He, one day, fent for a famous fculptor of my country, and ordered him to make a beautiful ftatue of Beelzebub. The fculptor fucceeded to admiration. Never was there fuch a handfome devil. But, unhappily, our Praxiteles had only given five clutches to his animal, whereas the Boutaniers always gave him fix. This capital blunder of the artift was aggravated, by the grand mafter of the ceremonies to the devil, with all the zeal of a man juftly jealous of his mafter's rights, and of the facred and immemorial cuftom of the kingdom of Boutan. He infifted that the fculptor fhould atone for his crime by the lofs of his head. The fculptor replied, that his five clutches were exactly equal in weight to fix ordinary clutches; and the king of Boutan, who was a prince of great clemency, granted him a pardon. From that time the people of Boutan were undeceived with regard to the devil's fix clutches.

The fame day his majefty needed to let blood.

A

A furgeon of Gafcony, who had come to his court
in a fhip belonging to our Eaft-India company, was
appointed to take from him five ounces of his precious blood. The aftrologer of that quarter cried
out, that the king would be in danger of lofing his
life, if he opened a vein while the heavens were in
their prefent ftate. The Gafcon might have told
him, that the only queftion was about the ftate of
the king's health; but he prudently waited a few
minutes; and then taking an Almanac in his hand,
" You was in the right, great man!" faid he to the
aftrologer of the quarter; " the king would have
died, had he been blooded at the inftant you mention: the heavens have fince changed their afpect;
and now is the favourable moment." The aftrologer affented to the truth of the furgeon's obfervation. The king was cured; and by degrees it became an eftablifhed cuftom among the Boutaniers,
to bleed their kings whenever it was neceffary.

A bluftering Dominican at Rome faid to an
Englifh philofopher, " You are a dog; you fay
it is the earth that turns round, never reflecting
that Jofhua made the fun to ftand ftill." " Well!
my reverend father," replied the other; " and
fince that time the fun hath been immoveable."
The dog and the Dominican embraced each other;
and even the Italians were, at laft, convinced that
the earth turns round.

An augur and a fenator, in the time of Cæfar,
lamented the declining ftate of the republic. " The
times, indeed, are very bad," faid the fenator;
" we have reafon to tremble for the liberty of
Rome." " Ah!" faid the augur, " that is not the
greateft evil; the people now begin to lofe the
refpect which they formerly had for our order:
we feem barely to be tolerated; we ceafe to be neceffary

ceffary.   Some Generals have the affurance to give battle without confulting us ; and, to compleat our misfortunes, thofe who fell us the facred pullets begin to reafon. " Well, and why don't you reafon likewife ?" replied the fenator, " and fince the dealers in pullets in the time of Cæfar are more knowing than they were in the time of Numa, ought not you modern augurs to be better philofophers than thofe who lived in former ages ?"

The Two Comforters.

ONE day the great philofopher Citofile faid to a woman who was difconfolate, and who had good reafon to be fo, "Madam, the queen of England, daughter to Henry IV. was as wretched as you: fhe was banifhed from her kingdoms; was in the utmoft danger of lofing her life in a ftorm at fea; and faw her royal fpoufe expire on a fcaffold." "I am forry for her," faid the lady; and began again to lament her own misfortunes.

"But, faid Citofile, remember the fate of Mary Stuart. She loved, but with a moft chafte and virtuous affection, an excellent mufician, who played admirably on the bafs-viol. Her hufband killed her mufician before her face; and, in the fequel, her good friend and relation, queen Elizabeth, who called herfelf a virgin, caufed her head to be cut off on a fcaffold covered with black, after having confined her in prifon for the fpace of eighteen years." "That was very cruel," replied the lady, and prefently relapfed into her former melancholy.

"Perhaps, faid the comforter, you have heard of the beautiful Joan of Naples, who was taken prifoner and ftrangled." "I have a confufed remembrance of her ftory." faid the afflicted lady.

"I muft relate to you, added the other, the adventure of a foverign princefs, who, within my memory, was dethroned after fupper, and who died

in

in a defert ifland." "I know her whole hiftory," replied the lady.

" Well then, I will tell you what happened to another great princefs whom I inftructed in philo-fophy. She had a lover, as all great and beautiful princeffes have: her father entered the chamber, and furprifed the lover, whofe countenance was all on fire, and his eyes fparkling like a carbuncle. The lady too had a very florid complexion. The father was fo highly difpleafed with the young man's countenance, that he gave him one of the moft terrible blows that had ever been given in his province. The lover took a pair of tongs and broke the head of the father-in-law, who was cured with great difficulty, and ftill bears the mark of the wound. The lady in a fright leaped out of the window and diflocated her foot, in confequence of which fhe ftill halts, though poffeffed in other refpects of a very handfome perfon. The lover was condemned to death for having broken the head of a great prince: you can eafily judge in what a deplorable condition the princefs muft have been when her lover was led to the gallows. I have feen her long ago when fhe was in prifon: fhe always talked to me of her own misfortunes."

" And why will you not allow me to think of mine?" faid the lady. " Becaufe, faid the philo-fopher, you ought not to think of them; and fince fo many great ladies have been fo unfortunate, it ill becomes you to defpair. Think on Hecuba; think on Niobe." " Ah! faid the lady, had I lived in their time, or in that of fo many beautiful prin-ceffes, and had you endeavoured to confole them by a relation of my misfortunes, would they have liftened to you, do you imagine?"

Next day the philofopher loft his only fon, and

was

was like to have died with grief.   The lady caufed
a catalogue to be drawn up of all the kings who
had loft their children, and carried it to the philofopher.   He read it ; found it very exact ; and
wept neverthelefs.   Three months after, they re-
newed their vifits, and were furprifed to find each
other in fuch a gay and fprightly humour.   They
caufed to be erected a beautiful ftatue to Time,
with this infcription, *To him who comforts.*

THE

PRINCESS

OF

BABYLON.

THE aged Belus, king of Babylon thought himfelf the firft man upon earth ; for all his courtiers told him fo, and his hiftoriographers proved it. What might excufe this ridiculous vanity in him was, that, in fact, his predeceffors had built Babylon upwards of 30,000 years before him, and he had embellifhed it. We know that his palace and his park, fituated at a few parafangs from Babylon, extended between the Euphrates and the Tigris, which wafhed thofe enchanted banks. His vaft houfe, three thoufand feet in front, almoft reached the clouds. The platform was furrounded with a baluftrade of white marble, fifty feet high, which fupported coloffal ftatues of all the kings and great men of the empire. This platform, compofed of two rows of bricks, covered with a thick furface of lead from one extremity to the other, bore twelve feet of earth ; and upon this earth were raifed groves of olive, orange, citron, palm, cocoa, and cinnamon trees, and ftock gilliflowers, which formed alleys that the rays of the fun could not penetrate.

The

The waters of the Euphrates running by the aſſiſtance of pumps, in a hundred canals, into the vaſt marble baſons in this garden, and afterwards falling by other canals, formed caſcades of ſix thouſand feet in length in the park, and a hundred thouſand *jets d'eau,* whoſe height was ſcarce perceptible; they afterwards returned into the Euphrates, of which they were part. The gardens of Semiramis, which aſtoniſhed Aſia ſeveral ages after, were only a feeble imitation of theſe ancient prodigies; for in the time of Semiramis, every thing began to degenerate amongſt men and women.

But what was more admirable in Babylon, and eclipſed every thing elſe, was the only daughter of the King, named Formoſanta. It was from her pictures and ſtatues, that in ſucceeding times Praxiteles ſculptured his Aphrodita, and the Venus of Medicis. Heavens! what a difference between the original and the copies! ſo that Belus was prouder of his daughter than of his kingdom. She was eighteen years old: it was neceſſary ſhe ſhould have a huſband worthy of her; but where was he to be found? An ancient oracle had ordained, that Formoſanta could not belong to any but him who could bend the bow of Nembrod.

This Nembrod, the ſtrong hunter before the Lord, had left a bow ſeventeen Babylonian feet in length, made of ebony, harder than the iron of mount Caucaſus, which is wrought in the forges of Derbent; and no mortal ſince Nembrod could bend this aſtoniſhing bow.

It was again ſaid, that the arm which ſhould bend this bow would kill the moſt terrible and ferocious lion that ſhould be let looſe in the Circus of Babylon. This was not all; the bender of the bow,

bow, and the conqueror of the lion, fhould over-throw all his rivals : but he was above all things to be very fagacious, the moft magnificent and moft virtuous of men, and poffefs the greateft cu-riofity in the whole univerfe.

Three kings appeared, who were bold enough to claim Formofanta ; Pharaoh of Egypt, the Shah of India, and the great Khan of the Scythians. Belus appointed the day and place of combat, which was to be at the extremity of his park, in the vaft extent furrounded by the joint waters of the Euphrates and the Tigris. Round the lifts a marble amphitheatre was erected, which might con-tain five hundred thoufand fpectators. Oppofite the amphitheatre was placed the king's throne ; he was to appear with Formofanta, accompanied by the whole court; and on the right and left between the throne and the amphitheatre, there were other thrones and feats for the three kings, and for all the other fovereigns who were defirous to be pre-fent at this auguft ceremony.

The king of Egypt arrived the firft, mounted upon the bull Apis, and holding in his hand the cithern of Ifis. He was followed by two thoufand priefts clad in linen veftments whiter than fnow, two thoufand eunuchs, two thoufand magicians, and two thoufand warriors.

The king of India came foon after in a car drawn by twelve elephants. He had a train ftill more numerous and more brilliant than Pharaoh of Egypt.

The laft who appeared was the king of the Scy-thians. He had none with him but chofen war-riors, armed with bows and arrows. He was mount-ed upon a fuperb tyger, which he had tamed, and which was as tall as any of the fineft Perfian horfes.

The

The majeftic and important mien of this king effaced the appearance of his rivals ; his naked arms, as nervous as they were white, feemed already to bend the bow of Nembrod.

These three lovers immediately proftrated themfelves before Belus and Formofanta. The king of Egypt prefented the princefs with two of the fineft crocodiles of the Nile, two fea-horfes, two zebras, two Egyptian rats, and two mummies, with the books of the great Hermes, which he judged to be the fcarceft things upon earth.

The king of India offered her a hundred elephants, each bearing a wooden gilt tower, and laid at her feet the Vedam wrote by the hand of Xaca himfelf.

The king of the Scythians, who could neither write nor read, prefented a hundred warlike horfes with black fox-fkin houfings.

The princefs appeared with a down-caft look before her lovers, and reclined herfelf with fuch a grace as was at once modeft and noble.

Belus ordered the kings to be conducted to the thrones that were prepared for them. Would I had three daughters, faid he to them, I fhould make fix people this day happy ! He then made the competitors caft lots which fhould try Nembrod's bow firft. Their names infcribed were put into a golden cafque. That of the Egyptian king came out firft ; then the name of the king of India appeared. The king of Scythia, viewing the bow and his rivals, did not complain at being the third.

Whilft thefe brilliant trials were preparing, twenty thoufand pages and twenty thoufand youthful maidens diftributed, without any diforder, refrefhments to the fpectators between the rows of the feats. Every one acknowledged, that the gods had
infti-

inftituted kings for no other caufe than every day
to give feftivals, upon condition they fhould be di-
verfified ; that life is too fhort to be made any o-
ther ufe of; that law-fuits, intrigues, wars, the al-
tercations of theologifts, which confume human
life, are horrible and abfurd ; that man is born only
for happinefs ; that he would not paffionately and
inceffantly purfue pleafure, were he not defigned
for it ; that the effence of human nature is to
enjoy ourfelves, and all the reft is folly. This
excellent moral was never controverted but by
facts.

Whilft preparations were making for determin-
ing the fate of Formofanta, a young ftranger,
mounted upon an unicorn, accompanied by his
valet, mounted on a like animal, and bearing upon
his hand a large bird, appeared at the barrier.
The guards were furprifed to obferve in this equipage a figure that had an air of divinity. He had,
as hath been fince related, the face of Adonis upon
the body of Hercules ; it was majefty accompanied
by the graces. His black eye-brows and flowing
fair treffes wore a mixture of beauty unknown at
Babylon, and charmed all obfervers. The whole
amphitheatre rofe up, the better to view the ftranger : all the ladies of the court viewed him with
looks of aftonifhment. Formofanta herfelf, who
had hitherto kept her eyes fixed upon the ground,
raifed them and blufhed ; the three kings turned
pale ; all the fpectators, in comparing Formofanta
with the ftranger, cried out, There is no other in
the world but this young man who can be fo handfome as the princefs.

The ufhers, ftruck with aftonifhment, afked him
if he was a king ? The ftranger replied, that he

had not that honour, but that he had come very diſtant, excited by curioſity, to ſee if there were any king worthy of Formoſanta. He was introduced into the firſt row of the amphitheatre, with his valet, his two unicorns, and his bird. He ſaluted with great reſpect Belus, his daughter, the three kings, and all the aſſembly. He then took his ſeat, not without bluſhing. His two unicorns lay down at his feet, his bird perched upon his ſhoulder; and his valet, who carried a little bag, placed himſelf by his ſide.

The trials began. The bow of Nembrod was taken out of its golden caſe. The firſt maſter of the ceremonies, followed by fifty pages, and preceded by twenty trumpets, preſented it to the king of Egypt, who made his prieſts bleſs it; and ſupporting it upon the head of the bull Apis, he did not queſtion his gaining this firſt victory. He diſmounted, and came into the middle of the Circus; he tries, exerts all his ſtrength, and makes ſuch ridiculous contortions, that the whole amphitheatre re-echoes with laughter, and Formoſanta herſelf cannot help ſmiling.

His high almoner approached him: Let your majeſty give up this idle honour, which depends ſolely upon the nerves and muſcles; you will triumph in every thing elſe. You will conquer the lion, as you are poſſeſſed of the ſabre of Oſiris. The princeſs of Babylon is to belong to the prince who is moſt ſagacious, and you have ſolved ænigmas. She is to wed the moſt virtuous: you are ſuch, as you have been educated by the prieſts of Egypt. The moſt generous is to carry her, and you have preſented her with two of the handſomeſt crocodiles, and two of the fineſt rats in all Delta. You are poſſeſſed of the bull Apis and the books of Hermes,

Hermes, which are the fcarceft things in the univerfe. No one can difpute Formofanta with you. You are in the right, faid the king of Egypt, and refumed his throne.

The bow was then put into the hands of the king of India. It bliftered his hands for a fortnight; but he confoled himfelf in prefuming that the Scythian king would not be more fortunate than himfelf.

The Scythian handled the bow in his turn. He united fkill with ftrength : the bow feemed to have fome elafticity in his hands; he bent it a little, but he could never bring it any thing near a curve. The fpectators, who had been prejudiced in his favour by his agreeable afpect, lamented his ill fuccefs, and concluded that the beautiful princefs would never be married.

The unknown youth leaped into the area, and addreffing himfelf to the king of Scythia faid, Your Majefty need not be furprifed at not having entirely fucceeded. Thefe ebony bows are made in my country; there is only one peculiar twift to give them. Your merit is greater in having bent it, than if I were to curve it. He then took an arrow, and placing it upon the ftring, bent the bow of Nembrod, and made the arrow fly beyond the gates. A million of hands at once applauded the prodigy. Babylon re-echoed with acclamations, and all the women agreed how happy it was for fo handfome a youth to be fo ftrong.

He then took out of his pocket a fmall ivory tablet, and wrote upon it with a golden pencil, fixed the tablet to the bow, and prefented it all together to the princefs with fuch a grace as charmed every fpectator. He then modeftly returned to his place between his bird and his valet. All Babylon was i n astonishment, the three kings were confounded whilst the stranger did not seem to pay the least attention to what had happened.

Formosanta was still more surprised to read upon the ivory tablet tied to the bow, these verses written in good Chaldean :

> L'arc de Nembrod est celui de la guerre ;
> L'arc de l'amour est celui du bonheur ;
>   Vous le portez.   Par vous ce Dieu vainqueur
> Est devenu le maitre de la terre.
> Trois Rois puissants, trois rivaux aujourd'hui
> Osent pretendre a l'honneur de vous plaire.
> Je ne sais pas qui votre cœur prefere,
> Mais l'univers sera jaloux de lui *.

This little madrigal did not displease the princess. It was criticised by some of the lords of the ancient court, who said, that formerly, in good times, Belus would have been compared to the sun, and Formosanta to the moon ; his neck to a tower, and her breast to a bushel of wheat. They said the stranger had no sort of imagination, and that he had lost sight of the rules of true poetry, but all the ladies thought the verses very gallant. They were astonished that a man, who handled a bow so well, should have so much wit. The lady of honour to the princess said to her, Madam, what numerous talents are here entirely lost ? What benefit will this young man derive from his wit and Belus's bow ?

---

* Nembrod's is the warlike bow :—The bow of love is that of happiness :—This you bear. Through you the victorious god is become master of the earth. Three powerful kings, rivals of the day, have dared pretend to the honour of pleasing you. I know not which your heart prefers; but the whole universe must be jealous of him.

bow? Being admired, said Formofanta. Ah! said
the lady, one more madrigal, and he might very
well be beloved!

Neverthelefs, Belus, having confulted his fages,
declared, that though none of thefe kings could
bend the bow of Nembrod, his daughter was, neverthelefs, to be married, and that fhe fhould belong to him who could conquer the great lion, which
was purpofely in training in his great menagerie.
The king of Egypt, upon whofe education all the
wifdom of Egypt had been exhaufted, judged it
very ridiculous to expofe a king to the ferocity of
wild beafts in order to be married. He acknowledged, he confidered the poffeffion of Formofanta
of ineftimable value; but he imagined, that if the
lion fhould ftrangle him, he could never wed this
fair Babylonian. The king of India was of the
fame way of thinking with the Egyptian; they both
concluded that the king of Babylon was laughing
at them, and that they fhould fend for armies to
punifh him; that they had many fubjects, who
would think themfelves highly honoured to die in
the fervice of their mafters, without its cofting
them a fingle hair of their facred heads; that they
could eafily dethrone the king of Babylon, and
then they would draw lots for the fair Formofanta.

This agreement being made, the two kings fent
each an exprefs into his refpective country, with
orders to affemble three hundred thoufand men to
carry off Formofanta.

However, the king of Scythia defcended alone
into the area with his fcymetar in hand. He was
not diftractedly enamoured with Formofanta's
charms; glory till then had been his only paffion,
and it had led him to Babylon. He was willing
to

to shew, that if the kings of India and Egypt were so prudent as not to tilt with lions, he was courageous enough not to decline the combat, and he would repair the honour of diadems. His uncommon valour would not even allow him to avail himself of the assistance of his tyger. He advanced singly, slightly armed with a shell casque ornamented with gold, shaded with three horses tails as white as snow.

One of the most enormous and ferocious lions, that fed upon the Antilibanian mountains, was let loose upon him. His tremendous talons appeared capable of tearing the three kings to pieces at once, and his gullet to devour them. The two proud champions flew with the utmost precipitancy and in the most rapid manner at each other. The couragious Scythian plunged his sword into the lion's throat; but the point meeting with one of those thick teeth that nothing can penetrate, was broke to shatters; and the monster of the woods, more furious from his wound, had already impressed his bleeding claws into the monarch's sides.

The unknown youth, touched with the peril of so brave a prince, leapt into the area swift as lightning; when he cut off the lion's head with as much dexterity, as we have lately seen, in our carousals, youthful knights knock off the heads of black images.

Then drawing out a small box, he presented it to the Scythian king, saying to him, Your majesty will there find the genuine dittany, which grows in my country. Your glorious wounds will be healed in a moment. Accident alone prevented your triumph over the lion; your valour is not the less to be admired.

The Scythian king, animated more with gratitude

jude than jealousy, thanked his benefactor; and after having tenderly embraced him, returned to his seat to apply the dittany to his wounds.

The stranger gave the lion's head to his valet, who having washed it at the great fountain which was beneath the amphitheatre, and drained all the blood, took an iron instrument out of his little bag, with which having drawn the lion's forty teeth, he supplied their place with forty diamonds of equal size.

His master, with his usual modesty returned to his place; he gave the lion's head to his bird: Beauteous bird, said he, carry this small homage, and lay it at the feet of Formosanta. The bird winged his way with the dreadful triumph in one of his pounces, and presented it to the princess, bending, with humility, his neck, and crouching before her. The sparkling diamonds dazzled the eyes of every beholder. Such magnificence was unknown even in superb Babylon; the emerald, the topaz, the saphire, and the pyrope, were as yet considered as the most precious ornaments. Belus and the whole court were struck with admiration. The bird which presented this present surprised them still more. It was of the size of an eagle, but its eyes were as soft and tender as those of the eagle are fierce and threatening. Its bill was rose-colour, and seemed somewhat to resemble Formosanta's handsome mouth. Its neck represented all the colours of Iris, but still more lively and brilliant; gold, in a thousand shades, glittered upon its plumage; its feet resembled a mixture of silver and purple, and the tails of those beautiful birds, which have since drawn Juno's car, did not come up to the splendor of this bird's.

The attention, curiosity, astonishment, and exta-

fy

fy of the whole court, were divided between the jewels and the bird. He had perched upon the baluftrade between Belus and his daughter Formofanta; fhe flattered it, careffed it, and kiffed it. It feemed to receive her embraces with a mixture of pleafure and refpect. When the princefs gave the bird a kifs, it returned to the embrace, and then looked upon her with languifhing eyes. She gave it bifcuits and piftachoes, which it received in its purple-filvered paw, and carried them to its bill with inexpreffible grace.

Belus, who had attentively confidered the diamonds, concluded, that fcarce any one of his provinces could repay fo valuable a prefent. He ordered that more magnificent gifts fhould be prepared for the ftranger than thofe that were deftined for the three monarchs. This young man, faid he, is doubtlefs fon to the king of China, or of that part of the world called Europe, which I have heard fpoken of; or of Africa, which, it is faid, is in the neighbourhood of the kingdom of Egypt.

He directly fent his firft equerry to compliment the ftranger, and afk him, whether he was himfelf the fovereign, or fon to the fovereign of one of thofe empires; and why, being poffeffed of fuch furprifing treafures, he had come with nothing but the valet and a little bag?

Whilft the equerry advanced towards the amphitheatre to execute his commiffion, another valet arrived upon an unicorn. This valet, addreffing himfelf to the young man, faid, Ormar, your father is approaching the end of his life: I am come to acquaint you with it. The ftranger raifed his eyes to heaven, whilft tears ftreamed from them, and anfwered only by faying, *Let us depart.*

The equerry, after having paid Belus's compliments
ments

ments to the conqueror of the lion, to the giver of the forty diamonds, and to the mafter of the beautiful bird, afked the valet, Of what kingdom was the father of this young hero fovereign ? The valet replied, His father is an old fhepherd, who is much beloved in the diftrict.

During this converfation, theftranger had already mounted his unicorn. He faid to the equerry, My lord, vouchfafe to proftrate me at the feet of Belus and his daughter. I muft entreat her to take particular care of the bird I leave with her, as it is a nonpareil like herfelf. In uttering thefe laft words he fet off, and flew like lightning ; the two valets followed him, and he was in an inftant out of fight.

Formofanta could not refrain from fhrieking. The bird turning towards the amphitheatre, where his mafter had been feated, feemed greatly afflicted to find him gone ; then viewing ftedfaftly the princefs, and gently rubbing her beautiful hand with his bill, he feemed to betrothe himfelf to her fervice.

Belus, more aftonifhed than ever, hearing that this very extraordinary young man was the fon of a fhepherd, could not believe it. He difpatched meffengers after him ; but they foon returned with advice, that the three unicorns, upon which thefe men were mounted, could not be come up with ; and that according to the rate they went, they muft go a hundred leagues a day.

§ 2.

Every one reafoned upon this ftrange adventure, and wearied themfelves with conjectures. How can the fon of a fhepherd make a prefent of forty large diamonds ? How comes it that he is mounted

upon an unicorn? This bewildered them, and Formosanta, whilst she caressed her bird, was sunk into a profound reverie.

Princess Aldea, her cousin-german, who was
very well shaped, and almost as handsome as Formosanta, said to her, Cousin, I know not whether
this demigod be the son of a shepherd; but methinks he has fulfilled all the conditions stipulated
for your marriage. He has bent Nembrod's bow,
he has conquered the lion, he has a great share of
sense, having wrote for you a very pretty extempore; and after having presented you with forty
large diamonds, you cannot deny that he is the
most generous of men. In his bird he possessed
the most curious thing upon earth. His virtue
cannot be equalled, since though he might have
staid with you, he departed without hesitation, as
soon as he heard his father was ill. The oracle is
fulfilled in every particular, except that wherein he
is to overcome his rivals; but he has done more,
he has saved the life of the only competitor he
had to fear; and when the object is beating the
other two, I believe you cannot doubt that he will
easily succeed.

All that you say is very true, replied Formosanta: but is it possible, that the greatest of men,
and perhaps the most amiable too, should be the
son of a shepherd?

The lady of honour joining in the conversation,
said, that the title of Shepherd was frequently given
to kings; that they were called Shepherds, because
they attended very closely their flocks; that this
was doubtless a piece of ill-timed pleasantry in his
valet; that this young hero had not come so badly
equipped, but to shew how much his personal merit alone was above the fastidious parade of kings.

The

The princess made no answer but in giving her
bird a thousand tender kisses.

A great festival was nevertheless prepared for
the three kings, and for all the princes who were
come to the feast. The king's daughter and niece
were to do the honours. The king received presents worthy the magnificence of Babylon. Belus,
during the time the repast was serving up, assembled his council upon the marriage of the beautiful
Formosanta, and this is the way he delivered himself as a great politician :

I am old : I know not what longer to do with my
daughter, or upon whom to bestow her. He who
deserved her is nothing but a mean shepherd ; the
kings of India and Egypt are cowards ; the king of
the Scythians would be very agreeable to me, but
he has not performed any one of the conditions im-
posed. I will again consult the oracle. In the mean
while, deliberate among you, and we will conclude
agreeable to what the oracle says; for a king should
follow nothing but the dictates of the immortal
gods.

He then repaired to the temple: the oracle answered in few words according to custom : *Thy
daughter shall not be married till she has traversed the
globe.* Belus returned in astonishment to the council, and related this answer.

All the ministers had a profound respect for
oracles ; they therefore all agreed, or at least appeared to agree, that they were the foundation of
religion ; that reason should be mute before them ;
that it was by their means that kings reigned over
their people ; that without oracles there would be
neither virtue nor repose upon earth.

At length, after having testified the most profound veneration for them, they almost all con-
F f 2   cluded

cluded that this oracle was impertinent, and that he should not be obeyed; that nothing could be more indecent for a young woman, and particularly the daughter of the great king of Babylon, than to run about, without any particular destination; that this was the most certain method to prevent her being married or else engage her in a clandestine, shameful, and ridiculous one; that, in a word, this oracle had not common sense.

The youngest of the ministers named Onadase, who had more sense than the rest, said, that the oracle doubtless meant some pilgrimage of devotion, and offered to be the princess's guide. The council approved of his opinion, but every one was for being her equerry. The king determined that the princess might go three hundred parasangs upon the road to Arabia, to the temple; whose saint had the reputation of procuring young women happy marriages, and that the dean of the council should accompany her. After this determination they went to supper.

§ 3.

In the centre of the gardens, between two cascades, was erected an oval saloon, three hundred feet in diameter, whose azure roof, intersected with golden stars, represented all the constellations and planets, each in its proper station; and this cieling turned about, as well as the canopy, by machines as invisible as those which direct the celestial motions. A hundred thousand flambeaux, inclosed in rich crystal cylinders, illuminated the out and inside of the dining-hall. A buffet with steps contained twenty thousand vases and golden dishes; and opposite the buffet, upon other steps, were seated a

great

great number of muficians.—Two other amphitheatres were decked out; the one with the fruits
of each feafon, the other with cryftal decanters, in
which fparkled every kind of wine upon earth.

The guefts took their feats round a table divided
into compartments, which refembled flowers and
fruits, all in precious ftones. The beautiful Formofanta was placed between the kings of India and
Egypt; the amiable Aldea next the king of Scythia.
There were about thirty princes, and each was feated next one of the handfomeft ladies of the court.
The king of Babylon, who was in the middle, oppofite his daughter, feemed divided between the
chagrin of being yet unable to marry her, and the
pleafure of ftill beholding her. Formofanta afked
leave to place her bird upon the table next her;
the king approved of it.

The mufic, which played, furnifhed every prince
with an opportunity of converfing with his female
neighbour. The feftival was as agreeable as it was
inagnificent. A ragout was ferved before Formofanta, which her father was very fond of. The
princefs faid it fhould be carried to his Majefty; the
bird immediately took hold of it, and carried it in
a miraculous manner to the king. Never was any
thing more aftonifhing at fupper. Belus careffed
it as much as his daughter had done. The bird
afterwards took its flight to return to her. It difplayed in flying fo fine a tail, and its extended
wings fet forth fuch a variety of brilliant colours,
the gold of its plumage made fuch a dazzling eclat,
that all eyes were fixed upon him. All the muficians were ftruck motionlefs, and their inftruments
afforded harmony no longer. None ate, no one
fpoke, nothing but a buzzing of admiration was to
be heard. The princefs of Babylon kiffed it dur-

ing

ing the whole ſupper, without conſidering whether
there were any kings in the world. Thoſe of India
and Egypt felt their ſpite and indignation rekindle
with double force, and they reſolved ſpeedily to ſet
their three hundred thouſand men in motion to
obtain revenge.

As for the king of Scythia, he was engaged in
entertaining the beautiful Aldea : his haughty ſoul
deſpiſing, without malice, Formoſanta's inattention,
had conceived for her more indifference than re-
ſentment. She is handſome, ſaid he, I acknowledge ; but ſhe appears to me one of thoſe women
who are entirely taken up with their own beauty,
and who fancy that mankind are greatly obliged to
them when they deign to appear in public. I
ſhould prefer an ugly complaiſant woman, that teſ-
tified ſome regard, to that beautiful ſtatue. You
have, Madam, as many charms as ſhe poſſeſſes, and
you condeſcend to converſe, at leaſt, with ſtrangers. I acknowledge to you with the ſincerity of
a Scythian, that I prefer you to your couſin. He
was, however, miſtaken in regard to the character
of Formoſanta ; ſhe was not ſo diſdainful as ſhe appeared ; but his compliments were very well received by princeſs Aldea. Their converſation became very intereſting ; they were very well contented, and already certain of one another before
they left table.

After ſupper the gueſts walked in the groves.
The king of Scythia and Aldea did not fail ſeeking
for a place of retreat. Aldea, who was ſincerity
itſelf, thus declared herſelf to the prince :

I do not hate my couſin though ſhe be handſo-
mer than myſelf, and is deſtined for the throne of
Babylon ; the honour of pleaſing you may very
well ſtand in the ſtead of charms. I prefer Scythia
with

with you, to the crown of Babylon without you.
But this crown belongs to me by right, if there be
any right in the world; for I am the elder branch
of Nembrod, and Formofanta is only of the younger. Her grandfather dethroned mine, and put him
to death.

Such, then, is the force of blood in the houfe of
Babylon! faid the Scythian. What was your
grandfather's name? He was called Aldea like me;
my father bore the fame name; he was banifhed
to the extremity of the empire with my mother;
and Belus, after their death, having nothing to fear
from me, was willing to bring me up with his
daughter. But he has refolved that I fhall never
marry.

I will avenge the caufe of your father, of your
grandfather, and your caufe, faid the king of Scythia. I am refponfible for your being married: I
will carry you off the day after to-morrow by day-
break; for we muft dine to-morrow with the king
of Babylon; and I will return and fupport your
rights with three hundred thoufand men. I agree
to it, faid the beauteous Aldea; and after having
exchanged their words of honour, they feparated.

The incomparable Formofanta had been for a
long time retired to reft. She had ordered a little
orange tree, in a filver cafe, to be placed by the fide
of her bed, that her bird might perch upon it. Her
curtains were drawn, but fhe was not in the leaft
difpofed to fleep: her heart and her imagination
were too much awake. The charming ftranger
was ever before her fight; fhe fancied fhe faw him
fhooting an arrow with Nembrod's bow; fhe con-
templated him in the action of cutting off the lion's
head; fhe repeated his madrigal; at length, fhe faw
him retiring from the crowd upon his unicorn:—

tears,

tears, sighs, and lamentations, overwhelmed her at
this reflection.—At intervals she cried out, Shall
I then never see him more? Will he never return?

He will return, Madam, replied the bird from
the top of the orange tree. Can one once have
seen you, and not desire to see you again?

Heavens! eternal powers! my bird speaks the
purest Chaldean. In uttering these words she drew
back the curtain, put out her hand to him, and
knelt upon her bed, saying, Art thou a god descended upon earth? Art thou the great Orosmades
concealed under this beautiful plumage? If thou
art, restore me this charming young man.

I am nothing but a winged animal, replied the
bird; but I was born at the time when all animals
still spoke; when birds, serpents, asses, horses, and
griffins, conversed familiarly with man. I would
not speak before company, lest your ladies of honour should have taken me for a sorcerer; I would
not discover myself to any but you.

Formosanta was speechless, bewildered, and intoxicated with so many wonders: desirous of putting a hundred questions to him at once, she at
length asked him how old he was? Twenty-seven
thousand nine hundred years and six months, Madam; I date my age from the little revolution of
heaven which your magi call the precession of the
equinoxes, and which is accomplished in about
twenty-eight thousand of your years. There are
revolutions of a much greater extent, so are there
beings much older than me. It is twenty-two thousand years since I learnt Chaldean in one of my
travels. I have always had a very great taste for
the Chaldean language, but my brethren, the other
animals, have renounced speaking in your climate.

And

And why fo, my divine bird? Alas! becaufe men have accuftomed themfelves to eat us, inftead of converfing and inftructing themfelves with us. Barbarians! fhould they not have been convinced, that having the fame organs with them, the fame fentiments, the fame wants, the fame defires, we had what is called a Soul, the fame as them; that we were their brothers, and that none fhould be dreffed and ate but the wicked? We are fo far your brothers, that the Supreme Being, the Omnipotent and Eternal Being, having made a compact with men, exprefsly comprehended us in the treaty. He forbad you to nourifh yourfelves with our blood, and we to fuck yours *.

The fables of your ancient Locman, tranflated into fo many languages, will be a teftimony eternally fubfifting of the happy commerce you formerly carried on with us. They all begin with thefe words; *In the time when beafts fpoke*. It is true, there are many families among you who keep up an inceffant converfation with their dogs; but they have refolved not to anfwer, fince they have been compelled by whipping to go a-hunting, and become accomplices in the murder of our ancient and common friends, ftags, deers, hares, and partridges.

You have ftill fome ancient poems in which horfes fpeak, and your coachmen daily addrefs them in words; but in fo barbarous a manner, and in uttering fuch infamous expreffions, that horfes, which formerly entertained fo great a kindnefs for you, now deteft you.

The country which is the refidence of your charm-

VOL. I.   G g   †   · ing

---

* See chapter ix. of Genefis, and chap. iii. xviii. and xix. of Ecclefiaft.

ing stranger, the most perfect of men, is the only
one in which your species has continued to love
ours, to converse with us; and this is the only
country of the world where men are just.

And where is this country of my dear incognito? what is the name of his empire? for I will no
more believe he is a shepherd than that you are a
bat.

His country, madam, is that of the Gangarids,
a virtuous and invincible people, who inhabit the
eastern shore of the Ganges. The name of my
friend is Amazan. He is no king; and I know
not whether he would so much humble himself as
to be one; he has too great a love for his fellow-
countrymen; he is a shepherd like them. But do
not imagine that those shepherds resemble yours;
who, covered with rags and tatters, watch their
sheep, far better clad than themselves; who groan
under the burthen of poverty, and who pay to an
extortioner half the miserable stipend of wages
which they receive from their masters. The Gangaridian shepherds are all born equal, are the masters of innumerable herds, which cover their fields
in constant verdure. They are never killed; it is
a horrid crime towards the Ganges to kill and eat
one's fellow creature. Their wool is finer and
more brillant than the finest silk, and constitutes the
greatest traffic of the East. Besides, the land of the
Gangarids produces all that can flatter the desires
of man. Those large diamonds which Amazan
had the honour of presenting you with, are from a
mine which belongs to him. An unicorn, on which
you saw him mounted, is the usual animal the
Gangarids ride upon. It is the finest, the proud-
est, most terrible, and at the same time most gentle
animal, that ornaments the earth. A hundred
Gangarids,

Gangarids, with as many unicorns, would be suf-
ficient to difperfe innumerable armies. About two
centuries ago, a king of India was mad enough to
want to conquer this nation: he appeared, followed
by ten thoufand elephants and a million of warriors.
The unicorns pierced the elephants, juft as I have
feen upon your table beads pierced in golden bro-
chets. The warriors fell under the fabres of the
Gangarids, like crops of rice mowed by the people
of the Eaft. The king was taken prifoner, with
upwards of fix thoufand men. He was bathed in the
falutary water of the Ganges, followed the regimen
of the country, which confifts only of vegetables,
and in which nature there hath been amazingly li-
beral to nourifh every breathing creature. Men
who are fed with carnivorous aliments, and drenched with fpirituous liquors, have a fharp aduft blood,
which turns their brains a hundred different ways.
Their chief rage is a fury to fpill their brother's
blood, and laying wafte fertile plains to reign over
church-yards. Six full months were taken up in
curing the king of India of his diforder; when the
phyficians judged that his pulfe was in a greater
ftate of tranquillity, they certified this to the council of the Gangarids. The council having followed the advice of the unicorns, humanely fent back
the king of India, his filly court, and impotent warriors, to their own country. This leffon made
them wife, and from that time the Indians refpected the Gangarids, as ignorant men, willing to be
inftructed, revere the Chaldean philofophers they
cannot equal. Apropos, my dear bird, faid the
princefs to him, do the Gangarids profefs any religion? have they one? Madam, we meet to return
thanks to God on the days of the full moon: the
men in a great temple made of cedar, and the wo-

men

men in another, to prevent their devotion being diverted: all the birds assemble in a grove, and the quadrupeds on a fine down. We thank God for all the benefits he has bestowed upon us. We have in particular some parrots that preach wonderfully well.

Such is the country of my dear Amazan; there I reside: my friendship for him is as great as the love with which he has inspired you. If you will credit me, we will set out together, and you shall pay him a visit.

Really, my dear bird, this is a very pretty profession of yours, replied the princess smiling, and who flamed with desire to undertake the journey, but did not dare say so. I serve my friend, said the bird; and, after the happiness of loving you, the greatest is to be an assistant in your amours.

Formosanta was quite fascinated; she fancied herself transported from earth. All she had seen that day, all she then saw, all she heard, and particularly what she felt in her heart, so ravished her, as far to surpass what those fortunate Mussulmen now feel, who, disencumbered from their terrestrial ties, find themselves in the ninth heaven in the arms of their Houris, surrounded and penetrated with glory and celestial felicity.

§ 4.

She passed the whole night in speaking of Amazan. She no longer called him any thing but her shepherd; and from this time it was that the names of Shepherd and Lover were indiscriminately used throughout every nation.

Sometimes she asked the bird whether Amazan had had any other mistresses. He answered No,
and

and she was at the summit of felicity. Sometimes she asked how he passed his life; and she, with transport, learnt, that it was employed in doing good, in cultivating arts, in penetrating into the secrets of nature, and improving himself. She at times wanted to know if the soul of her lover was of the same nature as that of her bird; how it happened that he had lived twenty thousand years, when her lover was not above eighteen or nineteen. She put a hundred such questions, to which the bird replied with such discretion as excited her curiosity. At length sleep closed their eyes, and yielded up Formosanta to the sweet delusion of dreams sent by the gods, which sometimes surpass reality itself, and which all the philosophy of the Chaldeans can scarce explain.

Formosanta did not wake till very late. The day was far advanced, when the king her father entered her chamber. The bird received his majesty with respectful politeness, went before him, fluttered his wings, stretched his neck, and then replaced himself upon his orange tree. The king seated himself upon his daughter's bed, whose dreams had made her still more beautiful. His large beard approached her lovely face, and after having twice embraced her, he spoke to her in these words:

My dear daughter, you could not yesterday find a husband agreeable to my wishes; you nevertheless must marry; the prosperity of my empire requires it. I have consulted the oracle, which you know never errs, and which directs all my conduct. His commands are, that you should traverse the globe: You must therefore begin your journey.—Ah! doubtless, to the Gangarids, said the princess; and in uttering these words, which escaped her, she was

sensible

of her indiscretion. The king, who was utterly
ignorant of geography, asked her what she meant
by the Gangarids? She easily diverted the question.
The king told her she must go upon a pilgrimage,
that he had appointed the persons who were to attend her, the dean of the counsellors of state, the
high almoner, a lady of honour, a physician, an
apothecary, her bird, and all necessary domestics.

Formosanta, who had never been out of her father's palace, and who till the arrival of the three
kings and Amazan had led a very insipid life, according to the *etiquette* of rank and the parade of
pleasure, was charmed at setting out upon a pilgrimage. Who knows, said she, whispering to her
heart, if the gods may not inspire Amazan with the
like desire of going to the same chapel, and I may
have the happiness of again seeing the pilgrim? She
affectionately thanked her father, saying, she had
always entertained a secret devotion for the saint
she was going to visit.

Belus gave an excellent dinner to his guests,
who were all men. They formed a very ill assort-
ed company; kings, princes, ministers, pontiffs, all
jealous of each other; all weighing their words,
and equally embarrassed with their neighbours and
themselves. The repast was very gloomy, though
they drank pretty freely. The princesses remained
in their apartments, each meditating upon their
respective journey. They dined at their little cover. Formosanta afterwards walked in the gardens
with her dear bird, who, to amuse her, flew from
tree to tree, displaying his superb tail and divine
plumage.

The king of Egypt, who was heated with wine,
not to say drunk, asked one of his pages for a bow
and arrow. This prince was, in truth, the most
un-

unskilful archer in his whole kingdom.   When he
aimed at a mark, the place of the greatest safety was
generally the spot he hit.   But the beautiful bird,
flying as swiftly as the arrow, seemed to court it,
and fell bleeding in the arms of Formosanta.   The
Egyptian, bursting into a foolish laugh, retired to
his place.   The princess rent the skies with her
moans; melted into tears, tore her hair and beat
her breast.   The dying bird said to her in a low
voice, Burn me, and fail not to carry my ashes to
the east of the ancient city of Aden or Eden, and
expose them to the sun upon a little pile of cloves
and cinnamon : after having uttered these words he
expired.   Formosanta was for a long time in a
swoon, and saw the light again only to burst in sighs
and groans.   Her father partaking of her grief,
and imprecating the king of Egypt, did not doubt
but this accident foretold some fatal event.   He
went hastily to consult the oracle of his chapel.
The oracle replied, *A mixture of every thing; life
and death, infidelity and constancy, loss and gain, calamities and good fortune.*   Neither he nor his council could comprehend any meaning in this reply;
but, at length, he was satisfied with having fulfilled
the duties of devotion.

His daughter was bathed in tears, whilst he consulted the oracle ; she paid the funeral obsequies to
the bird, which he had directed, and resolved to
carry its remains into Arabia at the risk of her life.
He was burnt in incombustible flax, with the o-
range-tree on which he used to perch.   She gather-
ed up the ashes in a little golden vase, set with rubies, and the diamonds taken from the lion's mouth.
Oh! that she could, instead of fulfilling this melancholy duty, have burnt alive the detestable king of
Egypt! This was her sole wish.   She, in spite, put

to

to death the two crocodiles, his two fea horfes; his two zebars, his two rats, and had his two mummies thrown into the Euphrates. Had fhe been pofleff-ed of his bull Apis, fhe would not have fpared him.

The king of Egypt, enraged at this affront, fet out immediately to forward his three hundred thoufand men. The king of India, feeing his ally depart, fet off alfo upon his return the fame day, with a firm intention of joining his three hundred thoufand Indians to the Egyptian army. The king of Scythia decamped in the night with the princefs Aldea, fully refolved to fight for her at the head of three hundred thoufand Scythians, and to reftore her the inheritance of Babylon, which was her right, as fhe was defcended from the elder branch.

As for the beautiful Formofanta, fhe fet out at three in the morning with her caravan of pilgrims, flattering herfelf that fhe might go into Arabia, and execute the laft will of her bird; and that the juftice of the gods would reftore her the dear Amazan, without whom life was become infupportable.

When the king of Babylon awoke, he found all his company gone. How mighty feftivals terminate! faid he; and what a furprifing vacuum they leave in the foul, when the hurry is over! But he was tranfported with a rage truly royal, when he found that princefs Aldea was carried off. He ordered all his minifters to be called up, and the council to be convened. Whilft they were dreffing, he failed not to confult the oracle; but he could never get from it any other than thefe words, fo celebrated fince throughout the univerfe: *When girls are not married by their relations, they marry themfelves.*

Orders were immediately iffued to march three hundred thoufand men againft the king of Scythia. Thus was the torch of the moft dreadful war lighted up, which was produced by the amufements of the fineft feftival ever given upon earth. Afia was upon the point of being over-run by four armies of three hundred thoufand men each. It is plain, that the war of Troy, which aftonifhed the world fome ages after, was mere childrens play in comparifon to this; but it fhould alfo be confidered, that in the Trojans quarrel, the object was nothing more than a very libidinous old woman, who had contrived to be twice run away with; whereas, in this cafe, the caufe was tripartite—two girls and a bird.

The king of India went to meet his army upon the large fine road which then led ftraight to Babylon, at Cachemir. The king of Scythia flew with Aldea by the fine road which led to mount Immaus. All thefe fine roads have difappeared in a feries of time, by reafon of bad government. The king of Egypt had marched to the weft, along the coaft of the little Mediterranean fea, which the ignorant Hebrews have fince called the Great Sea.

As to the charming Formofanta, fhe purfued the road of Baffora, planted with lofty palm trees, which furnifhed a perpetual fhade, and fruits at all feafons. The temple, in which fhe was to perform her pilgrimage, was in Baffora itfelf. The faint, to whom this temple had been dedicated, was pretty nearly in the ftyle of him who was afterwards adored at Lampfacus. He not only procured young women hufbands, but he often fupplied the hufband's place. He was the holieft faint in all Afia.

Formofanta had no fort of inclination for the faint of Baffora; fhe only invoked her dear Gangaridian fhepherd, her charming Amazan. She propofed embarking at Baffora, and landing in Arabia Felix, to perform what her deceafed bird had commanded.

At the third ftage, fcarce had fhe entered into a fine inn, where her harbingers had made all the neceffary preparations for her, when fhe learnt that the king of Egypt was arrived there alfo. Informed by his emiffaries of the princefs's route, he immediately altered his courfe, followed by a numerous efcort. Having alighted, he placed centinels at all the doors; then repaired to the beautiful Formofanta's apartment, when he addreffed her by faying, Mifs, you are the lady I was in queft of; you paid me very little attention when I was at Babylon; it is juft to punifh fcornful capricious women: you will, if you pleafe, be kind enough to fup with me to-night; you will have no other bed than mine, and I fhall behave to you according as I am fatisfied with you.

Formofanta faw very well that fhe was not the ftrongeft; fhe judged that good fenfe confifted in knowing how to conform to one's fituation; fhe refolved to get rid of the king of Egypt by an innocent ftratagem: fhe looked to him through the corners of her eyes, which after-ages has called ogling; and thus fhe fpoke to him, with a modefty, grace, and fweetnefs, a confufion, and a thoufand other charms, which would have made the wifeft man a fool, and deceived the moft difcerning:

I acknowledge, Sir, I always appeared with a downcaft look when you did the king my father the honour of vifiting him. I had fome apprehenfions for my heart, I dreaded my too great fimplicity;

city ; I trembled left my father and your rivals
should observe the preference I gave you, and which
you so highly deserved.   I can now declare my
sentiments.   I swear by the bull Apis, which after
you is the thing I respect the most in the world,
that your proposals have enchanted me.   I have
already supped with you at my father's, and I will
sup again here with you, without his being of the
party ; all that I request of you is, that your high
almoner should drink with us : he appeared to me
at Babylon to be an excellent guest ; I have some
Chiras wine remarkably good, I will make you
both taste it.   As to your second proposition, it is
very engaging ; but a girl well brought up should
not dwell upon it ; satisfy yourself with being informed, that I consider you as the greatest of kings,
and the most amiable of men.

  This discourse turned the king of Egypt's head ;
he agreed to have the almoner's company.   I have
another favour to ask you, said the princess, which
is to allow me to speak to my apothecary : women
have always some little ails that require attention,
such as vapours in the head, palpitations of the
heart, colics, and the like, which at particular times
require some assistance ; in a word, I at present
stand in need of my apothecary, and I hope you
will not refuse me this slight testimony of love.

  Miss, replied the king of Egypt, though the de-
signs of an apothecary are directly opposite to mine,
and the objects of his art are directly contrary to
those of mine, I know life too well to refuse you so
just a demand ; I will order him to attend you
whilst supper is preparing.   I imagine you must be
somewhat fatigued by the journey ; you will also
have occasion for a chamber-maid, you may order
her you like best to attend you ; I will afterwards

wait your commands and conveniency. He retired, and the apothecary, and chamber-maid, named
Irla, entered. The princefs had an entire confidence in her; fhe ordered her to bring fix bottles
of Chiras wine for fupper, and to make all the centinels, who had her officers under arreft, drink the
fame; then fhe recommended her apothecary to
infufe in all the bottles certain pharmaceutic drugs,
which made thofe who took them fleep twenty-four
hours, and with which he was always provided:
She was punctually obeyed. The king returned
with his high almoner in about half an hour's time;
the converfation at fupper was very gay; the king
and the prieft emptied the fix bottles, and acknow-
leged there was no fuch good wine in Egypt: the
chamber-maid was attentive to make the fervants
in-waiting drink. As for the princefs, fhe took
great care not to drink any herfelf, faying, that fhe
was ordered by her phyfician a particular regimen.
They were all prefently afleep.

The king of Egypt's almoner had one of the fineft beards that a man of his rank could wear. Formofanta lopt it off very fkilfully; then fewing it to
a ribbon, fhe put it on her own chin. She then
dreffed herfelf in the prieft's robes, and decked herfelf in all the marks of his dignity, and her waiting-
maid clad herfelf like the facriftan of the goddefs
Ifis; at length, having furnifhed herfelf with his
urn and jewels, fhe fet out from the inn amidft the
centinels, who were afleep like their mafter. Her
attendant had taken care to have two horfes ready
at the door. The princefs could not take with her
any of the officers of her train; they would have
been ftopt by the great guards.

Formofanta and Irla paffed through feveral ranks
of foldiers, who, taking the princefs for the high-
prieft,

prieft, called her, My moft Reverend Father in
God, and afked his blelfing. The two fugitives
arrived in twenty-four hours at Baffora, before the
king awoke. They then threw off their difguife,
which might have created fome fufpicion. They
fitted out with all poffible expedition a fhip, which
carried them by the Streights of Ormus, to the beautiful banks of Eden in Arabia Felix. This was
that Eden, whofe gardens were fo famous, that
they have fince been the refidence of the jufteft of
mankind; they were the model of the Elyfian
fields, the gardens of the Hefperides, and thofe of
the Fortunate Iflands; for in thofe warm climates
men imagined there could be no greater felicity
than fhades and murmuring brooks. To live eternally in heaven with the Supreme Being, or to walk
in the garden of paradife, was the fame thing to
thofe who inceffantly fpoke without underftanding
one another, and who could fcarce have any diftinct
ideas or juft expreffions.

As foon as the princefs found herfelf in this land,
her firft care was to pay her dear bird the funeral
obfequies he had required of her. Her beautiful
hands prepared a fmall pile of cloves and cinnamon. What was her furprize, when, having fpread
the afhes of the bird upon this pile, fhe faw it blaze
of itfelf! They were all prefently confumed. In
the place of the afhes there appeared nothing but a
large egg, from whence fhe faw her bird iffue more
brilliant than ever. This was one of the moft
happy moments the princefs had ever experienced
in her whole life; there was but another that could
ever be dearer to her; it was the object of her
wifhes, but almoft beyond her hopes.

I plainly fee, faid fhe to the bird, you are the
phœnix which I have heard fo much fpoken of.

I am

I am almoſt ready to expire with joy and aſtoniſhment. I did not believe in your reſurrection; but it is my good fortune to be convinced of it. Reſurrection, Madam, ſaid the phœnix to her, is one of the moſt ſimple things in the world. There is nothing more aſtoniſhing in being born twice than once. Every thing in this world is the effect of reſurrection; caterpillars are regenerated into butterflies; a kernel put into the earth is regenerated into a tree. All animals buried in the earth regenerate into vegetations, herbs, and plants, and nouriſh other animals, of which they ſpeedily compoſe part of the ſubſtance; all particles which compoſed bodies are transformed into different beings. It is true, that I am the only one to whom Oroſmade has granted the favour of regenerating in my own form.

Formoſanta, who from the moment ſhe firſt ſaw Amazan and the phœnix, had paſſed all her time in a round of aſtoniſhment, ſaid to him, I can eaſily conceive that the Supreme Being may form out of your aſhes a phœnix nearly reſembling yourſelf; but that you ſhould be preciſely the ſame perſon, that you ſhould have the ſame ſoul, is a thing, I acknowledge, I cannot very clearly comprehend. What became of your ſoul when I carried you in my pocket after your death?

Good heavens, Madam! is it not as eaſy for the great Oroſmade to continue action upon a ſingle atom of my being, as to begin afreſh this action? He had before granted me ſenſation, memory, and thought; he grants them to me again; whether he united this favour to an atom of elementary fire latent within me, or the aſſemblage of my organs, is, in reality, of no conſequence; men, as well as phœnixes, are equally ignorant how things come

come to pass ; but the greatest favour the Supreme
Being has bestowed upon me, is to regenerate me
for you.   Oh! that I may pass the twenty-eight
thousand years which I have still to live before my
next resurrection, with you and my dear Amazan!

My dear phœnix, remember what you first told
me at Babylon, which I shall never forget, and
which flattered me with the hope of again seeing
my dear shepherd, whom I idolize ; we must abso-
lutely pay the Gangarids a visit together, and I must
carry him back with me to Babylon.   This is precisely my design, said the phœnix ; there is not a
moment to lose.   We must go in search of Amazan by the shortest road, that is, thro' the air.   There
are in Arabia Felix two griffins, who are my particular friends, who live only a hundred and fifty
thousand leagues from hence ; I am going to write
to them by the pigeons post, and they will be here
before night.   We shall have time to work you a
little convenient canopy with drawers, in which
you may place your provisions.   You will be quite
at your ease in this vehicle, with your maid.   These
two griffins are the most vigorous of their kind ;
each of them will support one of the poles of the
canopy between their claws.   But, once for all,
time is very precious.   He immediately went with
Formosanta to order the canopy at an upholsterer's
of his acquaintance.   It was made complete in
four hours.   In the drawers were placed small fine
loaves, biscuits superior to those of Babylon, large
lemons, pine-apples, cocoa and pistachio nuts, Eden
wine, which is as superior to that of Chiras, as Chiras is to that of Surinam.

The canopy was as light as it was commodious
and solid.   The two griffins arrived at Eden by the
appoint.

appointed time. Formofanta and Irla placed themfelves in the vehicle. The two griffins carried it
off like a feather. The phœnix fometimes flew
after it, and fometimes perched upon its back. The
two griffins winged their way towards the Ganges
with the velocity of an arrow which rends the air.
They never ftopt but a moment at night, for the
travellers to make fome refrefhment, and the car-
riers to take a draught of water.

They at length reached the country of the Gangarids. The princefs's heart palpitated with hope,
love, and joy. The phœnix ftopt the vehicle before the Amazan's houfe; he defired to fpeak with
him; but he had been abfent from home three
hours, without any one knowing whether he was
gone.

There are no words, even in the Gangaridian
language, that could exprefs Formofanta's extreme
defpair. Alas! this is what I dreaded, faid the
phœnix: the three hours which you paffed at the
inn upon the road to Baffora with that wretched
king of Egypt, have perhaps been at the price of
the happinefs of your whole life; I very much fear
we have loft Amazan, without the poffibility of re-
covering him.

He then afked the fervants, if they could falute
the lady his mother? She anfwered, Her hufband
had died only two days before, and fhe could fpeak
to no one. The phœnix, who was not without
influence in the houfe, introduced the princefs of
Babylon into a faloon, the walls of which were covered with orange-tree-wood inlaid with ivory.
The inferior fhepherds and fhepherdeffes, who were
dreffed in long white garments with gold-coloured
trimmings, ferved her up, in a hundred plain porcelain bafkets, a hundred various delicious meats,
amongft

amongst which no difguifed carcaffes were to be feen; they confifted of rice, fago, vermicelli, macaroni, omelets, milk-eggs, cream, cheefe, paftry of every kind, vegetables, fruit peculiarly odoriferous and grateful to the tafte, of which no idea can be formed in other climates; and they were accompanied with a profufion of refrefhing liquors fuperior to the fineft wine.

Whilft the princefs regaled herfelf, feated upon a bed of rofes, four peacocks, who were luckily mute, fanned her with their brilliant wings; two hundred birds, one hundred fhepherds and fhepherdeffes, warbled a concert in two different choirs; the nightingales, thiftlefinches, linnets, chaffinches, fung the higher notes with the fhepherdeffes, and the fhepherds fung the tenor and the bafs. The princefs acknowledged, that if there was more magnificence at Babylon, nature was infinitely more agreeable among the Gangarids; but whilft this confolatory and voluptuous mufic was playing, tears flowed from her eyes, whilft fhe faid to the damfel Irla, Thefe fhepherds and fhepherdeffes, thefe nightingales, thefe linnets, are making love; and for my part, I am deprived of the Gangaridian hero, the worthy object of my moft tender and impatient defires.

Whilft fhe was taking this collation, and tears and admiration kept pace with each other, the phœnix addreffed himfelf to Amazan's mother, faying: Madam, you cannot avoid feeing the princefs of Babylon; you know—I know every thing, faid fhe, even her adventure at the inn upon the road to Baffora; a black-bird related the whole to me this morning; and this cruel black-bird is the caufe of my fon's going mad, and leaving his paternal abode.---You do not know, then, that the

princess regenerated me ?---No, my dear child, the
black bird told me that you were dead, and this
made me inconfolable. I was fo afflicted at this
lofs, the death of my hufband, and the precipitate
flight of my fon, that I ordered my door to be fhut
to every one. But fince the princefs of Babylon
has done me the honour of paying me a vifit, I beg
fhe may be immediately introduced; I have matters of the laft importance to acquaint her with,
and I chufe you fhould be prefent. She then went
to meet the princefs in another faloon. She could
not walk very well; this lady was about three
hundred years old; but fhe had ftill fome agreeable
veftiges of beauty; it might be difcovered, that
about her two hundred and thirtieth, or two hundred and fortieth year, fhe muft have been a moft
charming woman. She received Formofanta with
a refpectful noblenefs, blended with an air of intereft and chagrin, which made a very lively impreffion upon the princefs.

Formofanta immediately paid her the compliments of condolence upon her hufband's death.
Alas! faid the widow, you have more reafon to
lament his death than you imagine. I am, doubtlefs, greatly afflicted, faid Formofanta, he was father to——here a flood of tears prevented her
from going on. For his fake only I undertook
this journey, amidft many perils, and narrowly efcaped many dangers. For him I left my father,
and the moft fplendid court in the univerfe. I was
detained by a king of Egypt, whom I deteft. Having efcaped from this ravifher, I have traverfed the
air, in fearch of the only man I love. When I arrive, he flies from me!----Here fighs and tears ftopt
her farther harangue.

His mother then faid to her, Madam, when the
king

king of Egypt carried you off when you supped with him at an inn upon the road to Bassora, when your beautiful hands filled him bumpers of Chiras wine, did you observe a black-bird that flew about the room? Yes, really, said the princess, I do now recollect there was such a bird, though I did not then pay it any kind of attention; but in collecting my ideas, I now remember well, that at the instant when the king of Egypt got up from table to give me a kiss, the black-bird flew out at the window in giving a loud cry, and never appeared after.

Alas! Madam, resumed Amazan's mother, this is precisely the cause of all our misfortunes: my son had dispatched this black-bird to gain intelligence of your health, and all that past at Babylon. He proposed speedily to return, throw himself at your feet, and consecrate to you the remainder of his life. You know not to what a pitch he adores you. All the Gangarids are both amorous and faithful; but my son is the most passionate and constant of them all. The black-bird found you at an inn, drinking very chearfully with the king of Egypt and a vile priest; he afterwards saw you give this monarch, who had killed the phœnix, a fond embrace;---the man my son holds in utter detestation. The black-bird, at the sight of this, was seized with a just indignation; he flew away imprecating your fatal amours: he returned this day, and has related every thing; but, just Heaven, at what a juncture! at the very time that my son was deploring with me the loss of his father, and that of the phœnix, the very instant I had informed him he was your cousin-german!

Oh heavens! my cousin, Madam, is it possible? how can this be? And am I so happy as to be thus ———— I i ———— allied!

allied! and yet so miserable as to have offended
him!

My son is, I tell you, said his mother, your cousin, and I shall presently convince you of it ; but in
becoming my relation, you rob me of my son ; he
cannot survive the grief which the embrace you
gave to the king of Egypt has occasioned him.

Ah! my dear aunt, cried the beautiful Formosanta, I swear by him and the all-powerful Orosmades, that this embrace, so far from being criminal, was the strongest proof of love your son could
receive from me. I disobeyed my father for his
sake. For him I went from the Euphrates to the
Ganges. Fallen into the hands of the worthless
Pharaoh of Egypt, I could not escape his clutches,
but by artifice. I call the ashes and soul of the
phœnix, which were then in my pocket, to witness;
he can do me justice. But how can your son, born
upon the banks of the Ganges, be my cousin? I,
whose family have reigned upon the banks of the
Euphrates for so many centuries?

You know, said the venerable Gangaridian lady
to her, that your grand-uncle, Aldea, was king of
Babylon, and that he was dethroned by Belus's
father?---Yes, Madam.---You know that this Aldea had in marriage a daughter named Aldea,
brought up in your court. It was this prince, who,
being persecuted by your father, took refuge in our
happy country under another name: he married
me: by him I bore young prince Aldea Amazan;
the most beautiful, the most courageous, the
strongest, and most virtuous of mortals;---and at
this hour the maddest. He went to the Babylonian festival upon the credit of your beauty; since
that time he idolizes you, and, perhaps, I shall never again set eyes upon my dear son.

She

She then displayed to the princess all the titles of the house of the Aldeas. Formosanta scarce deigned to look at them. Ah! Madam, do we examine what is the object of our desire? My heart sufficiently believes you. But where is Aldea Amazan? where is my kinsman, my lover, my king? where is my life? what road has he taken? I will seek for him in every sphere the Eternal Being has framed, and of which he is the greatest ornament: I will go into the star Canope, into Sheath, into Aldebaran; I will go and convince him of my love and my innocence.

The phœnix justified the princess with regard to the crime that was imputed to her by the black-bird, fondly embracing the king of Egypt; but it was necessary to undeceive Amazan and recal him. Birds are dispatched on every side, unicorns set forward on every road : news at length arrives that Amazan took that towards China. Well, then, said the princess, let us set out for China; the journey is not long, and I hope I shall bring you back your son in a fortnight at farthest. At these words the tears of affection streamed from his mother's eyes and those of the princess ;---they most tenderly embraced in the great effusion of their hearts.

The phœnix immediately ordered a coach with six unicorns. Amazan's mother furnished two thousand horsemen, and made the princess her niece a present of some thousands of the finest diamonds of her country. The phœnix, afflicted at the evil occasioned by the black-bird's indiscretion, ordered all the black-birds to quit the country; and from that time none have been met with upon the banks of the Ganges.

§ 5.

§ 5.

The unicorns, in lefs than eight days, carried
Formofanta, Irla, and the phœnix, to Cambalu, the
capital of China. This city was larger than that of
Babylon, and its magnificence very different. Thefe
frefh objects, thefe new manners, would have amufed Formofanta could any thing but Amazan have
engaged her.

As foon as the emperor of China learnt that the
princefs of Babylon was at one of the city gates,
he difpatched to her four thoufand Mandarines in
ceremonial robes: they all proftrated themfelves before her, and prefented her with a compliment
written in golden letters upon a fheet of purple filk.
Formofanta told them, that if fhe were poffeffed of
four thoufand tongues, fhe would not omit replying
immediately to every Mandarin; but that having
only one, fhe hoped they would be fatisfied with
her general thanks. They conducted her, in a
refpectful manner, to the emperor.

He was the moft juft, the politeft, and wifeft
monarch upon earth. It was he who firft tilled a
fmall field with his own imperial hands, to make
agriculture refpectable to his people. He firft
allotted premiums to virtue: laws in all other countries were fhamefully confined to the punifhment of
crimes. This emperor had juft banifhed from his
dominions a gang of foreign Bonzes, who had come
from the extremities of the Weft, with the frantic
hope of compelling all China to think like themfelves; and who, under pretence of teaching truths,
had already acquired honours and riches. In ex-
pelling them, he delivered himfelf in thefe words,
which are recorded in the annals of the empire:

" You may here do as much harm as you have
elfe-

elfewhere; you are come to preach dogmas of in-
tolerance, in the moft tolerating nation upon earth.
I fend you back, that I may never be compelled to
punifh you. You will be honourably conducted
to my frontiers; you will be furnifhed with every
thing neceffary to return to the confines of the
hemifphere from whence you came. Depart in
peace, if you can be at peace, and never return."

The princefs of Babylon learnt with pleafure this
fpeech and determination; fhe was the more certain of being well received at court, as fhe was
very far from entertaining any dogmas of intole-
rance. The emperor of China, in dining with her
tete-a tete, had the politenefs to banifh all difagreeable *etiquettes :* fhe prefented the phœnix to him,
who was greatly careffed by the emperor, and who
perched upon his chair. Formofanta, towards the
end of the repaft, ingenuoufly acquainted him with
the caufe of her journey, and intreated him to
fearch for the beautiful Amazan in the city of Cambalu ; and in the mean while fhe acquainted the
emperor with her adventures, without concealing
the fatal paffion with which her heart burnt for
this youthful hero. Who do you mention him to?
faid the emperor of China; he did me the pleafure
of coming to my court: I was enchanted with this
amiable Amazan. It is true, that he is deeply
afflicted; but his graces are thereby the more affecting. No one of my favourites has more wit
than him, there is not a gown Mandarin who has
more knowledge, not a military one who has a more
martial or heroic air. His extreme youth adds an
additional value to all his talents. If I were fo
unfortunate, fo abandoned by the Tien and Chang-
ti, as to defire being a conqueror, I would defire
Amazan to put himfelf at the head of my armies,
and

and I should be sure of conquering the whole universe. It is a great pity that his melancholy sometimes disconcerts him.

Ah! Sir, said Formosanta, with much agitation
and grief, blended with an air of reproach, why did
you not make me dine with him? This is a mortal
stroke you have given me!—send for him immediately. Madam, replied the emperor, he set out
this very morning, without acquainting me with
his destination. Formosanta, turning towards the
phœnix, said to him, Did you ever know so unfortunate a damsel as myself? But, resuming, she said,
Sir, how came he to quit so polite a court, and in
which, methinks, one might pass one's life, in so
abrupt a manner?

This was the case, Madam, said he: One of the
most amiable of the princesses of the blood, falling
desperately in love with him, fixed a rendezvous to
meet him at noon; he set out at day-break, leaving
this billet for my kinswoman, whom it hath cost a
deluge of tears:

" Beautiful princess of the blood of China, you
are deserving of a heart that was never offered up
to any other altar; I have sworn to the immortal
gods, never to love any other than Formosanta
princess of Babylon, and to teach her how to conquer one's desires in travelling. She has had the
misfortune to yield to a worthless king of Egypt;
I am the most unfortunate of men; I have lost my
father and the phœnix, and the hope of being loved by Formosanta. I left my mother in affliction,
and my country, unable to live a moment in that
spot where I learnt that Formosanta loved another
than me. I swore to traverse the earth, and be
faithful: You would despise me, and the gods
punish

punish me, if I violated my oath : chuse another lover, Madam, and be as faithful as I am."

Ah! give me that miraculous letter, said the beautiful Formosanta, it will afford me some consolation : I am happy in the midst of my misfortunes. Amazan loves me ; Amazan for me renounces the embraces of princesses of China ; there is no one upon earth but himself endowed with so much fortitude ; he sets me a most brilliant example ; the phœnix knows I did not stand in need of it : how cruel it is to be deprived of one's lover for the most innocent embrace given through pure fidelity! But, in fine, whither is he gone ? what road has he taken ? Deign to inform me, and I will set out.

The emperor of China told her, that, according to the reports he had received, her lover had taken the road towards Scythia. The unicorns were immediately harnessed, and the princess, after the most tender compliments, took leave of the emperor, with the phœnix, her chamber-maid Irla, and all her train.

As soon as she arrived in Scythia, she was more convinced than ever how much men and governments differed, and would differ, till such time as some more enlightened people should by degrees remove that cloud of darkness which had covered the earth for so many ages ; and till there should be found in barbarous climes, heroic souls, who would have strength and perseverance enough to transform brutes into men. There are no cities in Scythia, consequently no agreeable arts ; nothing was to be seen but extensive fields, and whole nations whose sole habitations were tents and chars. Such an appearance struck her with terror. Formosanta enquired in what tent or char the king was lodged? She was informed that he had set out eight days before with three hundred thousand cavalry to attack the king of Babylon, whose niece, the beautiful princess Aldea, he carried off.

What! hath he run away with my cousin, cried Formosanta? I could not have imagined such an incident. What! is my cousin, who was too happy in paying her court to me, become a queen, and I am not yet married? She was immediately conducted, by her desire, to the queen's tent.

Their unexpected meeting in such distant climes; the uncommon occurrences they mutually had to impart to each other, gave such charms to this interview, as made them forget they never loved one another : they saw each other with transport ; and a soft illusion supplied the place of real tenderness : they embraced with tears ; and there was a cordiality and frankness on each side that could not have taken place in a palace.

Aldea remembered the phœnix and the waiting-maid Irla. She presented her cousin with zibelin skins, who in return gave her diamonds. The war between the two kings was spoken of. They deplored the state of men, the victims of the caprice of princes, when two honest men might settle the difference, without a single throat being cut, in less than an hour : but the principal topic was the handsome stranger, who had conquered lions, given the largest diamonds in the universe, the writer of madrigals, now become the most miserable of men from the intelligence of a black-bird. He is my dear brother, said Aldea. He is my lover, cried Formosanta: you have, doubtless, seen him ; is he still here? for, cousin, he knows he is your brother ; he cannot have left you so abruptly as he did the king of China.

Have I seen him? good heaven! Yes, he passed
four

four whole days with me. Ah! coufin, how much
my brother is to blame! A falfe report has abfolutely turned his brain; he roams about the world,
without knowing whither he is deftined. Image
to yourfelf, that his phrenfy is fo great, that he has
refufed the favours of the handfomeft Scythian lady
in all Scythia. He fet out yefterday, after writing
her a letter which has thrown her into defpair. As
for him, he is gone to vifit the Cimmerians. God
be thanked! cried Formofanta; another refufal in
my favour! My good fortune is beyond my hope,
as my misfortunes furpaffed my greateft apprehenfions. Procure me this charming letter, that I may
fet out and follow him, loaded with his facrifices.
Farewell, coufin! Amazan is among the Cimmerians, and I fly to meet him.

Aldea judged that the princefs her coufin was
ftill more frantic than her brother Amazan. But
as fhe had herfelf been fenfible of the effects of this
epidemic contagion, having given up the delights
and magnificence of Babylon for a king of Scythia;
and as the women always excufe thofe follies that
are the effects of love, fhe felt for Formofanta's
affliction, wifhed her a happy journey, and promifed to be her advocate with her brother, if ever fhe
was fo fortunate as to fee him again.

§ 6.

From Scythia the princefs of Babylon, with her
phœnix, arrived foon at the empire of the Cimmerians, a country indeed much lefs populous than
Scythia, but of far greater extent.

After a few days journey, fhe entered a very
large city, which has of late been greatly improved
by the reigning emprefs: fhe herfelf was not there

at that time, but was making a progress through
her dominions, on the frontiers of Europe and
Asia, in order to judge of their state and condition
with her own eyes, to enquire into their grievances,
and to provide the proper remedies for them.

The principal magistrate of that antient capital,
as soon as he was informed of the arrival of the
Babylonian lady and the phœnix, lost no time in
paying her all the honours of the country; being
certain that his mistress, the most polite and generous princess in the world, would be extremely
well pleased to find that he had received so illustrious a lady with all that respect which she herself,
if on the spot, would have shewed her.

The princess was lodged in the palace, and entertained with great splendor and elegance. The
Cimmerian lord, who was an excellent natural
philosopher, diverted himself in conversing with
the phœnix, at such times as the princess chose to
retire to her own apartment. The phœnix told
him, that he had formerly travelled among the
Cimmerians, but that he should not have known
the country again. How comes it, said he, that
such prodigious changes have been brought about
in so short a time? Formerly, when I was here,
about three hundred years ago, I saw nothing but
savage nature in all her horrors; at present, I perceive industry, arts, splendor, and politeness. This
mighty revolution, replied the Cimmerian, was begun by one man, and is now carried to perfection
by one woman; a woman who is a greater legisla-
tor than the Isis of the Egyptians, or the Ceres of
the Greeks. Most lawgivers have been unhappy
in a narrow genius and an arbitrary disposition,
which confined their views to the countries, they
governed: each of them looked upon his own, as

the

the only people exifting upon the earth, or as if
they ought to be at enmity with all the reft: they
have formed inftitutions, introduced cuftoms, and
eftablifhed a religion for them alone. Thus the
Egyptians, fo famous for thofe heaps of ftones called
Pyramids, have difhonoured and befotted themfelves with their barbarous fuperftitions. They
defpife all other nations as profane; refufe all manner of intercourfe with them; and, excepting thofe
converfant in the court, who now and then rife
above the prejudices of the vulgar, there is not an
Egyptian who will eat off a plate that had ever been
ufed by a ftranger. Their priefts are equally cruel and abfurd. It were better to have no laws at
all, and to follow thofe notions of right and wrong
engraven on our hearts by nature, than to fubject
fociety to inftitutions fo inhofpitable.

Our emprefs has adopted a quite different fyftem;
fhe confiders her vaft dominions, under which all
the meridians on the globe are united, as under an
obligation of correfpondence with all the nations
dwelling under thofe meridians. The firft and moft
fundamental of her laws, is an univerfal toleration
of all religions, and an unbounded compaffion for
every error. Her penetrating genius perceives, that
though the modes of religious worfhip differ, yet
morality is every where the fame: by this principle, fhe has united her people to all the nations on
earth, and the Cimmerians will foon confider the
Scandinavians and the Chinefe as their brethren.
Not fatisfied with this, fhe has refolved to eftablifh
this invaluable toleration, the ftrongeft link of fociety among her neighbours: by thefe means, fhe
has obtained the title of the Parent of her country;
and, if fhe perfeveres, will acquire that of the Be-
nefactrefs of mankind.

Before

Before her time, the men, who were unhappily possessed of power, sent out legions of murderers to ravage unknown countries, and to water with the blood of the children the inheritance of their fathers. Those assassins were called Heroes, and their robberies accounted glorious atchievements. But our sovereign courts another sort of glory; she has sent forth her armies to be the messengers of peace; not only to prevent men from being the destroyers, but to oblige them to be the benefactors, of one another. Her standards are the ensigns of public tranquillity.

The phœnix was quite charmed with what he heard from this nobleman; he told him, that though he had lived twenty-seven thousand nine hundred years and seven months in this world, he had never seen any thing like it. He then enquired after his friend Amazan. The Cimmerian gave the same account of him that the princess had already heard from the Chinese and the Scythians. It was Amazan's constant practice to run away from all the courts he visited, the instant any lady made him an assignation, apprehending he might be prevailed upon to give some proofs of human frailty. The phœnix soon acquainted Formosanta with this fresh instance of Amazan's fidelity; a fidelity so much the more surprising, since he could not imagine his princess would ever hear of it.

Amazan had set out for Scandinavia, where he was entertained with sights still more surprising. In this place, he beheld monarchy and liberty subsisting together in a manner thought incompatible in other states; the labourers of the ground shared in the legislature with the grandees of the realm. In another place he saw what was still more extraordinary; a prince equally remarkable for his extreme

treme youth and uprightnefs, who poffeffed a fovereign authority over his country, acquired by a folemn contract with his people.

Amazan beheld a philofopher on the throne of
Sarmatia, who might be called a king of anarchy;
for he was the chief of a hundred thoufand petty
kings, one of whom with his fingle voice could render ineffectual the refolutions of all the reft. Eolus
had not more difficulty to keep the warring winds
within their proper bounds, than this monarch to
reconcile the tumultuous difcordant fpirits of his fubjects. He was the mafter of a fhip furrounded with
eternal ftorms; but the veffel did not founder, for
he was an excellent pilot.

In traverfing thofe various countries, fo different
from his own, Amazan perfevered in rejecting all
the favourable advances made to him by the ladies,
though inceffantly diftracted with the embrace given
by Formofanta to the king of Egypt, being refolved
to fet Formofanta an amazing example of an un-
fhaken and unparalleled fidelity.

The princefs of Babylon was conftantly clofe at
his heels, and fcarce ever miffed of him but by
a day or two; without the one being tired of
roaming, or the other lofing a moment in purfuing
him.

Thus he traverfed the immenfe continent of Germany, where he beheld with wonder, the progrefs
which reafon and philofophy had made in the North;
even their princes were enlightened, and were
become the patrons of freedom of thought. Their
education had not been trufted to men who had an
intereft in deceiving them, or who were themfelves
deceived; they were brought up in the knowledge
of univerfal morality, and in the contempt of fu-
perftition; they had banifhed from all their eftates
a fenfe-

a fenfelefs cuftom which had enervated and depopulated the fouthern countries; this was to bury alive in immenfe dungeons, infinite numbers of both fexes who were eternally feparated from one another, and fworn to have no communication together. This madnefs had contributed more than the moft cru.l wars to lay wafte and ravage the earth.

The princefs of the North had at laft found out, that if they wanted a good breed of horfes, they muft not feparate the fineft ftallions from the mares. They had likewife exploded other errors equally abfurd and pernicious; in fhort, men had at laft ventured to make ufe of their reafon in thofe immenfe regions; whereas it was ftill believed almoft every where elfe, that they could not be governed but in proportion to their ignorance.

§ 7.

From Germany, Amazan arrived at Batavia; where his perpetual chagrin was in a good meafure alleviated, by preferving among the inhabitants a faint refemblance of his happy countrymen the Gangarids. There he faw liberty, property, equality, plenty, with toleration in religion; but the ladies were fo indifferent, that not one made him any amorous advances; a thing he had never met with before. It is true, had he been inclined to addrefs them, they would have yielded one after another; though, at the fame time, not one would have been the leaft in love; but he was far from any thoughts of making conquefts.

Formofanta had nearly caught him in this infipid nation: he had fet out but a moment before her arrival.

Amazan

Amazan had heard so much among the Batavians in praise of a certain island called Albion, that
he was led by curiosity to embark with his unicorns on board a ship, which, with a favourable
easterly wind, carried him in four hours to that
celebrated country, more famous than Tyre, or the
Atlantic island.

The beautiful Formosanta, who had followed
him, as it were on the scent, to the banks of the
Wolga, the Vistula, the Elbe, and the Weser, and
had never been above a day or two behind him,
arrived soon after at the mouths of the Rhine,
where it disembogues its waters into the German
Ocean.

Here she learned that her beloved Amazan had
just set sail for Albion. She thought she saw the
vessel on board of which he was, and could not
help crying out for joy: at which the Batavian
ladies were greatly surprised, not imagining that a
young man could possibly occasion so violent a transport. They took, indeed, but little notice of the
phœnix, as they reckoned his feathers would not
fetch near so good a price as those of their own
ducks, and other water-fowl. The princess of Babylon hired two vessels to carry herself and her retinue to that happy island, which was soon to possess
the only object of her desires, the soul of her life,
and the god of her heart.

An unpropitious wind from the west arose of a
sudden, just as the faithful and unhappy Amazan
landed on the Albion shore, and detained the ships
of the Babylonian princess, just as they were going
to put to sea. Seized with a deep melancholy, she
betook herself to bed, determined to remain there
till the wind should change; but it blew for the
space of eight days, with an unremitting violence.

The princess, during this age of eight days, employed her maid of honour Irla in reading romances; which were not indeed written by the Batavians; but as they are the factors of the universe, they traffick in the wit as well as commodities of other nations.—The princess purchased of Mark Michael Rey, the bookseller, all the novels which had been written by the Ausonians and the Welches, the sale of which had been wisely prohibited among those nations, to enrich their neighbours the Batavians. She expected to find in those histories some adventure similar to her own, which might alleviate her grief.—The maid of honour read, the phœnix gave his advice, and the princess, finding nothing in the Fortunate Country Maid, in Tanſai, or in the Sopha, that had the least resemblance to her own affairs, interrupted the reader every moment, by asking how the wind stood?

§ 8.

In the mean time Amazan was on the road to the capital of Albion, in his coach and six unicorns, all his thoughts employed on his dear princess: at a small distance he perceived a carriage overturned in a ditch; the servants had gone different ways in quest of assistance, but the owner kept his seat, smoaking his pipe with great tranquillity, without testifying the smallest impatience: his name was My Lord What then, in the language from which I translate these memoirs.

Amazan made all the haste possibly to help him, and with his simple arm set the carriage to rights, so much was his strength superior to that of other men. My Lord What-then took no other notice of him, than saying, A stout fellow, by G—d! in the

mean

mean time the country people, being come up, flew into a great paffion at being called out to no pur-pofe, and fell upon the ftranger. They abufed him, called him outlandifh dog, and challenged him to ftrip and box.

Amazan feized a brace of them in each hand, and threw them twenty paces from him; the reft feeing this, pulled off their hats, and bowing with great refpect, afked his honour for fomething to drink. His honour gave them more money than they had ever feen in their lives before. My Lord What-then now expreffed great efteem for him, and afked him to dinner at his country-houfe, about three miles off. His invitation being accepted, he went into Amazan's coach, his own being out of order by the accident.

After a quarter of an hour's filence, My Lord What-then looking upon Amazan for a moment, faid, How d'ye do? which, by the way, is a phrafe without any meaning; adding, You have got fix fine unicorns there. After which he fell a fmoak-ing as ufual.

The traveller told him his unicorns were at his fervice, and that he had brought them from the country of the Gangarids: from thence he took occafion to inform him of his affair with the prin-cefs of Babylon, and the unlucky kifs fhe had given the king of Egypt: to which the other made no reply, being very indifferent whether there were any fuch people in the world, as a king of Egypt or a princefs of Babylon. He remained dumb for another quarter of an hour; after which he afked his companion a fecond time how he did, and whe-ther they had any good roaft beef among the Gan-garids. Amazan anfwered with his wonted polite-nefs, That they did not eat their brethren on the

banke

banks of the Ganges; he then explained to him
that fyftem which many ages afterwards was fur-
named the Pythagorean philofophy. But My
Lord fell afleep in the mean time, and made but
one nap of it till he came to his own houfe.

He was married to a young and charming woman, on whom nature had beftowed a foul as lively
and fenfible as her hufband's was dull and ftupid.
Several gentlemen of Albion had that day come
to dine with her; among whom there were characters of all forts; for that country having been
almoft always under the government of foreigners,
the families that had come over with thefe princes
had imported their different manners. There were
in this company fome perfons of a very amiable difpofition, others of a fuperior genius, and a few of
very profound learning.

The miftrefs of the houfe had none of that auk-
ward affected ftiffnefs, that falfe modefty, with
which the young Albion ladies were then reproached; fhe did not conceal, by a fcornful look and an
affected taciturnity, her deficiency of ideas; and
the embarraffing humility of having nothing to fay.
Never was a woman more engaging. She received Amazan with a grace and politenefs that were
quite natural to her. The extreme beauty of this
young ftranger, and the fudden comparifon fhe
could not help making between him and her hufband, immediately ftruck her in a moft fenfible
manner.

Dinner being ferved, fhe placed Amazan at her
fide, and helped him to all fort of puddings, having learned from himfelf that the Gangarids never
fed upon any thing which had received from the
gods the celeftial gift of life. His beauty and
ftrength, the manners of the Gangarids, the progrefs
of

of arts, religion, and government, were the subjects of a conversation equally agreeable and inftructive all the time of the entertainment, which lafted till night: during which My Lord What-then did nothing but push the bottle about, and call for the toaft.

After dinner, while my lady was pouring out the tea, ftill feeding her eyes on the young ftranger, he entered into a long converfation with a member of parliament; for every one knows that there was, even then, a parliament called Wittenagenot, or the Affembly of wife men. Amazan enquired into the conftitution, laws, manners, cuftoms, forces, and arts; which made this country fo refpectable; and the member anfwered him in the following manner:

For a long time we went ftark naked, though our climate is none of the hotteft. We were likewife for a long time enflaved by a people come from the ancient country of Saturn, watered by the Tiber, But the mifchiefs we have done one another have greatly exceeded all that we ever fuffered from our firft conquerors. One of our princes carried his daftardlinefs to fuch a pitch, as to declare himfelf the fubject of a prieft, who dwells alfo on the banks of the Tiber, and is called the Old Man of the Seven Mountains: it has been the fate of thefe feven mountains to domineer over the greateft part of Europe, then inhabited by brutes in human fhape.

To thofe times of infamy and debafement fucceeded the ages of barbarity and confufion. Our country, more tempeftuous than the furrounding ocean, has been ravaged and drenched in blood by our civil difcords; many of our crowned heads have perifhed by a violent death: above a hundred
dred

.dred princes of the royal blood have ended their
days on the scaffold, whilst the hearts of their ad-
herents have been torn from their breasts, and
thrown in their faces. In short, it is the province
of the hangman to write the history of our island,
seeing this personage has finally determined all our
affairs of moment.

But to crown these horrors, it is not very long
since some fellows wearing black mantles, and o-
thers who cast white shirts over their jackets, having been bitten by mad dogs, communicated their
madness to the whole nation. Our country was
then divided into two parties, the murderers and
the murdered, the executioners and the sufferers,
plunderers and slaves; and all in the name of God,
and whilst they were seeking the Lord.

Who would have imagined, that from this horrible abyss, this chaos of dissension, cruelty, ignorance, and fanaticism, a government should at last
spring up, the most perfect, it may be said, now in
the world; yet such has been the event. A prince,
honoured and wealthy, all-powerful to do good,
without any power to do evil, is at the head of a
free, warlike, commercial, and enlightened nation.
The nobles on one hand, and the representatives of
the people on the other, share the legislature with
the monarch.

We have seen, by a singular fatality of events,
disorder, civil wars, anarchy and wretchedness, lay
waste the country, when our kings aimed at arbitrary power: whereas tranquillity, riches, and universal happiness, have only reigned among us, when
the prince has remained satisfied with a limited authority. All order has been subverted whilst we
were disputing about mysteries, but was re-establish-
ed the moment we grew wise enough to despise
them.

them. Our victorious fleets carry our glory over
all the ocean ; our laws place our lives and fortunes in security ; no judge can explain them in an
arbitrary manner, and no decision is ever given
without the reasons assigned for it. We should punish a judge as an affassin, who should condemn a
citizen to death without declaring the evidence
which accused him, and the law upon which he
was convicted.

It is true, there are always two parties among
us, who are continually writing and intriguing a-
gainst each other ; but they constantly re-unite,
whenever it is needful to arm in defence of liberty
and our country. These two parties watch over
one another, and mutually prevent the violation of
the sacred *deposit* of the laws : they hate one another, but they love the state ; they are like those
jealous lovers, who pay court to the same mistress
with a spirit of emulation.

From the same fund of genius by which we
discovered and supported the natural rights of mankind, we have carried the sciences to the highest
pitch to which they can attain among men. Your
Egyptians, who pass for such great mechanics ;
your Indians, who are believed to be such great
philosophers ; your Babylonians, who boast of having observed the stars for the course of four hundred and thirty thousand years ; the Greeks, who
have written so much, and said so little, know in
reality nothing in comparison of our shallowest
scholars, who have studied the discoveries of our
great masters. We have ravished more secrets
from Nature, in the space of an hundred years, than
the human species has been able to discover in as
many ages.

This is a true account of our present state. I
have

have concealed from you neither the good nor the
bad ; neither our shame nor our glory ; and I have
exaggerated nothing.

At this difcourfe Amazan felt a ftrong defire
to be inftructed in thofe fublime fciences his friend
fpoke of ; and if his paffion for the princefs of Babylon, his filial duty to his mother whom he had
quitted, and his love for his native country, had
not made ftrong remonftrances to his diftempered
heart, he would willingly have fpent the remainder
of his life in Albion. But that unfortunate kifs
his princefs had given the king of Egypt, did not
leave his mind at fufficient eafe to ftudy the ab-
ftrufe fciences.

I confefs, faid he, having made a folemn vow to
roam about the world, and to efcape from myfelf.
I have a curiofity to fee that ancient land of Saturn,
that people of the Tiber and of the Seven Mountains, who have been heretofore their mafters ;
they muft undoubtedly be the firft people on earth.
I advife you by all means, anfwered the member,
to take that journey, if you have the fmalleft tafte
for mufic or painting. Even we ourfelves frequently carry our fpleen and melancholy to the Seven
Mountains. But you will be greatly furprifed
when you fee the defcendants of our conquerors.

This was a long converfation, and Amazan was
a little touched in the head. He fpoke in fo agrec-
able a manner, his voice was fo charming, his
whole behaviour fo noble and engaging, that the
miftrefs of the houfe could not refift the pleafure of
having a little private chat with him in her turn.
She tenderly fqueezed his hand as fhe fpoke, and
darted fuch looks at him, from her wary and fparkling eyes, that they fhot defire through every move-
ment of the foul. She kept him to fupper, and to
sleep

sleep there that night. Every moment, every word, every look, inflamed her passion. When all were retired to rest, she sent him a little billet-doux, not doubting he would come to entertain her in bed, whilst My Lord What-then was asleep in his. Amazan had once more the courage to resist; such marvellous effects does a grain of folly produce in an exalted and deeply-wounded mind!

Amazan, according to custom, wrote the lady an answer full of respect, representing to her the sacredness of his oath; and the strict obligation he was under to teach the princess of Babylon to conquer her passions by his example; after which he harnessed his unicorns and departed for Batavia; leaving all the company in deep admiration of him, and the lady in profound despair. In the agonies of her grief she dropt Amazan's letter. My Lord What-then read it next morning: Damn it, said he, shrugging up his shoulders, what stuff and nonsense have we got here? and then rode out a foxhunting with some of his drunken neighbours.

Amazan was already failing upon the sea, possessed of a geographical chart, with which he had been presented by the learned Albion he had conversed with at Lord What-then's. He was extremely astonished to find the greatest part of the earth upon a single sheet of paper.

His eyes and imagination wandered over this little space; he observed the Rhine, the Danube, the Alps of Tyrol there specified under different names; and all the countries through which he was to pass before he arrived at the city of the Seven Mountains; but he more particularly fixed his eyes upon the country of the Gangarids; upon Babylon, where he had seen his dear princess, and upon the fatal country of Bassora, where she had given a fa-

tal kifs to the king of Egypt. He fighed, and tears
ftreamed from his eyes; but he agreed with the
Albion who had prefented him with the univerfe in
epitome, when he averred that the inhabitants of
the banks of the Thames were a thoufand times
better inftructed than thofe upon the banks of the
Nile, the Euphrates, and the Ganges.

As he returned into Batavia, Formofanta flew towards Albion with her two fhips that went at full
fail. Amazan's fhip and the princefs's croffed one
another, and almoft touched; the two lovers were
clofe to each other, which they could not doubt of.
—Ah! had they but known it! but tyrannic deftiny would not allow it.

§ 9.

No fooner had Amazan landed on the flat mud-
dy fhore of Batavia, than he flew like lightning towards the city of the Seven Mountains. He was
obliged to traverfe the fouthern part of Germany.
At every four miles he met with a prince and princefs, maids of honour and beggars. He was aftonifhed every where at the coquetries of thefe ladies and maids of honour, which they difplayed
with German good faith; and he only anfwered
with modeft refufals. After having cleared the
Alps he embarked upon the fea of Dalmatia, and
landed in a city that had no refemblance to any
thing he had heretofore feen. The fea formed the
ftreets, and the houfes were erected in the water.
The few public places with which this city was ornamented were filled with men and women with
double faces; that which nature had beftowed upon them, and a pafteboard one, ill painted, with
which they covered their natural vifage; fo that
·this

this people feemed compofed of fpectres. Upon
the arrival of ftrangers in this counttry, they immediately purchafe thefe vifages, in the fame manner
as people elfewhere furnifh themfelves with hats
and fhoes. Amazan defpifed a fafhion fo contrary
to nature ; he appeared juft as he was. There
were in the city twelve thoufand girls regiftered in
the great book of the Republic ; thefe girls were
ufeful to the ftate, being appointed to carry on the
moft advantageous and agreeable trade that ever
enriched a nation. Common traders ufually fend,
at great rifk and expence, merchandizes of various
kinds to the Eaft ; but thefe beautiful merchants
carried on a conftant traffic without rifk, which
conftantly fprung from their charms. They all
came to prefent themfelves to the handfome Amazan, and offer him his choice. He fled with the
utmoft precipitancy, uttering the name of the incomparable princefs of Babylon, and fwearing by
the immortal gods, that fhe was far handfomer than
all the twelve thoufand Venetian girls. Sublime
traitrefs, he cried in his tranfports, I will teach
you to be faithful !

Now the yellow furges of the Tiber, peftiferous
fens, a few pale emaciated inhabitants, clothed in
tatters which difplayed their dry tanned hides, appeared to his fight, and befpoke his arrival at the
gate of the city of the Seven Mountains, that city
of heroes and legiflators who conquered and polifhed a great part of the globe.

He expected to have feen at the triumphal gate,
five hundred battalions commanded by heroes, and
in the fenate an affembly of demi-gods giving laws
to the earth ; but the only army he found confifted of about thirty tatterdemalions, mounting guard
with umbrellas for fear of the fun. Being arrived

at a temple which appeared to him very fine, but
not so magnificent as that of Babylon, he was greatly astonished to hear a concert performed by men
with female voices.

This, said he, is a mighty pleasant country, which
was formerly the land of Saturn. I have been in
a city where no one shewed his own face; here is
another where men have neither their own voices
nor beards. He was told that these singers were
no longer men; that they had been divested of
their virility that they might sing the more agreeably the praises of a great number of persons of
merit. Amazan could not comprehend the meaning of this. These gentlemen desired him to sing;
he sung a Gangaridian air with his usual grace. His
voice was a fine *counter-tenor*. Ah Signior, said they,
what a delightful *soprano* you would have, if——If
what, said he; what do you mean?——Ah! Signior,
if you were---If I were what?---If---you were---with-
out a beard! They then explained to him very plea-
santly, and with the most comic gesticulations, according to the custom of their country, the point
in question. Amazan was quite confounded. I
have travelled a great way, said he, but I never before heard such a whim.

After they had sung a good while, the Old Man
of the Seven Mountains went with great ceremony
to the gate of the temple; he cut the air in four
parts with his thumb raised, two fingers extended
and two bent, in uttering these words in a language
no longer spoken: *To the city and to the universe* *.
The Gangarid could not comprehend how two
fingers could extend so far.

He presently saw the whole court of the master
                                                    of

---

* Urbi & Orbi.

of the world file off. This court confifted of grave
perfonages, fome in fcarlet, and others in violet
robes: they almoft all eyed the handfome Amazan
with a tender look; they bowed to him, and faid
to one another, *San Martino, che bel' ragazzo !. San
Pancratio, che bel' fanciullo !*

The zealots, whofe vocation was to fhew the
curiofities of the city to ftrangers, very eagerly offered to conduct him to feveral ruins, in which a
muleteer would not chufe to pafs a night, but
which were formerly worthy monuments of the
grandeur of a royal people. He moreover faw
pictures of two hundred years ftanding, and ftatues
that had remained twenty ages, which appeared to
him mafter-pieces in their kind. Can you ftill produce fuch works? No, your Excellency, replied one
of the zealots; but we defpife the reft of the earth,
becaufe we preferve thefe rarities. We are a kind
of old cloaths-men, who derive our glory from the
caft-off garbs in our warehoufes.

Amazan was willing to fee the prince's palace,
and he was accordingly conducted thither. He faw
men dreffed in violet-coloured robes, who were
reckoning the money of the revenues of the do-
mains of lands, fituated fome upon the Danube,
fome upon the Loire, others upon the Guadalquivir,
or the Viftula. Oh! oh! faid Amazan, after having confulted his geographical map, your mafter,
then, poffeffes all Europe, like thofe ancient heroes of the Seven Mountains? He fhould poffefs
the whole univerfe by divine right, replied a violet-
livery man; and there was even a time when his
predeceffors nearly compaffed univerfal monarchy;
but their fucceffors are fo good as to content themfelves at prefent with fome monies which the kings
their fubjects pay to them in the form of a tribute.

Your

Your mafter is, then, in fact, the king of kings; is that his title ? faid Amazan. No, your Excellency, his title is *the fervant of fervants* ; he was originally a fifherman and porter, wherefore the emblems of his dignity confift of keys and nets ; but he at prefent iffues orders to every king in Chriftendom. It is not a long while fince he fent one hundred and one mandates to a king of the Celtes, and the king obeyed.

Your fifherman muft then have fent five or fix hundred thoufand men to put thefe orders in execution ?

Not at all, your Excellency; our holy mafter is not rich enough to keep ten thoufand foldiers on foot; but he has five or fix hundred thoufand divine prophets difperfed in other countries. Thofe prophets of various colours are, as they ought to be, fupported at the expence of the people : they proclaim from heaven, that my mafter may, with his keys, open and fhut all locks, and particularly thofe of ftrong boxes. A Norman prieft, who held the poft of confidant of this king's thoughts, convinced him he ought to obey, without replying, the hundred and one thoughts of my mafter ; for you muft know that one of the prerogatives of the Old Man of the Seven mountains, is never to err, whether he deigns to fpeak or deigns to write.

In faith, faid Amazan, this is a very fingular man ; I fhould be curious to dine with him. Were your Excellency even a king, you could not eat at his table ; all that he could do for you, would be to allow you to have one ferved by the fide of his, but fmaller and lower. But if you are inclined to have the honour of fpeaking to him, I will afk an audience for you on condition of the *buena mancia*, which you will be kind enough to give me. Very
readily,

readily, faid the Gangarid.   The violet-livery man
bowed : I will introduce you to-morrow, faid he ;
you muft make three very low bows, and you muft
kifs the Old Man of the Seven Mountains' feet.
At this information Amazan burft into fo violent a
fit of laughing that he was almoft choaked ; which,
however, he furmounted, holding his fides, whilft
the violent emotions of the rifible mufcles forced
the tears down his cheeks, till he reached the inn,
where the fit ftill continued upon him.

At dinner, twenty beardlefs men and twenty
violins produced a concert.   He received the compliments of the greateft lords of the city during the
remainder of the day ; thefe made him propofals
ftill more extravagant than that of kiffing the Old
Man of the Seven Mountains feet.   As he was extremely polite, he at firft imagined that thefe gentlemen took him for a lady, and informed them of
their miftake with great decency and circumfpec-
tion ; but being fomewhat clofely preffed by two
or three of thofe violet-coloured gentry, who were
the moft forward, he threw them out of the window, without fancying he had made any great facrifice to the beautiful Formofanta.   He left with
the greateft precipitation this city of the mafters of
the world, where he found himfelf neceffitated to
kifs an old man's toe, as if his cheek were at the
end of his foot, and where young men are accofted
in a more whimfical manner.

§ 10.

In all the provinces through which he paffed,
having conftantly repulfed every amorous overture
of every fpecies, being ever faithful to the princefs
of Babylon, though inceffantly enraged at the king
of

of Egypt, this model of conftancy at length arrived at the new capital of the Gauls. This city, like
many others, had alternately fubmitted to barbarity, ignorance, folly, and mifery. The firft name
it bore was Dirt and Mire; it then took that of
Ifis, from the worfhip of Ifis, which had reached
even here. Its firft fenate confifted of a company of watermen. It had long been in bondage,
and fubmitted to the ravages of the heroes of
the Seven Mountains; and fome ages after, fome
other heroic thieves, who came from the farther
banks of the Rhine, had feized upon its little
lands.

Time, which changes all things, had formed it
into a city, half of which was very noble and very
agreeable, the other half fomewhat barbarous and
ridiculous : this was the emblem of its inhabitants.
There were within its walls at leaft a hundred
thoufand people, who had no other employment
than play and diverfion. Thefe idlers were the
judges of thofe arts which the others cultivated.
They were ignorant of all that paffed at court ;
though they were only four fhort miles diftant
from it :--but it feemed to be at leaft fix hundred
thoufand miles off. Agreeablenefs in company,
gaiety and frivolity, formed the important and fole
confiderations of their lives : they were governed
like children, who are extravagantly fupplied with
gewgaws to prevent their crying. If the horrors
which had, two centuries before, laid wafte their
country, or thofe dreadful periods when one half
of the nation maffacred the other for fophifms,
came upon the carpet, they, indeed, faid, This was
not well done ; then they fell a-laughing, or finging of catches.

In proportion as the Idlers were polifhed, agreeable,

able, and amiable, it was obferved there was a greater and more fhocking contraft between them and
thofe who were engaged in bufinefs.

Among the latter, or fuch as pretended fo to be,
there was a gang of melancholy fanatics, whofe
abfurdity and knavery divided their character,
whofe appearance alone diffufed mifery, and who
would have overturned the world, had they been
able to gain a little credit. But the nation of Idlers,
by dancing and finging, forced them into obfcurity in their caverns, as the warbling birds drive
the creaking bats back to their holes and ruins.

A fmaller number of thofe who were occupied
were the prefervers of ancient barbarous cuftoms,
againft which, nature terrified, loudly exclaimed;
they confulted nothing but their worm-eaten regifters.   If they there difcovered a foolifh horrid cuftom, they confidered it as a facred law.   It was
from this vile practice of not daring to think for
themfelves, but extracting their ideas from the ruins
of thofe times when no one thought at all, that in
the metropolis of pleafure there ftill remained fome
fhocking manners.   Hence it was that there was
no proportion between crimes and punifhments.   A
thoufand deaths were fometimes inflicted upon an
innocent victim, to make him acknowledge a crime
he had not committed.

The extravagancies of youth were punifhed with
the fame feverity as murder or parricide.   The
Idlers fcreamed loudly at thefe exhibitions, and the
next day thought no more about them, but were
buried in the contemplation of fome new fafhion.

This people faw a whole age elapfe, in which the
fine arts attained a degree of perfection that far
furpaffed the moft fanguine hopes: foreigners then
repaired thither, as they did to Babylon, to admire

the great monuments of architecture, the wonders
of gardening, the sublime efforts of sculpture and
painting. They were charmed with a species of music
that reached the heart without astonishing the ears.

True poetry, that is to say, such as is natural and
harmonious, that which addresses the heart as well
as the mind, was unknown to this nation before
this happy period. New kinds of eloquence displayed sublime beauties. The theatres in particular
re-echoed with master-pieces that no other nation
ever approached. In a word, good taste prevailed
in every profession, to that degree, that there were
even good writers among the Druids.

So many laurels, that had branched even to the
skies, soon withered in an exhausted soil. There
remained but a very small number, whose leaves
were of a pale dying verdure. This decay was occasioned by the facility of producing laziness
preventing good productions, and by a satiety
of the brilliant, and a taste for the whimsical.
Vanity protected arts that brought back times of
barbarity; and this same vanity, in persecuting
real talents, forced them to quit their country; the
hornets banished the bees.

There was scarce any real arts, scarce any real
genius; merit now consisted in reasoning right or
wrong upon the merit of the last age. The daub-
er of a sign-post criticised with an air of sagacity
the works of the greatest painters; and the blotters
of paper disfigured the works of the greatest writers.
Ignorance and a bad taste had other daubers in
their pay; the same things were repeated in a hundred volumes, under different titles. Every work
was either a dictionary or a pamphlet. A Druid
gazetteer wrote twice a week the obscure annals of
an unknown people possessed with the devil, and
celestial

celeftial prodigies operated in garrets by little beggars of both fexes : other Ex-Druids, drefled in
black, ready to die with rage and hunger, fet forth
their complaints in a hundred different writings,
that they were no longer allowed to cheat mankind, this privilege being conferred on fome goats
clad in grey ; and fome Arch-Druids were employed in printing defamatory libels.

Amazan was quite ignorant of all this, and even
if he had been acquainted with it, he would have
given himfelf very little concern about it, having his
head filled with nothing but the princefs of Babylon,
the king of Egypt, and the inviolable vow he had
made to defpife all female coquetry, in whatever
country his defpair fhould drive him.

The gaping ignorant mob, whofe curiofity ex-
ceeds all the bounds of nature and reafon, for a
long time thronged about his unicorns ; the more
fenfible women forced open the doors of his *hotel* to
contemplate his perfon.

He at firft teftified fome defire of vifiting thecourt;
but fome of the Idlers who conftituted good company, and cafually went thither, informed him that
it was quite out of fafhion, that times were greatly
changed, and that all amufements were confined to
the city. He was invited that very night to fup
with a lady, whofe fenfe and talents had reached
foreign climes, and who had travelled in fome
countries through which Amazan had paffed. This
lady gave him great pleafure, as well as the fociety
he met at her houfe. Here reigned a decent liberty, gaiety without tumult, filence without pedantry,
and wit without afperity. He found that *good company* was not quite ideal, though the title was frequently ufurped by pretenders. The next day he
dined in a fociety far lefs amiable, but much more

voluptu-

voluptuous. The more he was satisfied with the
guests, the more they were pleased with him. He
found his soul soften and dissolve, like the aroma-
tics of his country, which gradually melt in a moderate heat, and exhale in delicious perfumes.

After dinner he was conducted to a place of public entertainment which was enchanting; condemned, however, by the Druids, because it deprived them of their auditors, which the most excited
their jealousy. The representation here consisted
of agreeable verses, delightful songs, dances which
expressed the movements of the soul, and perspec-
tives that charmed the eye in deceiving it. This
kind of pastime, which included so many kinds,
was known only under a foreign name; it was called an *Opera*, which formerly signified, in the language of the Seven Mountains, work, care, occu-
pation, industry, enterprize, business. This business enchanted him. A female singer, in particular, charmed him by her melodious voice, and the
graces that accompanied her: this girl of *business*,
after the performance, was introduced to him by
his new friends. He presented her with a handful
of diamonds; for which she was so grateful, that
she could not leave him all the rest of the day. He
supped with her, and during the repast he forgot
his sobriety; and after the repast he also forgot his
vow of being ever insensible to beauty, and all the
blandishments of coquetry. What an instance of
human frailty!

The beautiful princess of Babylon arrived at this
juncture, with her phœnix, her chamber-maid
Irla, and her two hundred Gangaridian cavaliers
mounted on their unicorns. It was a long while
before the gates were opened. She immediately
asked, If the handsomest, the most courageous, the
most

most sensible, and the most faithful of men was still
in that city? The magistrates readily concluded that
she meant Amazan. She was conducted to his
hotel.—How great was the palpitation of her heart!
the powerful operation of the tender passion; her
whole soul was penetrated with inexpressible joy, to
see once more in her lover the model of constancy.
Nothing could prevent her entering his chamber;
the curtains were open; and she saw the beautiful
Amazan sleeping in the arms of a handsome *brunette.* They both stood in great need of rest.

Formosanta expressed her grief with such screams
as made the house echo, but which could neither
wake her cousin nor the girl of *business.* She swoon-
ed into the arms of Irla. As soon as she had recovered her senses, she retired from this fatal chamber with grief blended with rage. Irla gained intelligence of the young lady who passed such sweet
hours with the handsome Amazan. Irla was told
she was a girl of *business,* very complaisant, who
united to her other talents that of singing very
gracefully. Oh! just heaven, oh powerful Orof-
mades! cried the beautiful princess of Babylon
bathed in tears, By whom, and for whom am I thus
betrayed? He that could reject for my sake so many princesses, to abandon me for a strolling Gaul!
No—I can never survive this affront.

Madam, said Irla to her, this is the disposition
of all young people, from one end of the world to
the other; were they enamoured with a beauty
descended from heaven, they would at certain moments be unfaithful to her for the sake of an ale-
house girl.

It is done, said the princess, I will never see him
again whilst I live: let us depart this instant, and
let the unicorns be harnessed. The phœnix con-

jured her to stay at least till Amazan awoke, and
he might speak to him. He does not deserve it,
said the princess; you would cruelly offend me; he
would think that I had desired you to reproach
him, and that I am willing to be reconciled to him:
if you love me, do not add this injury to the insult
he has offered me. The phœnix, who after all
owed his life to the daughter of the king of Babylon, could not disobey her. She set out with all
her attendants. Whither are you going, Madam?
said Irla to her. I do not know, replied the princess; we will take the first road we find; provided
I fly from Amazan for ever, I am contented. The
phœnix, who was wiser than Formosanta, because
he was divested of passion, consoled her upon the
road. He gently remonstrated to her that it was
shocking to punish one's self for the faults of another;
that Amazan had given her proofs sufficiently strik-
ing and numerous of his fidelity; so that she should
forgive him for having forgot himself for one moment; that this was the only one, in which he had
been wanting of the grace of Orosmades; that it
would render him only the more constant in love
and virtue for the future; that the desire of expiat-
ing his fault would raise him beyond himself; that
it would be the means of increasing her happiness;
that many great princesses before her had forgiven
such slips, and had no reason to be sorry afterwards:
and he was so thoroughly possessed of the art of
persuasion, that Formosanta's mind grew more calm
and peaceable; she was now sorry she had set out
so soon; she thought her unicorns went too fast,
but she did not dare return: great was the conflict
between her desire of forgiving and that of shewing
her rage, between her love and vanity.—However,
her unicorns pursued their pace; and she traversed
the

the world, according to the prediction of her father's oracle.

When Amazan awoke, he was informed of the arrival and departure of Formosanta and the phœnix : He was informed of the rage and diftraction of the princefs ; that fhe had fworn never to forgive him. Then, faid he, there is nothing left for me to do, but follow her, and kill myfelf at her feet.

The report of this adventure drew together his feftive companions, who all remonftrated to him, that he had much better ftay with them ; that nothing could equal the pleafant life they led in the center of arts and peaceable delicate voluptuoufnefs ; that many ftrangers, and even kings, had preferred fuch an agreeable enchanting repofe, to their country and their thrones : moreover, his vehicle was broke, and that another was making for him according to the neweft fafhion ; that the beft tailor of the whole city had already cut out for him a dozen fuits in the laft tafte ; that the moft vivacious and moft amiable ladies in the whole city, at whofe houfes dramatic performances were reprefented, had each appointed a day to give him a regale. The girl of bufinefs was in the mean while drinking her chocolate at her toilet, laughing, finging, and ogling the beautiful Amazan, who by this time perceived fhe had no more fenfe than a goofe.

A fincerity, cordiality, and franknefs as well as magnanimity and courage, conftituted the character of this great prince ; he related his travels and misfortunes to his friends. They knew that he was coufin-german to the princefs ; they were informed of the fatal kifs fhe had given the king of Egypt. Such little tricks, faid they, are forgiven between relations, otherwife one's whole life would

pafs

pass in perpetual uneasiness. Nothing could shake his design of pursuing Formosanta; but his carriage was not ready, and he was compelled to remain three days among the Idlers, in feasting and pastimes: he, at length, took his leave of them, in embracing them, and making them accept of the diamonds of his country that were the best mounted, and recommending to them a constant pursuit of frivolity and pleasure, since they were thereby more agreeable and happy. The Germans, said he, are the grey-heads of Europe; the people of Albion are men formed; the inhabitats of Gaul are the children, and I love to play with children.

§ 11.

His guides had no difficulty in following the route the princess had taken; there was nothing else talked of but her and her large bird. All the inhabitants were still in a state of fascination. The people of Dalmatia and the Mark of Ancona were lately surprised in a manner less agreeable, when they saw a house fly in the air; the banks of the Loire, of the Dordogne, the Garonne, and the Gironde, still echoed with acclamations.

When Amazan reached the foot of the Pyrenees, the magistrates and Druids of the country made him dance whether he would or not, a *Tambourin;* but as soon as he cleared the Pyrenees, nothing presented itself that was either gay or joyous. If he here and there heard a peasant sing, it was a doleful ditty: the inhabitants stalked with much gravity, having a few strung beads and a girted poniard. The nation, cloathed in black, appeared to be in mourning. If Amazan's servants asked passengers any questions, they were answered by

signs;

ſigns; if they went into an inn, the hoſt acquainted his gueſts in three words, that there was nothing
in the houſe; but that the things they ſo preſſing-
ly wanted, might be fetched a few miles off.

When thoſe votaries to taciturnity were aſked if
they had ſeen the beautiful princeſs of Babylon
paſs, they anſwered with leſs brevity than uſual,
We have ſeen her; ſhe is not ſo handſome; there
are no beauties that are not tawny; ſhe diſplays a
boſom of alabaſter, which is the moſt diſguſting
thing in the world, and which is ſcarce known in
our climate.

Amazan advanced towards the province watered by the Betis. The Tyrians had not diſcovered
this country above twelve thouſand years, about the
time they diſcovered the great Atlantide Iſle, in-
undated ſo many centuries after. The Tyrians
cultivated Betica, which the natives of the country
had never done, being of opinion that it was not
their place to meddle with any thing, and that
their neighbours the Gauls ſhould come and cultivate their lands. The Tyrians had brought with
them ſome Paleſtines, who, from that time, wandered through every clime where money was to be
got.   The Paleſtines, by extraordinary uſury, at
fifty per cent. had poſſeſſed themſelves of almoſt all
the riches of the country.   This made the people
of Betica imagine the Paleſtines were ſorcerers;
and all thoſe who were accuſed of witchcraft were
burnt without mercy by a company of Druids, who
were called the Inquiſitors, or the *Anthropokaies*.
Theſe prieſts immediately put them in a maſquerade
habit, ſeized upon their effects, and devoutly repeated the Paleſtines own prayers, whilſt they were
baking by a ſlow fire, *por l'amor de Dios*.

The princeſs of Babylon alighted in that city

which has since been called Sevilla.   Her design
was to embark upon the Betis to return by Tyre
to Babylon, and see again king Belus her father;
and forget, if possible, her perfidious lover, or at
least to ask him in marriage.   She sent for two Palestines, who transacted all the business of the court.
They were to furnish her with three ships.   The
phœnix made all the necessary contracts with them,
and settled the price after some little dispute.

The hostess was a great devotee, and her husband, who was no less religious, was a Familiar ;
that is to say, a spy of the Druid Inquisitors *Anthropokaies.*   He failed not to inform them, that in
his house was a Sorceress and two Palestines, who
were entering into a compact with the devil, dis-
guised like a large gilt bird.   The Inquisitors having learned that the lady was possessed of a large
quantity of diamonds,   swore point blank that she
was a Sorceress :   they waited till night to imprison
the two hundred cavaliers and the unicorns, which
slept in very extensive stables ;   for the Inquisitors
are cowards.

Having strongly barricaded the gates, they seized
the princess and Irla ;   but they could not catch the
phœnix, who flew away with great swiftness ;   he
did not doubt of meeting with Amazan upon the
road from Gaul to Sevilla.

He met him upon the frontiers of Betica, and
acquainted him with the disaster that had befallen
the princess.   Amazan was struck speechless with
rage ;   he armed himself with a steel cuirass damas-
quined with gold, a lance twelve feet long, two
javelins, and an edged sword called the Thunderer,
which at one single stroke would rend trees, rocks,
and Druids :   he covered his beautiful head with a
golden casque, shaded with heron and ostrich feathers.

thers.----This was the ancient armour of Magog, which his fifter Aldea gave him when upon his journey in Scythia. The few attendants he had with him all mounted their unicorns.

Amazan, in embracing his dear phœnix, uttered only thefe melancholy expreffions : I am guilty ! Had I not flept with a girl of *bufinefs* in the city of the Idlers, the princefs of Babylon would not have been in this alarming fituation ; let us fly to the *Anthropokaies.* He prefently entered Sevilla. Fifteen hundred Alguazils guarded the gates of the inclofure in which the two hundred Gangarids and their unicorns were fhut up, without being allowed any thing to eat : all the neceffary preparations were making for the facrifice of the princefs of Babylon, her chamber-maid Irla, and the two rich Paleftines.

The high *Anthropokaie,* furrounded by his fubaltern *Anthropokaies,* was already feated upon his facred tribunal : a crowd of Sevillians, wearing ftrung beads at their girdles, joined their two hands without uttering a fyllable ; when the beautiful Princefs, Irla, and the two Paleftines, were brought forth with their hands tied behind their back, and dreffed in mafquerade habits.

The phœnix entered the prifon by a dormer window, whilft the Gangarids had begun to break open the doors. The invincible Amazan fhattered them without. They fallied forth all armed upon their unicorns, and Amazan put himfelf at their head. He had no difficulty in overthrowing the Alguazils, the Familiars, or the priefts called *Anthropokaics ;* each unicorn pierced dozens at a time. The thundering Amazan cut to pieces all he met ; the people flew away in black cloaks and dirty frize, always

keeping

keeping faft hold of their bleft beads *por l'amor de Dios*.

Amazan collared the high Inquifitor upon his tribunal, and threw him upon the pile, which was prepared about forty paces diftant; and he alfo caft upon it the other Inquifitors, one after the other. He then proftrated himfelf at Formofanta's feet. Ah! how amiable are you, faid fhe; and how I fhould adore you, if you had not been faithlefs to me with a girl of *bufinefs!*

Whilft Amazan was making his peace with the princefs, whilft his Gangarids caft upon the pile the bodies of all the *Anthropokaies*, and the flames afcended to the clouds, Amazan faw an army that approached him at a diftance. An aged monarch with a crown upon his head advanced upon a car, drawn by eight mulcs, harneffed with ropes; an hundred other cars followed. They were accompanied by grave looking men in black cloaks or frize, mounted upon very fine horfes; a multitude of people, with greafy hair, followed filently on foot.

Amazan immediately drew up his Gangarids about him, and advanced with his lance couched. As foon as the king perceived him, he took off his crown, alighted from his car, and embraced Amazan's ftirrup, faying to him: Man, fent by the gods, you are the avenger of human kind, the deliverer of my country. Thefe facred monfters, of which you have purged the earth, were my mafters, in the name of the Old Man of the Seven Mountains: I was forced to fuffer their criminal power. My people would have deferted me, if I had only been inclined to moderate their abominable crimes. From this moment I breathe, I reign, and am indebted to you for it.

He

He afterwards refpectfully kiffed Formofanta's hand, and entreated her to get into his coach (drawn by fix mules) with Amazan, Irla, and the phœnix. The two Paleftine bankers, who ftill remained proftrate on the ground through fear and acknowledgment, now raifed their heads ; and the troop of unicorns followed the king of Betica into his palace.

As the dignity of a king who reigned over a people of characteriftic brevity, required that his mules fhould go at a very flow pace, Amazan and Formofanta had time to relate to him their adventures. He alfo converfed with the phœnix, admiring and frequently embracing him. He eafily comprehended how brutal and barbarous the people of the Weft fhould be confidered, who ate animals, and did not underftand their language ; that the Gangarids alone had preferved the nature and dignity of primitive man ; but he particularly agreed, that the moft barbarous of mortals were the *Anthropokaies*, of whom Amazan had juft purged the earth. He inceffantly bleffed and thanked him. The beautiful Formofanta had already forgot the girl of *bufinefs*, and had her foul filled with nothing but the valour of the hero who had preferved her life. Amazan being acquainted with the innocence of the embrace fhe had given the king of Egypt, and the refurrection of the phœnix, tafted the pureft joy, and was intoxicated with the moft violent love.

They dined at the palace, but had a very indifferent repaft. The cooks of Betica were the worft in Europe. Amazan advifed the king to fend for fome from Gaul. The king's muficians performed, during the repaft, that celebrated air which has fince been

been called *the Follies of Spain.* After dinner matters of bufinefs came upon the carpet.

The king enquired of the handfome Amazan,
the beautiful Formofanta, and the charming phœnix, what they propofed doing. For my part, faid
Amazan, my intention is to return to Babylon, of
which I am the prefumptive heir, and to requeft of
my uncle Belus my coufin-german, the incomparable Formofanta, unlefs fhe would rather chufe to
live with me among the Gangarids.

My defign certainly is, faid the princefs, never to
feparate from my coufin-german. But I imagine
he will agree with me, that I fhould return firft to
my father, becaufe he only gave me leave to go upon a pilgrimage to Baffora, and I have wandered
all over the world. For my part, faid the phœnix,
I will every where follow thefe two tender generous
lovers.

You are in the right, faid the king of Betica ;
but your return to Babylon is not fo eafy as you
may imagine. I receive daily intelligence from
that country by Tyrian fhips, and my Paleftine
bankers, who keep a correfpondence with all the
people of the earth. The people are all in arms
towards the Euphrates and the Nile. The king of
Scythia claims the inheritance of his wife, at the
head of three hundred thoufand warriors on horfeback. The kings of Egypt and India are alfo laying wafte the banks of the Tygris and the Euphrates, each at the head of three hundred thoufand
men, to revenge themfelves for being laughed at.
Whilft the king of Egypt is abfent from his country, his foe the king of Ethiopia is ravaging Egypt
with three hundred thoufand men ; and the king
of Babylon has as yet only fix hundred thoufand
men to defend himfelf.

I ac-

I acknowledge to you, continued the king, when I hear of those prodigious armies which are disembogued from the East, and their astonishing magnificence; when I compare them to my trifling bodies of twenty or thirty thousand soldiers, which it is so difficult to clothe and nourish; I am inclined to think the Eastern subsisted long before the Western hemisphere. It should seem that we sprung only yesterday from chaos and barbarity.

Sire, said Amazan, the last comers frequently outstrip those who first began the career. It is thought in my country that man was first created in India; but this I am not certain of.

And, said the king of Betica to the phœnix, what do you think? Sire, replied the phœnix, I am as yet too young, to have any knowledge concerning antiquity. I have lived only about twenty-seven thousand years; but my father, who had lived five times that age, told me he had learnt from his father, that the countries of the East had always been more populous and richer than the others. It had been transmitted to him from his ancestors, that the generation of all animals had begun upon the banks of the Ganges. For my part, said he, I have not the vanity to be of this opinion. I cannot believe that the foxes of Albion, the marmots of the Alps, and the wolves of Gaul, are descended from my country: in the like manner, I do not believe that the firs and oaks of your country descended from the palm and cocoa trees of India.

But whence are we descended, then? said the king, I do not know, said the phœnix; all I want to know is, whither the beautiful princess of Babylon and my dear Amazan may repair. I very much question, said the king, whether with his two hundred unicorns he will be able to destroy so many

ny

ny armies of three hundred thoufand men each. Why not? faid Amazan.

The king of Betica felt the force of this fublime queftion, Why not? but he imagined fublimity alone was not fufficient againft innumerable armies. I advife you, faid he, to feek the king of Ethiopia; I am related to that black prince through my Paleftines. I will give you recommendatory letters to him: as he is at enmity with the king of Egypt, he will be but too happy to be ftrengthened by your alliance. I can affift you with two thoufand fober brave men; and it will depend upon yourfelf to engage as many more of the people who refide, or rather fkip about the foot of the Pyrenees, and who are called Vafques or Vafcons. Send one of your warriors upon an unicorn with a few diamonds, there is not a Vafcon that will not quit the caftle, that is, the thatched cottage of his father, to ferve you. They are indefatigable, courageous, and agreeable; and whilft you wait their arrival, we will give you feftivals, and prepare your fhips. I cannot too much acknowledge the fervice you have done me.

Amazan enjoyed the happinefs of having recovered Formofanta, and tafted in tranquillity her converfation, and all the charms of reconciled love, which are almoft equal to growing paffion.

A troop of proud joyous Vafcons foon arrived, dancing a tambourin. The other haughty grave troop of Beticans were ready. The old fun-burnt king tenderly embraced the two lovers; he fent great quantities of arms, beds, chefts, boards, black cloaths, onions, fheep, fowls, flour, and particularly garlic, on board the fhips, in wifhing them a happy voyage, invariable love, and many victories. The fleet approached the fhore, where it is faid

that

that many ages after, the Phœnician lady Dido, sister to one Pygmalion, and wife to one Sicheus, having left the city of Tyre, came and founded the superb city of Carthage, in cutting a bull's hide into thongs, according to the testimony of the gravest authors of antiquity, who never related fables, and according to the professors who have written for young boys; though, after all, there never was a person at Tyre named Pygmalion, Dido, or Sicheus, which names are entirely Greek; and though, in fine, there was no king in Tyre in those times.

Proud Carthage was not then a sea-port; there were at that time only a few Numidians there, who dried fish in the sun. They coasted along Biza-cenes, the Syrthes, the fertile banks where since arose Cyrene and the great Cherfonese.

They at length arrived towards the first mouth of the sacred Nile. It was at the extremity of this fertile land that the Ships of all commercial nations were already received in the port of Canope, without knowing whether the god Canope had founded this port, or whether the inhabitants had manufac-tured the god; whether the star Canope had given its name to the city, or whether the city had be-stowed it upon the star: all that was known of this matter was, the city and the star were both very ancient; and this is all that can be known of the origin of things, of what nature soever they may be.

It was here that the king of Ethiopia, having ravaged all Egypt, saw the invincible Amazan and the adorable Formosanta come on shore. He took one for the god of war, and the other for the god-dess of beauty. Amazan presented to him the let-ter of recommendation from the king of Spain. The king of Ethiopia immediately entertained them with fome admirable feftivals, according to the indifpenfable cuftom of heroic times. They then conferred about their expedition to exterminate the three hundred thoufand men of the king of Egypt, the three hundred thoufand of the emperor of the Indies, and the three hundred thoufand of the great Kan of the Scythians, who laid fiege to the immenfe, proud, voluptuous city of Babylon.

The two hundred Spaniards whom Amazan had brought with him, faid, that they had nothing to do with the king of Ethiopia's fuccouring Babylon; that it was fufficient their king had ordered them to go and deliver it; and that they were formidable enough for this expedition.

The Vafcons faid, they had performed many other exploits; that they would alone defeat the Egyptians, the Indians, and the Scythians; and that they would not march with the Spaniards unlefs thefe were in the rear-guard.

The two hundred Gangarids could not refrain from laughing at the pretenfions of their allies, and they maintained, that with only one hundred unicorns they could put to flight all the kings of the earth. The beautiful Formofanta appeafed them by her prudence, and by her enchanting difcourfe. Amazan prefented to the black monarch his Gangarids, his unicorns, his Spaniards, his Vafcons, and his beautiful bird.

Every thing was foon ready to march by Memphis, Heliopolis, Arfinoe, Petra, Artemitis, Sora, and Apameus, to attack the three kings, and to profecute this memorable war, before which all the wars ever waged by man, were nothing more than mere cock-fights.

Every.

Every one knows how the king of Ethiopia became enamoured with the beautiful Formofanta,
and how he furprized her in bed when a gentle
fleep clofed her long eye lafhes. We remember
that Amazan, a witnefs of this fpectacle, thought
he faw day and night in bed together. It is no
fecret that Amazan, enraged at the infult, drew his
thundring fword, with which he cut off the perverfe
head of the infolent negro, and drove all the Ethi-
opians out of Egypt.---Are not thefe prodigies written in the book of the Chronicles of Egypt? Fame
has with her hundred tongues proclaimed the victories he gained over the three kings with his Spaniards, his Vafcons, and his unicorns. He reftored the beautiful Formofanta to her father. He fet
at liberty all his miftrefs's train, whom the king of
Egypt had reduced to flavery. The great Kan of
the Scythians declared himfelf his vaflal ; and his
marriage was confirmed with princefs Aldea. The
invincible and generous Amazan, acknowledged
the heir of the kingdom of Babylon, entered the
city in triumph with the phœnix, in the prefence
of a hundred tributary kings. The feftival of his
marriage far furpaffed that which king Belus had
given. The bull Apis was ferved up roafted at
table. The kings of Egypt and India were cup-
bearers to the married pair ; and thefe nuptials
were celebrated by five hundred capital poets of
Babylon.

Oh! Mufes, who are conftantly invoked at the
beginning of a work, I only implore you at the
end. It is needlefs to reproach me with faying
grace, without having faid *benedicite.* But, Mufes!
you will not be lefs my patroneffes. Prevent, I
befeech you, any fupplimental fcribblers fpoiling,

by their fables, the truths which I have taught
mortals in this faithful narrative; in the manner
they have falsified Candide, L'Ingenu, and the
chaste adventures of the chaste Jane, which have
been disfigured by an Ex-Capuchin, in verses worthy of Capuchins, in the Batavian editions. May
they not do this injury to my typographist, who
has a numerous family, and who is scarce capable
to obtain types, paper, and ink.

Oh! Muses, impose silence upon the detestable
Coge, chattering professor of the college of Maza-
rin, who, not contented with the moral discourses
of Belisarius and the emperor Justinian, has written
vile defamatory libels against these two great
men.

Gag that pedant Larcher, who, tho' entirely ignorant of the ancient Babylonian tongue, without
ever having travelled, as I have, upon the banks of
the Euphrates and the Tigris, has had the impudence to maintain, that the beautiful Formosanta,
daughter to the greatest king in the world, and
princess Aldea, and all the women of this respectable court, prostituted themselves to the grooms of
Asia for money, in the great temple of Babylon.
This college libertine, the declared foe of you and
shame, accuses the beautiful Egyptians of Mendes,
of being enamoured with nothing but goats; secretly proposing to himself, from this example, to
make a tour to Egypt, and have some agreeable
intrigues.

Being as little acquainted with modern history as
antiquity, he insinuates, in order to ingratiate himself with some old dowager, that our incomparable
Ninon lay at the age of fourscore, with the Abbé
Gedouin, member of the French academy, and
that

that of Inſcriptions and Belles Lettres.　He never
heard of the Abbè Chateauneuf, whom he takes for
the Abbé Gedouin.　He is as little acquainted with
Ninon as he is with the ladies of Babylon.

Muſes, daughters of heaven, your foe Larcher
goes ſtill farther; he pens long eulogiums in favour
of pederaſty, and has the inſolence to ſay, that all
the Bambins of my country are addiſted to this infamous practice.　He thinks to eſcape by encreaſ-
ing the number of the guilty.

Chaſte and noble Muſes, who equally deteſt pedantry, and pederaſty, protect me againſt M. Larcher!

And you, Mr Aliboron, who call yourſelf Freron,
as you formerly did a Jeſuit; you, whoſe Parnaſſus
is ſometimes at the *Biſſetre*, and ſometimes at the
corner alehouſe; you, who have received ſo much
juſtice upon all the ſtages of Europe, in the decent
comedy of the *Ecoſſaiſe;* you, the worthy ſon of the
prieſt Desfontaines, the offspring of his amours with
thoſe beautiful children who carry an iron, and are
blind-folded like the ſon of Venus, and who like
him fly into the air, though they never go beyond
the tops of chimneys; my dear Aliboron, for whom
I always entertained ſo much affection, and who
made me laugh for a month inceſſantly at the time
of the repreſentation of the *Ecoſſaiſe ;* I recommend
to you my Princeſs of Babylon: ſay every thing
you can againſt it, that it may be read.

I ſhall not here forget you, Eccleſiaſtical Gazetteer, illuſtrious orator of the *Convulſionnaires*, father
of the church founded by the Abbe Becherand and
Abraham Chaumeix; fail not to ſay in your writings, equally pious, eloquent, and ſenſible that the
Princeſs of Babylon is a heretic, a deiſt, and an
athieſt.

atheift.   But above all, endeavour to prevail upon
the Sieur Riballier to have the Princefs of Babylon
condemned by the Sorbonne : you will, thereby,
afford my bookfeller much pleafure, to whom I
have given this little hiftory for his new year's
gift.

                                          MEMNON

MEMNON *the* PHILOSOPHER;

OR,

HUMAN WISDOM.

MEMNON one day took it into his head to become a great philofopher. There are few men who have not, at fome time or other, conceived the fame wild project. Says Memnon to himfelf, To be a perfect philofopher, and of courfe to be perfectly happy, I have nothing to do but to diveft myfelf entirely of paffions ; and nothing is more eafy, as every body knows. In the firft place, I will never be in love ; for, when I fee a beautiful woman, I will fay to myfelf, Thefe cheeks will one day grow wrinkled, thefe eyes be encircled with vermilion, that bofom become flabby and pendant, that head bald and palfied. Now I have only to confider her at prefent in imagination, as fhe will afterwards appear ; and certainly a fair face will never turn my head.

In the fecond place, I will be always temperate. It will be in vain to tempt me with good cheer, with delicious wines, or the charms of fociety. I will have only to figure to myfelf the confequences of excefs, an aching head, a loathing ftomach, the lofs of reafon, of health, and of time : I will then only eat to fupply the wafte of nature ; my health will be always equal, my ideas pure and luminous. All

this

this is fo eafy that there is no merit in accomplifh-
ing it.

But, fays Memnon, I muft think a little of how
I am to regulate my fortune : why, my defires are
moderate, my wealth is fecurely placed with the
Receiver General of the finances of Nineveh : I
have wherewithal to live independent ; and that is
the greateft of bleffings. I fhall never be under the
cruel neceffity of dancing attendance at court ; I
will never envy any one, and nobody will envy me :
ftill all this is eafy. I have friends, continued he,
and I will preferve them, for we fhall never have
any difference ; I will never take amifs any thing
they may fay or do ; and they will behave in the
fame way to me.——There is no difficulty in all
this.

Having thus laid his little plan of philofophy in
his clofet, Memnon put his head out of the window.
He faw two women walking under the plane trees
near his houfe. The one was old and appeared
quite at her eafe. The other was young, handfome,
and feemingly much agitated : fhe fighed, fhe
wept, and feemed on that account ftill more beautiful. Our philofopher was touched, not, to be
fure, with the beauty of the lady, (he was too much
determined not to feel any uneafinefs of that kind)
but with the diftrefs which he faw her in.--- He came
down ftairs and accofted the young Ninevite in the
defign of confoling her with philofophy. That
lovely perfon related to him, with an air of the
greateft fimplicity, and in the moft affecting manner, the injuries fhe fuftained from an imaginary
uncle ; with what art he had deprived her of fome
imaginary property, and of the violence which fhe
pretended to dread from him. You appear to me
(faid fhe) a man of fuch wifdom, that if you will
con-

condefcend to come to my houfe and examine into my affairs, I am perfuaded you will be able to draw me from the cruel embarraffment I am at prefent involved in." Memnon did not hefitate to follow her, to examine her affairs philofophically, and to give her found counfel.

The afflicted lady led him into a perfumed chamber, and politely made him fit down with her on a large fopha, where they both placed themfelves oppofite to each other, in the attitude of converfation, their legs croffed ; the one eager in telling her ftory, the other liftening with devout attention. The lady fpoke with downcaft eyes, whence there fometimes fell a tear, and which, as fhe now and then ventured to raife them, always met thofe of the fage Memnon. Their difcourfe was full of tendernefs, which redoubled as often as their eyes met. Memnon took her affairs exceedingly to heart, and felt himfelf every inftant more and more inclined to oblige a perfon fo virtuous and fo unhappy.—By degrees, in the warmth of converfation, they ceafed to fit oppofite ; they drew nearer; their legs were no longer croffed. Memnon counfelled her fo clofely, and gave her fuch tender advices, that neither of them could talk any longer of bufinefs, nor well knew what they were about.

At this interefting moment, as may eafily be imagined, who fhould come in but the uncle ; he was armed from head to foot, and the firft thing he faid was, that he would immediately facrifice, as was juft, the fage Memnon and his niece ; the latter, who made her efcape, knew that he was well enough difpofed to pardon, provided a good round fum were offered to him. Memnon was obliged to purchafe his fafety with all he had about him. In thofe days people were happy in getting fo eafily

quit. America was not then difcovered, and diftref-
fed ladies were not nearly fo dangerous as they are
now.

Memnon, covered with fhame and confufion,
got home to his own houfe: there he found a card
inviting him to dinner with fome of his intimate
friends. If I remain at home alone, faid he, I fhall
have my mind fo occupied with this vexatious adventure, that I fhall not be able to eat a bit, and I
fhall bring upon myfelf fome difeafe. It will therefore be prudent in me to go to my intimate friends,
and partake with them of a frugal repaft. I fhall
forget, in the fweets of their fociety, the folly I have
this morning been guilty of.   Accordingly he at-
tends the meeting; he is difcovered to be uneafy
at fomething, and he is urged to drink and banifh
care. A little wine, drunk in moderation, comforts the heart of god and man: fo reafons Memnon the philofopher, and he becomes intoxicated.
After the repaft, play is propofed. A little play,
with one's intimate friends, is a harmlefs paftime :--
he plays and lofes all that is in his purfe, and four
times as much on his word. A difpute arifes on
fome circumftance in the game, and the difputants
grow warm: one of his intimate friends throws a
dicebox at his head, and ftrikes out one of his eyes.
The philofopher Memnon is carried home to his
houfe, drunk and pennylefs, with the lofs of an
eye.

He fleeps out his debauch, and when his head
has got a little clear, he fends his fervant to the
Receiver-General of the finances of Nineveh to
draw a little money to pay his debt of honour to
his intimate friends. The fervant returns and informs him, that the Receiver-General had that
morning been declared a fraudulent bankrupt, and
that

that by this means an hundred families are reduced to poverty and defpair. Memnon, almoft befide himfelf, puts a plafter on his eye and a petition in his pocket, and goes to court to folicit juftice from the king againft the bankrupt. In the faloon he meets a number of ladies, all in the higheft fpirits, and failing along with hoops four and twenty feet in circumference. One of them, who knew him a little, eyed him afkance, and cried aloud, "Ah! what a horrid monfter!" Another, who was better acquainted with him, thus accofts him, "Good-morrow, Mr Memnon, I hope you are very well, Mr Memnon: La! Mr Memnon, how did you lofe your eye? and turning upon her heel, fhe tripped away without waiting an anfwer. Memnon hid himfelf in a corner, and waited for the moment when he could throw himfelf at the feet of the monarch. That moment at laft arrived. Three times he kiffed the earth, and prefented his petition. His gracious majefty received him very favourably, and referred the paper to one of his fatraps, that he might give him an account of it. The fatrap takes Memnon afide, and fays to him with a haughty air and fatyrical grin, "Hark ye, you fellow with the one eye, you muft be a comical dog indeed, to addrefs yourfelf to the king rather than to me; and ftill more fo, to dare to demand juftice againft an honeft bankrupt, whom I honour with my protection, and who is nephew to the waiting-maid of my miftrefs. Proceed no further in this bufinefs, my good friend, if you wifh to preferve the eye you have left."

Memnon having thus, in his clofet, refolved to renounce women, the exceffes of the table, play and quarreling, but efpecially having determined never to go to court, had been in the fhort fpace of four

and twenty hours duped and robbed by a gentle
dame, had got drunk, had gamed, had been engaged in a quarrel, had got his eye knocked out, and
had been at court, where he was fneered at and infulted.

Petrified with aftonifhment, and his heart broken
with grief, Memnon returns homeward in defpair.
As he was about to enter his houfe, he is repulfed
by a number of officers who are carrying off his
furniture for the benefit of his creditors ; he falls
down almoft lifelefs under a plane-tree. There he
finds the fair dame of the morning, who was walking
with her dear uncle ; and both fet up a loud laugh
on feeing Memnon with his plafter. The night
approached, and Memnon made his bed on fome
ftraw near the walls of his houfe. Here the ague
feized him, and he fell affeep in one of the fits,
when a celeftial fpirit appeared to him in a dream.

It was all refplendent with light ; it had fix beautiful wings, but neither feet, nor head, nor tail, and
could be likened to nothing. " What art thou ?"
faid Memnon. " Thy good genius," replied the
fpirit. " Reftore to me then my eye, my health,
my fortune, my reafon," faid Memnon ; and he
related how he had loft them all in one day.———
" Thefe are adventures which never happen to us
in the world we inhabit," faid the fpirit. " And
what world do you inhabit ?" faid the man of affliction. " My native country," replied the other,
" is five hundred millions of leagues diftant from
the fun, in a little ftar near Sirius, which you fee
from hence." " Charming country !" faid Memnon :
" And are there indeed with you no jades to dupe
a poor devil, no intimate friends that win his money and knock out an eye to him, no fraudulent
bankrupts, no fatraps, that make a jeft of you while
they

they refuſe you juſtice?" "No," ſaid the inhabitant of the ſtar, "we have nothing of what you
talk of; we are never duped by women, becauſe
we have none among us; we never commit ex-
ceſſes at table, becauſe we neither eat nor drink;
we have no bankrupts, becauſe with us there is
neither ſilver nor gold; our eyes cannot be knocked
out, becauſe we have not bodies in the form of
yours; and ſatraps never do us injuſtice, becauſe in
our world we are all equal." "Pray, my Lord,"
then ſaid Memnon, "without women and without
eating how do you ſpend your time?" "In watching," ſaid the genius, "over the other worlds that
are entruſted to us; and I am now come to give
you conſolation." "Alas!" replied Memnon,
"why did you not come yeſterday to hinder me
from committing ſo many indiſcretions?" "I was
with your elder brother Haſſan," ſaid the celeſtial
being. "He is ſtill more to be pitied than you
are. His moſt gracious Majeſty, the Sultan of the
Indies, in whoſe court he has the honour to ſerve,
has cauſed both his eyes to be put out for ſome
ſmall indiſcretion; and he is now in a dungeon,
his hands and feet loaded with chains." "'Tis a
happy thing truly," ſaid Memnon, "to have a
good genius in one's family, when out of two brothers one is blind of an eye, the other blind of both;
one ſtretched upon ſtraw, the other in a dungeon."
"Your fate will ſoon change," ſaid the animal of
the ſtar. "It is true, you will never recover your
eye but, except that, you may be ſufficiently happy if you never again take it into your head to
be a perfect philoſopher." "Is it then impoſſible?"
ſaid Memnon. "As impoſſible as to be perfectly
wiſe, perfectly ſtrong, perfectly powerful, perfectly
happy. We ourſelves are very far from it. There

is

is a world indeed where all this takes place ; but, in the hundred thousand millions of worlds difperf-ed over the regions of fpace, every thing goes on by degrees. There is lefs philofophy and lefs en-joyment in the fecond than in the firft, lefs in the third than in the fecond, and fo forth till the laft in the fcale, where all are completely fools." " I am afraid," faid Memnon, " that our little terraqueous globe here is the madhoufe of thofe hundred thou-fand millions of worlds, of which your Lordfhip does me the honour to fpeak." " Not quite," faid the fpirit, " but very nearly : every thing muft be in its proper place." " But are thofe poets and phi-lofophers wrong, then, who tell us that every thing is for the beft ?" " No, they are right, when we confider things in relation to the gradation of the whole univerfe." " Oh ! I fhall never believe it till I recover my eye again," faid the poor Memnon.

PLA

PLATO's DREAM.

PLATO was a great dreamer, as many others have been since his time. He dreamt that mankind were formerly double; and that, as a punishment for their crimes, they were divided into male and female.

He undertook to prove that there can be no more than five perfect worlds, because there are but five regular mathematical bodies. His republic was one of his principal dreams. He dreamt, moreover, that watching arises from sleep, and sleep from watching; and that a person who should attempt to look at an eclipse, otherwise than in a pail of water, would infallibly lose his sight. Dreams were, at that time, in great reputation.

Here follows one of his dreams, which is not one of the least interesting. He thought that the great Demiurgos, the eternal geometer, having peopled the immensity of space with innumerable globes, was willing to make a trial of the knowledge of the genii who had been witnesses of his works. He gave to each of them a small portion of matter to arrange, nearly in the same manner as Phidias and Zeuxis would have given their scholars a statue to

carve,

carve, or a picture to paint, if we may be allowed to compare small things to great.

Demogorgon had for his lot the lump of mould, which we call the Earth; and having formed it, such as it now appears, he thought he had executed a master-piece. He imagined he had silenced Envy herself, and expected to receive the highest panegyrics, even from his brethren: but how great was his surprise, when, at his next appearing among them, they received him with a general hiss.

One among them, more satirical than the rest, accosted him thus: " Truly you have performed mighty feats! you have divided your world into two parts; and, lest the one should have any communication with the other, you have carefully placed a vast collection of waters between the two hemispheres. The inhabitants must perish with cold under both your poles, and be scorched to death under the line. You have, in your great prudence, formed immense deserts of sands, for all who travel over them to die with hunger and thirst. I have no fault to find with your cows, your sheep, your cocks, and your hens; but can never be reconciled to your serpents and your spiders. Your onions and your artichokes are very good things, but I cannot conceive what whim took you in the head to scatter such an heap of poisonous plants over the face of your earth, unless it was to poison its inhabitants. Moreover, if I am not mistaken, you have created about thirty different kinds of monkeys, a still greater number of dogs, and only four or five species of the human race. It is true, indeed, you have bestowed on the latter of these animals a somewhat, by you called Reason; but, in truth, this same reason is a very ridiculous thing, and borders very near upon folly. Besides,

you

you do not feem to have fhown any very great regard to this two-legged creature, feeing you have
made him with fo few means of defence; fubjected
him to fo many diforders, and provided him with fo
few remedies; and formed him with fuch a multitude
of paffions, and fo fmall a portion of wifdom or prudence to refift them. You certainly was not willing that there fhould remain any great number of
thefe animals on the earth at once; for, without
reckoning the dangers to which you have expofed
them, you have fo ordered matters, that, taking
every day through the year, the fmall-pox will re-
gularly carry off the tenth part of the fpecies, and
its fifter malady will taint the fprings of life in the
nine remaining parts; and then, as if this was not
fufficient, you have fo difpofed things, that one-
half of thofe who furvive will be occupied in going
to law with each other, or cutting one another's
throats. Now, they muft doubtlefs have infinite
obligations to you, and it muft be owned you have
executed a mafter-piece."

Demogorgon blufhed: he was fenfible there was
much moral and phyfical evil in this affair; but
ftill he infifted there was more good than ill in it.
"It is an eafy matter to find fault, good folks!"
faid the genii; "but do you imagine it is fo eafy
to form an animal, who, having the gift of reafon
and free-will, fhall not fometimes abufe his liberty?
Do you think, that, in rearing between nine and
ten thoufand different plants, it is fo eafy to prevent
fome few from having noxious qualities? Do you
fuppofe, that with a certain quantity of water, fand,
and mud, you could make a globe that fhould have
neither feas nor deferts? As to you, my fneering
friend, I think you have juft finifhed the planet
Mars. Let us fee now what figure you make with

your two great belts, and your long nights, without
a moon to enlighten them. Let us examine your
world, and fee whether the inhabitants you have
made are exempt from follies or difeafes."

Accordingly the genii fell to examining the planet Mars, when the laugh went ftrongly againft
the laugher. The ferious genii who had made the
planet Saturn, did not efcape without his fhare of
cenfure, and his brother operators, the makers of
Jupiter, Mercury, and Venus, had each in their
turns fome reproaches to undergo.

Several large volumes, and a great number of
pamphlets, were written on this occafion; fmart
fayings and witty repartees flew about on all fides;
they railed againft and ridiculed each other; and,
in fhort, the difputes were carried on with all the
warmth of party heat, when the eternal Demiurgos
thus impofed filence on them all: "In your feveral performances there is both good and bad, becaufe you have a great fhare of underftanding, but
at the fame time fall fhort of perfection. Your
works will not endure above an hundred million of
years, after which you will acquire more knowledge, and perform better. It belongs to me alone
to create things perfect and immortal."

This was the doctrine Plato taught his difciples.
One of them, when he had finifhed his harangue,
cried out, *and fo then you awoke.*

B A B A B E C.

WHEN I was in the city of Benarez, on the borders of the Ganges, the country of the ancient Brachmans, I endeavoured to inftruct myfelf in their religion and manners. I underftood the Indian language tolerably well. I heard a great deal, and remarked every thing. I lodged at the houfe of my correfpondent Omri, who was the moft worthy man I ever knew. He was of the religion of the Bramins : I have the honour to be a Muffulman. We never exchanged one word higher than another about Mahomet or Brama. We performed our ablutions each on his own fide ; we drank of the fame fherbet, and we ate of the fame rice, as if we had been two brothers.

One day we went together to the pagoda of Gavani. There we faw feveral bands of Faquirs; fome of whom were Janguis. that is to fay, contemplative Faquirs ; and others difciples of the ancient Gymnofophifts, who led an active life. They have all a learned language peculiar to themfelves; it is that of the moft ancient Brachmans ; and they have a book written in this language, which they call the Hanfcrit. It is, beyond all contradiction, the moft ancient book in all Afia, not excepting the Zend.

I happened to crofs a Faquir, who was reading in this book. Ah! wretched Infidel! cried he, thou

haft

haft made me lofe a number of vowels that I was
counting, which will occafion my foul to pafs into
the body of a hare inftead of that of a parrot, with
which I had before the greateft reafon to flatter
myfelf.   I gave him a roupee to comfort him for
the accident.   In going a few paces farther, I had
the misfortune to fneeze ; the noife I made rouzed
a Faquir who was in a trance.   Heavens! cried he,
what a dreadful noife! Where am I? I can no longer fee the tip of my nofe * ! the heavenly light has
difappeared.   If I am the caufe, faid I, of your feeing further than the length of your nofe, here is a
roupee to repair the injury I have done you : fquint
again, and refume the heavenly light.

    Having thus brought myfelf off difcreetly enough,
I paffed over to the fide of the Gymnofophifts, feveral of whom brought me a parcel of mighty pretty nails to drive into my arms and thighs, in honour of Brama.   I bought their nails, and made ufe
of them to faften down my boxes.   Others were
dancing upon their hands, others cut capers on the
flack rope, and others went always upon one foot.
There were fome who dragged a heavy chain about
with them, and others carried a pack-faddle ; fome
had their heads always in a bufhel ; the beft people
in the world to live with.   My friend Omri carried me to the cell of one of the moft famous of thefe.
His name was Bababec : he was as naked as he was
born, and had a great chain about his neck, that
weighed upwards of fixty pounds.   He fat on a
wooden chair, very neatly decorated with little
points of nails, that run into his pofteriors ; and

---

* When the Faquirs have a mind to fee the heavenly light,
which very frequently happens with them, they turn their eyes
downwards towards the tip of their nofe.

you would have thought he had been fitting on a velvet cushion. Numbers of women flocked to him to consult him : he was the oracle of all the families in the neighbourhood ; and was, truly speaking, in great reputation. I was witness to a long conversation that Omri had with him. Do you think, father, said my friend, that, after having gone through seven metempsichofes, I may at length arrive at the habitation of Brama? That is as it may happen, said the Faquir. What sort of life do you lead? I endeavour, answered Omri, to be a good subject, a good husband, a good father, and a good friend : I lend money without interest to the rich who want it, and I give it to the poor ; I preserve peace amongst my neighbours. But have you ever run nails into your backside? demanded the Bramin. Never, reverend father. I am sorry for it, replied the father ; very sorry for it, indeed : It is a thousand pities ; but you will certainly not reach above the nineteenth heaven. No higher! said Omri. In troth, I am very well contented with my lot. What is it to me whether I go into the nineteenth or the twentieth, provided I do my duty in my pilgrimage, and am well received at the end of my journey? Is it not as much as one can desire, to live with a fair character in this world, and be happy with Brama in the next? And pray what heaven do you think of going to, good Master Bababec, with your nails and your chain? Into the thirty-fifth, said Bababec. I admire your modesty, replied Omri, to pretend to be better lodged than me : this is surely the mere effects of an exceffive ambition. How can you, who condemn others that covet honours in this world, arrogate such distinguished one's to yourself in the next? What right have you to be better treated than me? Know,

that

that I beſtow more alms to the poor in ten days, than the nails you run into your backſide coſt for ten years! What is it to Brama, that you paſs the whole day ſtark naked with a chain about your neck? This is doing a notable ſervice to your country, doubtleſs! I have a thouſand times more eſteem for the man who ſows pulſe or plants trees for all your tribe, than they who look at the tip of their noſes, or carry a pack-ſaddle to ſhew their magnanimity. Having finiſhed this ſpeech, Omri ſoftened his voice, embraced the Bramin, and, with an endearing ſweetneſs, beſought him to throw aſide his nails and his chain, to go home with him, and live with decency and comfort. The Faquir was perſuaded: he was waſhed clean, rubbed with eſſences and perfumes, and clad in a decent habit: he lived a fortnight in this manner, behaved with prudence and wiſdom, and acknowledged that he was a thouſand times more happy than before: but he loſt his credit among the people; the women no longer crouded to conſult him: he therefore quitted the houſe of the friendly Omri, and returned to his nails and his chain, to regain his reputation.

A

IN the year 1723, there was a Chinefe in Holland, who was both a learned man and a merchant, two things that ought by no means to be incompatible; but which, thanks to the profound refpect that is fhewn to money, and the little regard that the human fpecies do, and ever will, pay to merit, are become fo among us.

This Chinefe, who fpoke a little Dutch, happened to be in a bookfeller's fhop at the fame time that fome literati were affembled there. He afked for a book; they offered him Boffuet's Univerfal Hiftory, badly tranflated. At the title Univerfal Hiftory, how pleafed am I, cried the Oriental, to have met with this book; I fhall now fee what is faid of our great empire; of a nation that has fubfifted for upwards of fifty thoufand years; of that long dynafty of emperors who have governed us for fuch a number of ages. I fhall fee what thefe Europeans think of the religion of our literati, and of that pure and fimple worfhip we pay to the Supreme Being. What a pleafure will it be to me to find how they fpeak of our arts, many of which are of a more antient date with us than the æras of all the kingdoms of Europe! I fancy the author will be greatly miftaken in relation to the war we had about twenty-two thoufand five hundred and fifty-two years ago, with the martial people of Tonquin

quin and Japan, as well as the solemn ambaffy that
the powerful emperor of Mogulitan fent, to requeft
a body of laws from us in the year of the world
5000000000000079123450000. Lord blefs you,
faid one of the literati, there is hardly any mention
made of that nation in this book, it is too inconfiderable. Almoft the whole of it is taken up with
an account of the firft nation in the world, the only
nation, thofe great people the Jews.

The Jews! faid the Chinefe, thofe people then
muft certainly be mafters of three parts of the globe
at leaft. They hope to be fo one day, anfwered
the other; but at prefent they are thofe pedlars
that you fee going about here with toys and nick-
nacks, and that fometimes do us the honour to clip
our gold and filver. Surely you are not ferious,
faid the Chinefe, could thofe people ever have been
in poffeffion of a vaft empire? Here I joined in the
converfation, and told him, that for a few years
they were in poffeffion of a fmall country to themfelves; but that we were not to judge of a people
from the extent of their dominions, any more than
of a man by his riches.

But does not this book take notice of fome other
nations? demanded the man of letters. Undoubtedly, replied a learned gentleman who ftood at my
elbow; it treats largely of a fmall country about
fixty leagues wide, called Egypt, in which it is faid
that there is a lake of one hundred and fifty leagues
in circumference, made by the hands of man. My
god! exclaimed the Chinefe, a lake of one hundred and fifty leagues in circumference within a
fpot of ground only fixty leagues wide, this is very
curious! The inhabitants of that country continued
the doctor, were all fages. What happy times were
thofe, cry'd the Chinefe, but is that all? No, reply'd

the

the other, there is mention made of thoſe famous people the Greeks. Greeks! Greeks! ſaid the Aſiatic, who are thoſe Greeks? Why, reply'd the philoſopher, they were maſters of a little province, about the two hundredth part as large as China, but whoſe fame ſpread over the whole world. Indeed! ſaid the Chineſe, with an air of openneſs and ingenuouſneſs; I declare I never heard the leaſt mention of theſe people, either in the Mogul's country, in Japan, or in Great Tartary.

Oh, the barbarian! the ignorant creature! cry'd out our ſage, very politely. Why then, I ſuppoſe you know nothing of Epaminondas the Theban, nor of the Piræan Haven, nor the names of Achilles's two horſes, nor of Silenus's aſs? You have never heard ſpeak of Jupiter, nor of Diogenes, nor of Lais, nor of Cybele, nor of ——

I am very much afraid, ſaid the learned Oriental, interrupting him, that you know nothing of that eternally memorable adventure of the famous Xixofon Concochigramki, nor of the myſteries of the great Fi-pſi hi-hi. But pray tell me what other unknown things does this Univerſal Hiſtory treat of? Upon this my learned neighbour harangued for a quarter of an hour together about the Roman republic, and when he came to Julius Cæſar, the Chineſe ſtopped him, and very gravely ſaid, I think I have heard of him, was he not a Turk*?

How! cry'd our ſage in a fury, don't you ſo much as know the difference between Pagans, Chriſtians, and Mahometans? Did you never hear of Conſtantine? Do you know nothing of the hiſtory of the

---

* Not long ſince the Chineſe took all the Europeans to be Mahometans.

popes?

popes? We have heard fomething confufedly of one Mahomet, reply'd the Afiatic.

It is impoffible, fure, faid the other, but you muft have heard at leaft of Luther, Zuinglius, Bellarmin, and Oecolampadius. I fhall never remember all thofe names, faid the Chinefe; and fo faying he quitted the fhop, and went to fell a large quantity of Pekoa tea, and fine callicoe, with which he bought two fine girls, and a young lad, and fet fail for his own country, adoring *Tien*, and recommending himfelf to Confucius.

As to myfelf, the converfation I had been witnefs to plainly difcovered to me the nature of vainglory; and I could not forbear exclaiming, Since Cæfar and Jupiter are names unknown to the fineft, moft ancient, moft extenfive, moft populous, and moft civilized kingdom in the univerfe, it becomes ye well, O ye rulers of petty ftates! ye pulpit orators of a narrow parifh, or a little town! ye doctors of Salamanca, or of Bourges! ye trifling authors, and ye heavy commentators!—It becomes you well, indeed, to afpire at reputation.

The

THE adventure of the youthful Ruftan is generally known throughout the whole province of Candahar. He was the only fon of a mirza of that country : the title of Mirza there is much the fame with that of Marquis amongft us, or that of Baron amongft the Germans. The mirza his father had a handfome fortune. Young Ruftan was to be married to a mirzaffe, or young lady of his own rank ; the two families earneftly defired their union. Ruftan was to become the comfort of his parents, to make his wife happy, and to live bleft in her poffeffion.

But he had unfortunately feen the princefs of Cachemire at the fair of Kaboul, which is the moft confiderable fair in the world, and much more frequented than thofe of Baffora and Aftracan : the occafion that brought the old prince of Cachemire to the fair with his daughter was as follows :

He had loft the two moft precious curiofities of his treafury ; one of them was a diamond as thick as a man's thumb, upon which the figure of his daughter was engraved by an art which was then poffeffed by the Indians, and has fince been loft ; the other was a javelin, which went of itfelf where-

ever

ever its owner thought proper to fend it: this is nothing very extraordinary amongft us, but it was thought fo at Cachemire.

A faquir belonging to his highnefs ftole thefe two curiofities; he carried them to the princefs: Keep thefe two curiofities with the utmoft care, faid he, your deftiny depends upon them. Having fpoke thus, he departed, and was not afterwards feen. The duke of Cachemire, in defpair, refolved to vifit the fair of Kaboul, in order to fee whether there might not, amongft the merchants, who go thither from all the quarters of the world, be fome one poffeffed of his diamond and his weapon. He carried his daughter with him in all his travels. She carried her diamond well faftened to her girdle; but the javelin, which fhe could not fo eafily hide, fhe had carefully locked up at Cachemire in a large cheft.

Ruftan and fhe faw each other at Kaboul; they loved one another with all the fincerity of perfons of their age, and all the tendernefs of affection natural to thofe of their country. The princefs gave Ruftan her diamond as a pledge of her love, and he promifed at his departure to go incognito to Cachemire, in order to pay her a vifit.

The young mirza had two favourites, who ferved him as fecretaries, grooms, ftewards, and valets de chambre; the name of one was Topaze; he was handfome, well-fhaped, fair as a Circaffian beauty, as mild and ready to ferve as an Armenian, and as wife as a Guebra. The name of the other was Ebene; he was a very beautiful negro, more active and induftrious than Topaze, and one that thought nothing difficult. The young mirza communicated his intention of travelling to thefe. Topaze endeavoured to diffuade him from it with the

the circumfpect zeal of a fervant who was unwill-
ing to offend him ; he reprefented to him the great
danger to which he expofed himfelf; he afked him
how he could leave two families in defpair ? how
he could pierce the hearts of his parents? He fhook
the refolution of Ruftan ; but Ebene confirmed it
anew, and obviated all his objections.

The young man was not furnifhed with money
to defray the charge of fo long a voyage ; the prudent Topaze would not have lent him any ; Ebene
fupplied him ; he with great addrefs ftole his mafter's diamond, made a falfe one exactly like it, which
he put in its place, and pledged the true one to an
Armenian for feveral thoufand roupees.

As foon as the marquis was poffeffed of his rou-
pies, all things were in readinefs for his departure;
an elephant was loaden with his baggage, his attendants mounted on horfeback. Topaze faid to
his mafter, I have taken the liberty to expoftulate
with you upon your enterprize, but, after expoftu-
lating, it is my duty to obey ; I am devoted to you,
I love you, I will follow you to the extremity of
the earth ; but let us by the way confult the oracle
that is but two parafonges diftant from here : Ruftan confented. The anfwer returned by the oracle
was, " If you go to the eaft you will be at the
weft." Ruftan could not guefs the meaning of
this anfwer. Topaze maintained that it boded no
good. Ebene, always complaifant to his mafter,
perfuaded him that it was highly favourable.

There was another oracle at Kaboul ; they went
to it ; the oracle of Kaboul made anfwer in thefe
words, " If you poffefs, you will ceafe to poffefs ;
" if you are conqueror, you will not conquer ; if
" you are Ruftan, you will ceafe to be fo." This
oracle appeared ftill more unintelligible than the
former.

former. Take care of yourself, said Topaze : fear
nothing, said Ebene ; and this minifter, as may well
be imagined, was always thought in the right by
his mafter, whofe paffions and hopes he encouraged. Having left Kaboul, they paffed through a
vaft foreft ; they feated themfelves upon the grafs,
in order to take a repaft and left their horfes graz-
ing. The attendants were preparing to unload the
elephant which carried the dinner, the table, cloth,
plates, &c. when, all on a fudden, Topaze and
Ebene were perceived by the little caravan to be
miffing. They were called, the foreft refounded
with the names of Topaze and Ebene ; the lac-
quies feek them on every fide, and fill the foreft
with their cries ; they return without having feen
any thing, and without having received any anfwer.
We have, faid they to Ruftan, found nothing but
a vulture that fought with an eagle, and ftript it of
all its feathers. The mention of this combat excited the curiofity of Ruftan ; he went on foot to
the place, he perceived neither vulture nor eagle ;
but he faw his elephant, which was ftill loaden with
baggage, attacked by a huge rhinoceros : one ftruck
with its horn, the other with its probofcis. The
rhinoceros defifted upon feeing Ruftan ; his elephant was brought back, but his horfes were not
to be found. Strange things happen in forefts
to travellers, cried Ruftan. The fervants were
in great confternation, and the mafter in defpair,
for having at once loft his horfes, his dear negro,
and the wife Topaze, for whom he ftill had a
friendfhip, though he always differed from him in
opinion.

The hopes of being foon at the feet of the beauteous princefs of Cachemire confoled the mirza,
when he met with a huge ftreaked afs, which a vigorous

gorous two-handed country clown beat with an
oaken cudgel. The affes of this fort are extremely
beautiful, very fcarce, and beyond expreffion fwift
in running. The afs returned the reiterated blows
of the clown by kicks which might have rooted up
an oak. The young mirza, as was reafonable, took
upon him the defence of the afs, which was a
charming creature. The clown betook himfelf to
flight, crying to the afs, You fhall pay for this.

The afs thanked her deliverer in her own language, approached him, let herfelf be careffed, and
careffed him in her turn. After dinner, Ruftan
mounts her, and takes the road to Cachemire with
his fervants, who follow him fome on foot and fome
upon the elephant. Scarce was he got upon his
afs, when that animal turned towards Kaboul, inftead of proceeding to Cachemire. It was to no
purpofe for her mafter to turn the bridle, to kick,
to prefs the fides of the beaft with his knees, to
fpur, to flacken the bridle, to pull towards him. to
whip both on the right and the left, the obftinate
animal perfifted to run towards Kaboul.

Ruftan fweated, fretted, and raved, when he
met with a dealer in camels, who faid to him, Mafter, you have got a very malicious beaft, which
carries you where you do not chufe to go; if you
will give it to me, I will give you the choice of four
of my camels. Ruftan thanked providence for
having thrown fo good a bargain in his way. Topaze was very much in the wrong, faid he, to tell
me that my journey would prove unprofperous. He
mounts the handfomeft camel, the other three follow; he rejoins his caravan, and fees himfelf in the
road to his happinefs.

Scarce had he walked four parafonges, when he
was ftopped by a deep, broad, and impetuous torrent,

rent, which rolled upon rocks white with foam; the two banks were frightful precipices, which dazzled the fight and made the blood run cold: to pafs was impracticable; it was impoffible to go to the right or the left. I am beginning to be afraid, faid Ruftan, that Topaze was in the right in blaming my journey, and that I was in the wrong in undertaking it; if he was ftill here he might give me good advice; if I had Ebene with me, he would comfort me and find expedients; but every thing fails me. This perplexity was increafed by the confternation of his attendants: the night was dark, and they paffed it in lamentations. At laft fatigue and dejection made the amorous traveller fall afleep. He awakes at day-break, and fees a beautiful marble bridge built upon the torrent, which reached from fhore to fhore.

Nothing was heard but exclamations, cries of aftonifhment, and joy. Is it poffible? Is this a dream? What a prodigy is this! What an echantment! Shall we venture to pafs? The whole company kneeled, rofe up, went to the bridge, kiffed the ground, looked up to heaven, ftretched out their hands, fet their feet on it with trembling, went to and fro, fell into ecftacies; and Ruftan faid, At laft heaven favours me; Topaze did not know what he was faying; oracles were favourable to me; Ebene was in the right, but why is he not here?

Scarce had the company got beyond the torrent, when the bridge funk into the water with a prodigious noife. So much the better, fo much the better, cried Ruftan, praifed be God, bleffed be heaven; it would not have me return to my country, where I fhould be nothing more than a gentleman; the intention of heaven is, that I fhould wed

her

her I love; I fhall become prince of Cachemire; thus in " poffeffing" my miftrefs I fhall ceafe to " poffefs" my little marquifate at Candahar. " I fhall be Ruftan, and I fhall not be Ruftan," becaufe I fhall become a great prince: thus is a great part of the oracle clearly explained in my favour, the reft will be explained in the fame manner, I am too happy: but why is not Ebene with me? I regret him a thoufand times more than Topaze.

He proceeded a few parafonges farther with the greateft alacrity imaginable; but at the clofe of day, a chain of mountains, more rugged than a counterfcarp, and higher than the tower of Babel would have been if it had been finifhed, ftopped the paffage of the caravan, which was feized with dread.

All the company cried out, It is the will of God that we perifh here; he broke the bridge merely to take from us all hopes of returning; he raifed the mouutain for no other reafon but to deprive us of all means of advancing. Oh, Ruftan! oh, unhappy marquis! we fhall never fee Cachemire; we fhall never return to the land of Candahar.

The moft poignant anguifh, the moft infupportable dejection, fucceeded in the foul of Ruftan to the immoderate joy which he had felt, to the hopes with which he had intoxicated himfelf. He was by no means difpofed to interpret the prophecies in his favour. Oh, heavens! oh, God of my fathers! faid he, muft I then lofe my friend Topaze!

As he pronounced thefe words, fetching deep fighs, and fhedding tears in the midft of his difconfolate followers, the bafis of the mountain opens, a long gallery appears to the dazzled eyes in a vault lighted with a hundred thoufand torches: Ruftan immediately begins to lament, and his peo-

ple to throw themfelves upon their knees, and to
fall upon their backs in aftonifhment, and cry out,
A miracle! and fay, Ruftan is the favourite of
Witfnow, the well-beloved of Brama; he will become the mafter of mankind.   Ruftan believed it,
lie was quite befide himfelf, he was raifed above
himfelf.   Alas, Ebene, faid he, my dear Ebene,
where are you? Why are you not witnefs of all
thefe wonders? How did I lofe you? Beauteous
princefs of Cachemire, when fhall I again behold
your charms!

He advances with his attendants, his elephants,
and his camels, under the hollow of the mountain;
at the end of which he enters into a meadow enamelled with flowers and encompaffed with rivulets:
at the extremity of the meadows are walks of trees
to the end of which the eye cannot reach, and at
the end of thefe alleys is a river, on the fides of
which are a thoufand pleafure houfes with delicious
gardens.   He every where hears concerts of vocal
and inftrumental mufic; he fees dances; he makes
hafte to go upon one of the bridges of the river;
he afks the firft man he meets what fine country
that is?

He whom he addreffed himfelf to anfwered, You
are in the province of Cachemire; you fee the inhabitants immerfed in joy and pleafures; we cele-
brate the marriage of our beauteous princefs, who
is going to be married to the lord Barbabou, to
whom his father promifed her; may God perpetu-
ate their felicity! At thefe words Ruftan fainted
away, and the Cachemirian lord thought he was
troubled with the falling ficknefs; he caufed him
to be carried to his houfe, where he remained a
long time infenfible.   He fent in fearch of the two
moft able phyficians in that part of the country:
they

they felt the patient's pulfe, who having fomewhat recovered his fpirits, fobbed, rolled his eyes, and cried from time to time, Topaze, Topaze, you were entirely in the right !

One of the two phyficians faid to the Cachemi-rian lord, I perceive, by this young man's accent, that he is from Candahar, and that the air of this country is hurtful to him ; he muft be fent home : I perceive by his eyes that he has loft his fenfes ; entruft me with him, I will carry him back to his own country, and cure him. The other phyfician maintained, that grief was his only diforder ; and that it was proper to carry him to the wedding of the princefs, and make him dance. Whilft they were in confultation, the patient recovered his health ; the two phyficians were difmiffed, and Ruftan remained alone with his hoft.

My lord, faid he, I afk your pardon for having been fo free as to faint in your prefence ; I know it to be a breach of politenefs ; I intreat you to accept of my elephant, as an acknowledgment of the kindnefs you have fhewed me. He then relat-ed to him all his adventure, taking particular care to conceal from him the occafion of his journey. But, in the name of Witfnow and Brama, faid he to him, tell me who is this happy Barbabou, who is to marry the princefs of Cachemire ; why has her father chofen him for his fon-in-law, and why has the princefs accepted of him for an hufband ?

Sir, anfwered the Cachemirian, the princefs has by no means accepted of Barbabou ; fhe is, on the contrary, in tears, whilft the whole province joyful-ly celebrates her marriage : fhe has fhut herfelf up in a tower of her palace ; fhe does not chufe to fee any of the rejoicings made upon the occafion. Ruftan, at hearing this, perceived himfelf revive ;

the

the bloom of his complexion, which grief had caufed to fade, appeared again upon his counte, nance. Tell me, I intreat you, continued he, why the prince of Cachemire is obftinately bent upon giving his daughter to a Barbabou whom fhe does not like ?

This is the fact, anfwered the Cachemirian : Do you know that our auguft prince loft a large dia-mond and a javelin which he had a great value for? Ah! I very well know that, faid Ruftan. Know then, faid his hoft, that our prince being in def-pair at not having heard of his two precious curio-fities, after having caufed them to be fought for all over the world, promifed his daughter to whoever fhould bring him either the one or the other : a lord Barbabou came, who had got the diamond, and he is to marry the princefs to-morrow.

Ruftan turned pale, ftammered out a compliment, took his leave of his hoft, and galloped upon his dromedary to the capital city, where the ceremony was performed. He arrives at the palace of the prince, he tells him he has fomething of import-ance to communicate to him, he demands an au-dience ; he is told that the prince is taken up with the preparations for the wedding. It is for that very reafon, faid he, that I am defirous of fpeaking to him : fuch is his importunity, that he is at laft admitted. Prince, faid he, may God crown all your days with glory and magnificence! your fon-in-law is a knave.

What! a knave! how dare you fpeak in fuch terms ? Is that a proper way of fpeaking to a duke of Cachemire of a fon-in-law whom he has made choice of ? Yes, he is a knave, continued Ruftan ; and to prove it to your highnefs, I have brought you back your diamond.

The

The duke, furprized at what he heard, compared the two diamonds; and as he was no judge of precious ftones, he could not determine which was the true one. Here are two diamonds, faid he, and I have but one daughter; I am in a ftrange perplexity.

He fent for Barbabou, and afked him if he had not impofed upon him. Barbabou fwore he had bought his diamond from an Armenian: the other did not tell him who he had his from; but he propofed an expedient, which was, that his highnefs would pleafe to permit him to engage his rival in fingle combat. It is not enough for your fon-in-law to give a diamond, faid he, he fhould alfo give proofs of valour. Do not you think it juft that he who kills his rival fhould marry the princefs? Undoubtedly, anfwered the prince; it will be a fine fight for the court; fight directly: the conqueror fhall take the arms of the conquered, according to the cuftoms of Cachemire, and he fhall marry my daughter.

The two pretenders to the princefs immediately go down into the court. Upon the ftairs there was a pie and a raven; the raven cried, Fight, fight; the pie cried, Don't fight. This made the prince laugh; the two rivals fcarce took any notice of it; they begin the combat; all the courtiers made a circle round them. The princefs, who kept herfelf conftantly fhut up in her tower, did not chufe to behold this fight; fhe never dreamt of her lover's being at Cachemire, and fhe hated Barbabou to fuch a degree, that fhe could not bear the fight of him. The combat had the happieft event imaginable; Barbabou was killed outright; and this greatly rejoiced the people, becaufe he was ugly, and Ruftan was very handfome; the favour of the
public

public is almoſt always determined by this circum-
ſtance.

The conqueror put on the coat of mail, ſcarf, and
the caſque of the conquered, and came, followed
by the whole court, to preſent himſelf under the
windows of his miſtreſs. The multitude cried a-
loud, Beautiful princeſs, come and ſee your handſome lover, who has killed his ugly rival. Theſe
words we re-echoed by her women. The princeſs
unluckily looked out of the window, and ſeeing the
armour of a man ſhe hated, ſhe ran like one frantic to her ſtrong box, and took out the fatal javelin, which ſlew to pierce Ruſtan, notwithſtanding
his cuiraſs : he cried out loudly, and at this cry the
princeſs thought ſhe again knew the voice of her
unhappy lover.

She ran down ſtairs, with her hair diſhevelled,
and death in her eyes as well as her heart. Ruſtan
had alreeady fallen, all bloody, into the arms of his
father : ſhe ſees him. Oh, moment! oh, ſight! oh,
diſcovery of inexpreſſible grief, tenderneſs, and
horror! She throws herſelf upon him, and embraces him : You receive, ſaid ſhe, the firſt and laſt
kiſſes of your miſtreſs and your murderer. She
pulls the dart from the wound, plunges it in her
heart, and dies upon the body of the lover whom
ſhe adores. The father, terrified, in deſpair, and
ready to die like his daughter, tries in vain to
bring her to life ; ſhe was no more : he curſes the
fatal dart, breaks it to pieces, throws away the two
fatal diamonds ; and whilſt he prepared the funeral of his daughter, inſtead of her marriage, he
cauſed Ruſtan, who weltered in his blood, and
had ſtill ſome remains of life, to be carried to his
palace.

He was put into bed : the firſt objects he ſaw on
each

each fide of his death-bed were Topaze and Ebene. This furprize made him in fome degree recover his ftrength. Cruel men, faid he, why did you aban‑ don me? Perhaps the princefs would ftill be alive if you had been with the unhappy Ruftan. I have not forfaken you a moment, faid Topaze: I have been always with you, faid Ebene. Ah! what do you fay? why do you infult me in my laft mo‑ ments? anfwered Ruftan with a languifhing voice. You may believe me, faid Topaze; you know I never approved of this fatal journey, the dreadful confequences of which I forefaw. I was the eagle that fought with the vulture and ftript it of its fea‑ thers; I was the elephant that carried away the baggage, in order to force you to return to your own country; I was the ftreaked afs that carried you, whether you would or no, to your father; it was I that made your horfes go aftray; it was I that caufed the torrent that prevented your paffage; it was I that raifed the mountain which ftopped up a road fo fatal to you: I was the phyfician that advifed you to return to your own country; I was the pie that cried out to you not to fight.

And I, faid Ebene, was the vulture that he ftript of his feathers, the rhinoceros who gave him a hun‑ dred ftrokes with my horn, the clown that beat the ftreaked afs, the merchant who made you a prefent of camels to haften to your deftruction; I dug the cavern that you croffed, I am the phyfician that encouraged you to walk, the raven that cried out to you to combat.

Alas! faid Topaze, " Remember the oracles; " If you go to the eaft you will be at the weft." Yes, faid Ebene, here the dead are buried with their faces turned to the weft: the oracle was plain enough, though you did not underftand it. " You

poffef‑

poffeffed and you did not poffefs ;" for you had the
diamond, but it was a falfe one, though you did
not know it. " You are conqueror and you die,
" you are Ruftan and you ceafe to be fo ;" all has
been accomplifhed. Whilft he fpoke thus, four
white wings covered the body of Topaze, and four
black wings that of Ebene. What do I fee! cried
Ruftan. Topaze and Ebene anfwered together,
You fee your two geniufes. Good gentlemen,
cried the unhappy Ruftan, how came you to meddle? and what occafion had a poor man for two
geniufes? It is a law, anfwered Topaze; every man
has two geniufes. Plato was the firft man that faid
fo, and others have repeated it after him; you fee
that nothing can be more true: I, who now fpeak
to you, am your good genius; I was charged to watch
over you to the laft moment of your life; of this
tafk I have faithfully acquitted myfelf.

  But, faid the dying man, if your bufinefs was to
ferve me, I am of a nature much fuperior to yours;
and then how can you have the affurance to fay
you are my good genius, fince you have fuffered
me to be deceived in every thing I have undertaken,
and fince you fuffer both my miftrefs and me to die
miferably? Alas! faid Topaze, it was your deftiny.
If deftiny does all, anfwered the dying man, what is
a genius good for? And you, Ebene, with your four
black wings, you are, doubtlefs, my evil genius.
You have hit it, anfwered Ebene. Then I fuppofe you were the evil genius of my princefs likewife, faid Ruftan. No, replied Ebene, fhe had an
evil genius of her own, and I feconded him perfectly. Ah, curft Ebene! faid Ruftan, if you are fo malicious, you don't belong to the fame mafter with
Topaze: you have been formed by two different
principles, one of which is by nature good, the
                                              other

other evil. That does not follow, faid Ebene, this is a very knotty point. It is not poffible, anfwered the dying man, that a benevolent being could create fo deftructive a genius. Poffible or not poffible, replied the genius, the thing is juft as I fay. Alas, faid Topaze, my poor unfortunate friend, don't you fee that that rogue is fo malicious as to encourage you to difpute, in order to inflame your blood and haften your death? Get you gone, faid the melancholy Ruftan, I am not much better fatisfied with you than with him: he at leaft acknowledges that it was his intention to hurt me; and you, who pretended to defend me, have done me no fervice at all. I am very forry for it, faid the good genius. And I too, faid the dying man; there is fomething at the bottom of this which I cannot comprehend. Nor I neither, faid the good genius. I fhall know the truth of the matter in a moment, faid Ruftan. We fhall fee that, faid Topaze. The whole fcene then vanifhed. Ruftan again found himfelf in the houfe of his father, which he had not quitted, and in his bed, where he had flept an hour.

He awakes in aftonifhment, fweating all over, and quite wild; he rubs himfelf, he calls, he rings the bell. His valet-de-chambre, Topaze, runs in, in his night-cap, and yawning. Am I dead or alive, cried out Ruftan? fhall the beauteous princefs of Cachemire efcape? Does your lordfhip rave? anfwered Topaze, coldly.

Ah! cried Ruftan, what then is become of this barbarous Ebene, with his four black wings! it is he that makes me die by fo cruel a death. My lord, anfwered Topaze, I left him fnoring above ftairs, would you have me bid him come down? The villain, faid Ruftan, has perfecuted me for fix

months together: it was he who carried me to
the fatal fair of Kaboul ; it is he that cheated me of
the diamond with which the princefs prefented me ;
he is the fole caufe of my journey, of the death of my
princefs, and of the wound with a javelin, of which
I die in the flower of my age.

Take heart, faid Topaze, you were never at
Kaboul; there is no princefs of Cachemire ; her
father never had any children but two boys, who
are now at college : you never had a diamond :
the princefs cannot be dead, becaufe fhe is not
born ; and you are perfectly well in health.

What ! is it not then true that you attended me
whilft dying, and in the bed of the prince of Cachemire ? Did you not acknowledge to me, that,
in order to preferve me from fo many dangers, you
were an eagle, an elephant, a ftreaked afs, a phyfician, and a pie ? My lord, you have dreamt all this,
anfwered Topaze : our ideas are no more of our
own creating whilft we are afleep than whilft we
are awake : God has thought proper that this train
of ideas fhould pafs in your head, moft probably to
convey fome inftruction to you, of which you may
make a good ufe.

You make a jeft of me, replied Ruftan, how
long have I flept ? My lord, faid Topaze, you have
not yet flept an hour. Curft reafoner, returned
Ruftan, how is it poffible that I could be, in the
fpace of an hour, at the fair of Kaboul fix months
ago, that I could have returned from thence, have
travelled to Cachemire, and that Barbabou, the
princefs, and I, fhould have died ? My lord, faid
Topaze, nothing can be more eafy and more common ; and you might have travelled round the
world, and have met with a great many more adventures in much lefs time.

Is

Is it not true that you can, in an hour's time, read the abridgment of the Perfian hiftory, written by Zoroafter? yet this abridgment contains eight hundred thoufand years. All thefe events pafs before your eyes one after another, in an hour's time. Now you muft acknowledge, that it is as eafy to Brama to confine them to the fpace of an hour, as to extend them to the fpace of eight hundred thoufand years; it is exactly the fame thing. Imagine to yourfelf that time turns upon a wheel whofe diameter is infinite. Under this vaft wheel is a numerous multitude of wheels one within another: that in the center is imperceptible, and goes round an infinite number of times, whilft the great wheel performs but one revolution. It is evident, that all the events which have happened from the beginning of the world, to its end, might have happened in much lefs time than the hundred thoufandth part of a fecond; and one may even go fo far as to affert that the thing is fo.

I cannot comprehend all this, faid Ruftan. If you want information, faid Topaze, I have a parrot that will eafily explain it to you. He was born fome time before the deluge; he has been in the ark; he has feen a great deal; yet he is but a year and a half old: he will relate to you his hiftory, which is extremely interefting.

Go fetch your parrot, faid Ruftan, it will amufe me till I again find myfelf difpofed to fleep. It is with my fifter, the nun, faid Topaze; I will go and fetch it; it will pleafe you; its memory is faithful; it relates in a fimple manner, without endeavouring to fhew wit at every turn. So much the better, faid Ruftan, I like that manner of telling ftories. The parrot being brought to him, fpoke in this manner : —

N. B.

N. B. Mademoifelle Catherine Vadé could never find the hiftory of the parrot in the commonplace-book of her late coufin Anthony Vadé, author of that tale : this is a great misfortune, confidering what age that parrot lived in.

END OF VOLUME FIRST.

www.ingramcontent.com/pod-product-compliance
Lightning Source LLC
Chambersburg PA
CBHW021116270326
41929CB00009B/904